BUILDING TOWARD
CIVIL WAR

BUILDING TOWARD CIVIL WAR

Generational Rhythms in American Politics

Daniel J. Elazar

Center for the
Study of
Federalism

MADISON BOOKS
Lanham • New York • London

Published by Madison Books
4720 Boston Way
Lanham, Maryland 20706

3 Henrietta Street
London WC2E 8LU England

Distributed by National Book Network

The paper used in this publication meets the minimum
requirements of American National Standard for
Information Sciences—Permanence of Paper for
Printed Library Materials, ANSI Z39.48–1984. ∞™
Manufactured in the United States of America.

Library of Congress Cataloging-in-Publication Data

Elazar, Daniel Judah.
Building toward Civil War : generational rhythms
in American politics / Daniel J. Elazar.
p.   cm.
Includes bibliographical references and index.
1. United States—Politics and
government—1845–1861.   2. Political
culture—United States—History—19th century.
I. Title.
E415.7.E23   1992
973.6—dc20   91–35729 CIP

ISBN 0–8191–8349–0 (cloth : alk. paper)

British Cataloging in Publication Information Available

For the five generations of the Goldman clan,
past and present,
whose American beginnings were in Minnesota and
who in three generations have spread over the entire West.

CONTENTS

LIST OF TABLES, FIGURES, AND MAPS

PREFACE

Few historic events have captured the imagination of Americans as much as their Civil War. Indeed, the fascination of that irrepressible conflict has extended beyond the borders of the United States at the time and subsequently. The sources of the war's fascination have been primarily patriotic and dramatic. Occasionally they have been philosophic, rarely have they been scientific. Yet for all of its real patriotic meaning and dramatic character, the war and the events surrounding it deserve consideration from philosophic and scientific perspectives as well. To paraphrase Theodore Roosevelt, history is, among other things, a "bully teacher," even if there are few who will learn from its lessons.

For several generations immediately following the war, Americans in the North and the South shaped their political lives on the basis of what they learned from it, and to some degree what they learned shaped their social orders as well. Now that we have lost first-hand contact with the war generation, the impact of its teaching, however interpreted, on those aspects of American life has radically diminished. It is no accident that the solid South broke up at the same time that the last people who personally remembered the War Between the States were passing to their eternal rewards.

Today the conflict must speak in new ways to a new generation. While this does not diminish its patriotic importance or dramatic attraction, it does mean that its philosophic meaning and scientific lessons become important in a more universalistic way. While as Americans we no longer mold our politics or social relations on the basis of the war's scars, as people continually engaged in the quest for political and social comity, the war and its coming can teach us a great deal about political processes that promote or destroy comity.

This volume does not focus on the war itself, but on the fifteen years between 1846 and 1861 which brought the country from real, if flawed, union to civil conflict. By looking at those fifteen years we can examine a critical period in American history, a period whose import goes beyond the immediate questions of the coming of the war. In examining it, we can not only learn how the war came, but we can also learn something about how the breakdown of the political process is the prerequisite to the disruption of polities. The fifteen years before the Civil War can be examined as a chapter in American history and as a case study in the political life of a democratic polity. From both perspectives it is a fascinating period. In its most concrete historical sense, those fifteen years represented the first half of the first generation of industrial America, a country considerably different from the commercial and agrarian America of the eighteenth-century founders, one already on its way toward the metropolitan and technological America we know today. Insofar as such events can be isolated and localized, it was in those fifteen years that America "took off" along the road toward becoming an urban industrial society. This is true not only in connection with the spread of industrialization, but is also true in connection with the development of appropriate organizational mechanisms and accompanying political techniques to handle an industrializing and urbanizing society on a continental scale.

Looking back at that period from the vantage point of a later time, no less than looking at it from within, requires a careful effort to distinguish the truly fundamental changes that were occurring in the midst of the general claims of the times. Some revolutions come with total war and disruption, and are unmistakable in their presence. Most revolutionary experiences in the United States have been quite different. Even the Revolutionary War and the social and political revolution which accompanied it was probably viewed by most Americans living at the time as a distant occurrence, a matter of sporadic upset in the midst of what must have seemed to them simply an intensification of earlier trends. How much more hidden were the dramatic changes wrought by the great migrations which have been part and parcel of the American experience — the 30 million immigrants who crossed the Atlantic between 1830 and 1880, or the 70 million Americans who moved from town to city or central city to suburb between the end of World War II and the mid-1970s. The latter was probably the greatest migration in human history and certainly one which fundamentally changed the face of American society, yet it was even less dramatic for those involved in it than the events described here.

In a country that — until recently at least — has experienced little failure and less tragedy, those selfsame fifteen years offer one of the few opportunities for examining the breakdown of politics and political leadership that precipitates the collapse of both. In that respect, the experience of those fifteen years can be viewed as one paradigm of breakdown in democratic politics. As the book will show, the breakdown was not a simple unilinear matter. Not only did it require a very precise convergence of various social, economic and political factors, but it did not move in one direction only. Even as the political process was deteriorating, the foundations were being laid for new forms of political organization in the United States. Even as the country's political institutions were proving themselves incapable of handling the conflict over slavery, its governmental institutions were acquiring new tasks and undertaking new responsibilities to meet the demands of industrialization and of the American frontier.

The persistence of federal operations in the South until the firing on Fort Sumter is a story in itself. On one hand, it reflects the ability of bureaucracies to ignore the world around them and continue to conduct business as usual even as the walls come tumbling down (a phenomenon that has become even more visible in the twentieth century). On the other hand, it reveals how bureaucrats cannot rule alone, how they lack the ability to truly govern "in the clutch," reaffirming the classic distinction that administration is not government.

In many ways this book is a parallel to the author's *Cities of the Prairie: The Metropolitan Frontier and American Politics* which examines several aspects of the half generation following World War II (1946-1948 through 1961-1963) exactly a century after the events described in the following pages. Whereas *Cities of the Prairie* focuses on the opening of the metropolitan-technological frontier, this volume focuses on the opening of the urban-industrial frontier. In both cases the violent wrenching generated by the opening of new frontiers led to national crises of great seriousness — indeed, to the most intense crises the country has faced as a nation. The vitality of the republic enabled Americans to surmount both crises but not without paying a heavy price.

Despite the parallel, the two generations are not simply reflections of the same history in different guises. In each the crisis resulted from its own combination of circumstances and individuals. Nevertheless, each followed the same temporal course, the same generational rhythm. Perhaps therein lies the particular teaching of history.

* * *

Building Toward Civil War

This book is a product of the author's major study of the impact of the Civil War on American government, state and national, which is, in turn, part of a project launched in 1962 by the late Alan Nevins to provide a proper commemoration for the centenary of the American Civil War. The author wishes to acknowledge his great debt to Mr. Nevins for bringing him to the subject and allowing him to fulfill a lifelong ambition to contribute to the study of the American Civil War. Mr. Nevins was instrumental in making it possible for the author to do the bulk of the research in the Henry E. Huntington Library in San Marino, California, where Mr. Nevins was in residence after his retirement. The unparalleled resources of that library for Civil War research, intellectual companionship, and proper physical environment made the work a joy, and sharing in Mr. Nevins' table and in his famous walks around the library grounds were an inestimable privilege for a then young scholar.

The author wishes to specifically acknowledge the support of the Henry E. Huntington Library in the form of a research fellowship, the American Council for Learned Societies for a research grant, and the John Simon Guggenheim Foundation for a fellowship which made it possible for him to spend a year on the Civil War project. This combination of resources enabled him to undertake a serious project seriously and, for better or worse, to extend it beyond its immediate frame of reference to become part of his education.

With the prolongation of the overall project, it ultimately became part of the working agenda of the Center for the Study of Federalism at Temple University. Thus, the author benefited from the services of the Center and its capable staff. The author also wishes to thank Herbert Ershkowitz of the Temple University Department of History who read a draft of the manuscript and provided many helpful suggestions. Completion of the manuscript was made possible through the generous support of the Earhart Foundation of Ann Arbor, Michigan.

Daniel J. Elazar
Jerusalem and Philadelphia
October 1988

xiv

PART ONE:

A NEW GENERATION AND A NEW AGE

Chapter 1

REFORM TURNS TO THE SLAVERY QUESTION

Mr. Wilmot's Proviso

August 8, 1846, began as another hot summer day in Washington, notable to those caught up in the heat of the nation's capital that year only as the last Saturday of the second session of the Twenty-ninth Congress. In the manner of American legislative bodies, the pace of business in the House of Representatives was casually intense as the legislators concerned themselves with the press of last minute affairs common in the last days of a session. The still young war with Mexico, uppermost on everyone's mind, was apparently going well. There was already talk of peace and large scale acquisition of new territory in the far Southwest. The process of annexing Texas as a state and seating its representatives in Congress had been completed. Less than two months earlier, the Oregon question had been settled to American advantage, although the Yankees on the Northwestern frontier were dissatisfied with President Polk's concessions of the territory north of the forty-ninth parallel to the British, territory they had envisaged as future free soil to counterbalance the admission of Texas as a slave state. Although many amendments to the General Appropriations bill remained to be considered before the scheduled August 10 adjournment, they were in the nature of "little things," predominantly private claims, local matters really, advanced with little opposition in the already time-honored custom of congressional representation of local interests.

If any of the various representatives on the floor that Saturday afternoon were feeling pleased with their work, there was reason for their pleasure. Their Congress had taken the decisive steps toward rounding out the continental character of the American federal republic, completing the second great task of the American people. As if that were not sufficient, in a burst of activity stimulated by the most vigorous occupant in the White House in a decade, the Twenty-ninth Congress had also acted to settle several

3

of the other outstanding issues of their time. It had created an independent subtreasury system to handle federal funds and thus fill the void left by the demise of the National Bank a decade earlier. This action, which effectively put an end to the controversy over the National Bank that had occupied the attention of America's political and commercial leadership for two generations, set the basic pattern of the nation's fiscal organization until 1913 when the Federal Reserve System was created. Even in its details, it was to remain virtually unchanged until 1862.

Only a week earlier, Congress had completed work on the Walker Tariff that reversed the essentially protectionist thrust of the tariff measures enacted since 1816 and transformed the country's tariff policy in accord with the Democratic party's principle of tariff for revenue only. The revenue tariff was to last until the Democrats were replaced by the Lincoln administration in 1861. Congress had also created the Smithsonian Institution, reorganized the army, adopted a new policy with regard to the disposal of federally-owned mineral lands, and attended to many other details to tie up the loose ends left over from the days of Andrew Jackson. Now under the shadow of a war, which threatened to sharpen the nation's sectional divisions, its business was being brought to a close.

Congress was powerful in the 1840s, powerful because it was well led. In its ranks were senators such as Thomas Hart Benton of Missouri, the spokesman for the trans-Mississippi West; John C. Calhoun of South Carolina, the acknowledged leader of the South; Lewis Cass of Michigan, spokesman for the Northwest and its link with the party in power; Thomas Corwin of Ohio, a politician's politician; John J. Crittenden of Kentucky, who spoke for the absent Henry Clay; Sam Houston of Texas, a national hero newly arrived in the chamber but with the most powerful connections; and Daniel Webster of Massachusetts, the voice of New England and the Northeastern commercial interests. Among the representatives were men as diverse as John Quincy Adams, also of the Bay State, who had become the nation's conscience, and Stephen A. Douglas of Illinois, the very model of the new professional politician and rising spokesman for the West, who was shortly to assume Benton's mantle.

While the strength of Congress was apparent, the president's chair, for the first time in a decade, was also occupied by a strong figure. James K. Polk — "Young Hickory" as his supporters called him — was a Tennessean like his prototype and mentor, who believed in Jacksonian principles and who wielded Jacksonian power. His strong hand was additionally strengthened by a growing weakness in the Congress as the decade came to an end, a weakness not immediately apparent from reading the roster of its illustrious members. With one or two exceptions, the powerful leaders of the national legislature were men who stood at the twilight of their national careers, veterans who would shortly depart from the stage, men whose vigor was on the decline. Such men were still able to control their respective chambers and to lead the younger comers who were soon to succeed them, but they were in no position to dominate a vigorous president.

It was President Polk, seeking to expedite American acquisition of the Southwest and California, who came, in the waning hours of the 1846 session, with a request that was to generate an unexpected response and open the door for a new generation to be heard in the national political arena. Shortly before the afternoon recess, Speaker John W. Davis of Indiana presented a message from the president for his colleagues' consideration in which Mr. Polk requested the Congress to grant him a contingency fund of $2 million to be used to expedite the negotiation of a peace settlement with Mexico in such a way as to acquire certain parts of that unfortunate nation (particularly parts of California) for the United States. As Polk himself took care to point out, this action was not unprecedented. Thomas Jefferson himself had asked for and had been granted such contingency funds on two occasions. Mr. Polk's request fell upon the ears of a Congress hovering on the edge of the deepest and most catastrophic form of political cleavage — a moral cleavage reinforced by economics, culture, and geography — the slavery issue.

The territorial designs of the Polk administration were apparent from the very tone of the president's request. Since the territory in question lay due west of the South, the administration's chief supporters were Southerners, most of whom, though normally expansionist in any case, also hoped to add lands to which slavery could be transplanted. The Northern opponents of the war who feared that it would lead to the extension of Southern institutions were quick to move in an effort to bottle up the request in committee until the session's adjournment two days hence. The war party was equal to the occasion and a bill granting the president's request, apparently drafted earlier in preparation for the occasion, was introduced by James J. McKay of North Carolina, to be considered by the House sitting as a committee of the whole. In the uproar that ensued, the opposition was forced to concede a debate on the measure in the evening with a vote to follow. Shortly after 5 p.m. a quorum was assembled and the House was able to begin its debate on the McKay bill. Each representative was limited to ten minutes. Three representatives had already exhausted their time before David Wilmot, Democrat of Pennsylvania, was recognized for purposes of moving an amendment to the bill.

Wilmot, then thirty-two years old, was serving his first term in Congress and was just at the beginning of his long career in national politics. A resident of the northern tier of counties in Pennsylvania, the area settled by restless Yankees pushing westward, he had come to Washington without the prior experience in state legislative politics then customary in his native state. Thus, though a Democrat, he was untouched by the normative political culture of the Pennsylvania Democracy which viewed politics as a means for individual self-improvement and eschewed any serious concern with issues, especially divisive ones, as manifested by such men as James Buchanan and Simon Cameron. He was, rather, a pure Yankee Jacksonian of the type who, drawn by the demands of the frontier, entered the Democratic party after leaving New England while retaining Yankee-like conceptions of the moral purposes of politics.

Wilmot was anything but an abolitionist in 1846; indeed his motives for proposing what he proposed were mixed. He was a Free-Soiler, part of the moderate antislavery bloc whose first commitment was to the American constitutional compact as he understood it. Only a few years earlier he had been instrumental in preventing the abolitionists from using the courthouse in his home county for a rally, on the grounds that the abolitionist doctrine represented an invitation to violate that compact. In Congress he had been willing to accept the gag rule preventing the acceptance of abolitionist petitions rather than risk unconstitutional actions and had actively opposed any measures that even hinted of abolitionism. Indeed, by today's standards, he was a racist. Nevertheless, he was personally opposed to the slave system and was determined to urge every action consistent with the Constitution to limit the "peculiar institution" in the country as a whole.

As a Democrat, Wilmot had supported the Mexican War as necessary and just, despite the opposition of fellow-Yankee Whigs. He was further prepared to support President Polk's request, though he had grave reservations about his president's intentions. Opposed to territorial expansion through military conquest, he was, at the same time, eager to see the United States acquire the San Francisco Bay area as an outlet on the Pacific. He was unalterably opposed to any extension of slavery in the process. Thus he stood ready through a convergence of principles to take a stand that could possibly give him and his colleagues of the Northwestern Yankee democracy the best of both worlds.

Wilmot's solution was superficially an easy one — honor the president's request for a contingency fund with the proviso that any lands acquired from Mexico would be closed to slavery forever: "...as an express and fundamental condition to the acquisition of any territory from the Republic of Mexico...neither slavery nor involuntary servitude shall ever exist in any part of said territory, except for crime, whereof, the party shall first be duly convicted." His motion to that effect has been recorded in history as the Wilmot Proviso.

If there was any single turning point in the controversy that was to culminate in civil war, this spur of the moment action has best claim to that designation. The decision to introduce that amendment to McKay's bill and the preparation of the text had taken less than two hours during the recess that very afternoon. Though Wilmot made the motion, the resolution itself had been at least cleared with a number of his like-minded colleagues. If not the product of a conscious antislavery cabal, it was, nevertheless, a reasonable expression of the spirit of a majority of the members of the lower house.

After a heated debate, the House voted, more or less along sectional lines, to adopt the proviso that very same evening by a substantial margin. David Wilmot, the moderate, had apparently achieved a greater victory for the antislavery cause in one afternoon than had all the agitators in the twenty-six years since the adoption of the Missouri Compromise.

Wilmot's victory might have been complete but for a moment of confusion in the Senate on Monday, the tenth. That body took up consideration of the McKay Bill with the proviso in the last hour of the session. Senator Dixon H. Lewis of Alabama, floor manager of the measure, proposed immediate consideration and adoption of the bill without the proviso. This drew a protest from Senator John Davis of Massachusetts who gained the floor and, inadvertently or not, held it until the previously set hour for adjournment had come. Thus both the appropriation and the proviso died together with the session, and Davis earned a footnote in history for being the first legislator to filibuster a bill to death in the Senate.

Wilmot's proviso, like Polk's request, had ample precedent behind it, although it turned matters in a new direction. Such provisos had been used to limit the spread of slavery, or in efforts to do so, since the days of the Confederation Congress when Jefferson unsuccessfully submitted the first one, which was designed to prohibit slavery in all territory west of the original thirteen states. Jefferson's and others' had failed but some had succeeded. In any case, such provisos had been accepted as legitimate (some said noble) legislative gambits. The precedents are deceiving and actions which, in a different time, are justified on the grounds of precedent can sometimes be most revolutionary.

The Wilmot Proviso was just such a revolutionary action. Though it would be debated in Congress for two more years, it would never become law. But, more important in the long run, it would become the symbolic issue required to attract the public attention necessary to transform the slavery question into a burning political issue. The general public had paid little attention to congressional discussions of the gag rule or even to the problems of delivering the United States Mail in the South, even though these discussions had been advanced for a decade and had, along with the territorial questions, stamped the slavery issue as an important national concern. The Wilmot Proviso fell on willing ears that had been unwilling before. In short, while it was certainly not the first spark to have been generated by the slavery question, unlike the earlier ones that had fallen on stone, this one fell into the haystack.

The Politization of Moral Issues

Prior to August 8, 1846, the overwhelming majorities in Congress and among the nation's political leaders had given the slavery issue what might best be termed "negative attention." That is, they were invariably aware of the potential problem posed by slavery in a nation "half slave and half free" and consequently sought to keep the issue from coming to the surface politically. Hence, when forced by agitators or circumstances to take cognizance of the problem, they would act as swiftly as possible to bury it once again. They had been forced to do so several times in the seventy years since independence and had apparently been successful every time.

But slavery was not the kind of issue to stay buried, particularly in a nation that was founded through the substitution of a moral vision for the future — a mystique — in the place of an inherited myth of a common past. As long as the American people were occupied elsewhere, it could be pushed into the background but, by the summer of 1846, American concerns were shifting away from the preoccupations of the previous generation. In the years following the War of 1812, Americans were primarily concerned with filling out the nation's boundaries and extending its dominion to the Pacific while eliminating the vestiges of the colonial regime in the older sections of the country.

Both tasks were nearing completion by the mid-1840s. The Webster-Ashburton Treaty of 1842 settled the problems of the nation's northern borders in New England and Minnesota. That same year, the great migration to Oregon began, giving the country a continental character for the first time. Four years later, the question of who possessed what territory in Oregon was permanently settled and the Pacific Northwest came under American sovereignty. In the Southwest, the annexation of Texas was completed despite Northern opposition. Though Congress did not know it, by August 1846, the Americans in California had established their "Bear Flag Republic" and had effectively added that land to the United States.

Back in "the States," the events of the Jacksonian era had led to virtual elimination of property and religious qualifications as prerequisites for voting or holding office. Such vestiges of the old regime as the established church in New England and the neofeudal land tenure arrangements in New York were abolished. While eleven northern states still had a few slaves within their boundaries in 1840, survivors from before emancipation, by 1850 only a handful would be left, in New Jersey. Neomercantilism as a national economic policy began to give way to new notions of free capitalism and both the federal government and the state governments began to withdraw from direct participation in economic enterprises.

Politics moved out of the caucuses of the wellborn and into the hands of men claiming to represent the broad mass of "the people." The two party system had crystallized in the country as a whole and in most of the states as well, to an extent that would not be duplicated until the 1960s. Control of these new political parties was vested in the convention system from the township to the national arena and the conventions began to come under the dominance of professional politicians. Many more offices were made elective and the principle of rotation was introduced as a feature in the civil service. Congressional action on the tariff and fiscal questions in 1846 eliminated those issues as perennial concerns, which they had been for the previous thirty years.

The long period during which the issue smoldered beneath the surface, the immediacy of the problem of making political decisions for new lands, the growing economic and cultural differences between North and South and the growing public awareness of those differences, the newly found sense of morality and concern with reform generally, all these and perhaps other factors as well combined to hasten the hour when the slavery question could no longer be treated politically in order to keep it out of politics. After August 8, the nation's political leaders were forced to focus "positive attention" on the slavery issue. This, in turn, forced the nation to take sides on the question and demand an active politics whose only possible culmination would have to be some resolution of the issue. Thus it was that a new generation found itself with a moral issue that was to be the catchall, the touchstone, the shorthand symbol for so many other issues of lesser moral implications that were spreading among an aroused public.

After all is said and done, indications are that it was the moral impetus of reform that proved decisive in stimulating Northern antislavery sentiments. For many Americans — and particularly for New England Yankees highly susceptible to reformist ideas — it had been an easy step from the agitation over the democratic reforms of the 1820s and early 1830s to a concern for moral reform designed to improve mankind. This natural extension of the American moral mystique was manifested in the temperance movement, the drive for improved conditions designed to perfect man and usher in a modern millennium. The Jacksonian era was, in fact, the first call forth of a conscious reform movement in this country, in the sense of a congeries of individuals and groups who considered their main purpose to be that of reforming society for the sake of "man."

The emergence of reformers who recognized themselves, and were recognized by others, as such was a permanent and signal addition to American political life. Along with their emergence came the development of the idea that the people, operating through their elected representatives, could make major changes in the social order through the enactment of new laws. This notion is in its essence a modern innovation, a further rejection of the traditional conception of law as fundamental, ancient, and basically immutable; never changed except by those learned in the law who were able to "discover" new meanings or principles within it. It is one that was pioneered by Americans who, as citizens of the world's first modern society, were free to consciously shape their own laws because in settling a new world, they were emancipated from traditional law.

This new view of law found its first great expression in the development — theoretically from "scratch" — of written constitutions, state and national, in the last quarter of the eighteenth century. However, it was rarely used for other than procedural ends until the Jacksonian era which witnessed the enactment of important legislation, primarily in the states, creating new governmental institutions directed toward reform. It was not to be developed into a major tool for consciously attempting substantive social changes for yet another generation.

Reform in the Jacksonian era had been exclusively a white man's blessing. Yet, by the mid-1830s, at least a few of the Northern reformers had found it equally appropriate to transfer some of their concern to the slavery question. In doing so, they stepped into a virtual vacuum created by the demise of Southern abolitionism a decade earlier.

By the mid-1830s, the Missouri Compromise had become a part of history. Slave uprisings that had occurred in the Southern states in the interim had virtually killed the Southern antislavery sentiments that had helped convince antislavery Northerners to accept the settlement of 1820. As the plantation culture spread westward south of the Ohio River, the slave system was rapidly being canonized as the cornerstone of the Southern way of life. Those Southerners who persisted in opposing the peculiar institution had either migrated to the old Northwest or remained quietly at home avoiding any expression of their true sentiments.

The contrast between the industrializing North and the feudal-agricultural South had been growing more pronounced for several decades. It had already led to the great nullification controversy of the early 1830s which, in a fight over the use of the tariff to protect the development of Northern industry at the presumed expense of Southern agriculture, sharpened the breach between the sections even as a compromise preserving the Union was reached. As the antislavery cause became a sectional rather than national one, the growing rivalry between North and South took on the ominous aspect of a moral struggle, in addition to an economic one.

The abolitionism launched in the 1830s was of an entirely different character from anything which preceded it. With Garrison in the fore and a new moral fervor generated by revivalism and optimistic perfectionism in Christianity as exemplified by Charles G. Finney, abolitionism after 1830 really was a new movement. The American Antislavery Society was not merely an extension of old abolitionism into a regional mold; the difference between Jefferson, for example, and William Lloyd Garrison was enormous. The new nature of abolitionism and what it meant in terms of the intractability of the slavery issue, now phrased in such stridently moral terms, was to have the greatest political consequences.

By 1840, the antislavery spirit had become concentrated increasingly in the northernmost North: in the six states of New England proper and in the greater New England of upper New York State and the old Northwest, wherever Yankees came to settle, even more than in the areas fertilized by Quakers and ex-Southerners of antislavery inclinations where the abolitionist sentiment of earlier years had been manifest. The Yankees, in particular, carried the germ of that spirit. While most of them were not concerned with the slavery issue, except perhaps in some abstract way, wherever there were sons of the Puritans, there was bound to be a leavening of vociferous abolitionists; and where there were abolitionists, there was bound to be conflict with the easy-going public acceptance of the status quo.

The first clashes were not political in character. Local mobs assaulted and even lynched abolitionist speakers and editors, and street fights often developed between opposing groups. Nationally there were even debates in Congress over the rights of abolitionists to petition the national legislature to act against the slave system in the District of Columbia and to send their propaganda through the mails. In either case, the authority of government was invoked, at most, to keep the peace, not to deal with the issue as such. Even in Congress, men like John Quincy Adams who attempted to treat the problem directly were looked upon with some distaste by Northerners and Southerners alike. It was clearly, if implicitly, understood in the South that men could be elected to public office only if they supported the slave system, but this was hardly different than the expectation that the New England officeholders would support a protectionist tariff policy.

Before 1840 the new abolitionist societies themselves were curiously nonpolitical. Even though they sought a goal which could only be achieved politically, they remained divorced from serious political action other than waiting for candidates in the north to ascertain their views on slavery. Politics as a means of reform was still too new a notion to overcome their moral distaste for the political arena.

Exacerbating the Issue on the Frontier

Nevertheless, the political implications of the question continued to simmer beneath the surface of everyday politics, thrusting themselves upward from time to time. The primary force responsible for raising the slavery issue into active politics from the very first had been the advancing frontier. The settlement of the Western lands raised the issue just because new territories with new settlers require some a priori national decisions as to the course of their development. Twice before in the cases of the first trans-Appalachian frontier and Louisiana, the issue had been settled with a minimum amount of public excitement. In 1785 and 1787, there was general agreement as to the solution in all sections of the United States, in an atmosphere that was hostile to slavery and where the dictates of geography were clear. By 1820, the atmosphere surrounding slavery was changing but the eagerness for amicable settlement of the problem in an aura of mutual respect, produced by strong nationalist sentiment, led to compromise with a minimum of difficulty.

By the time the future status of Texas and Oregon were up for decision, the problem had been sufficiently complicated to make it very difficult to avoid the injection of the slavery issue into the political realm. In both cases the slavery question could be no less than a constitutional one, because the political decision that had to be made would not ratify a preexisting situation but would itself shape the constitution of the societies to be erected in the new lands.

The constitutional question was even more acute because its moral character extended beyond the immediate problem of holding human beings in bondage to touch upon fundamental choices in the very organization of new civil societies. For good or ill, the political decision regarding slavery, once made, was to spin out its consequences in ways which seemingly had no connection with questions of politics. A political decision opening or closing the gates of new territories to slaveholders would do much to determine whether future social organization in those territories would follow the pattern of the progressive, middle-class-dominating, capitalistic, commercial democracy developing in the North or the pattern of the conservative, aristocratic-dominated, quasi-formal, agrarian oligarchy entrenching itself in the South.

This is easily recognized in retrospect when the development of slave and free states admitted to the Union at the same time is comparable, namely:

Kentucky (1792) and Vermont (1791)
Tennessee (1976) and Ohio (1803)
Louisiana (1812) and Indiana (1816)
Mississippi (1817) and Illinois (1818)
Alabama (1819) and Maine (1820)
Arkansas (1836) and Michigan (1837)
Florida (1845) and Iowa (1846)
Texas (1845) and Wisconsin (1848)

Even at the time there were those who saw these different patterns of development and took notice of their consequences.

Abolitionist activity, with its monistic focus on slavery, tended to obscure the fact that the question of the social organization of American civil society was the real moral choice, one of even greater significance than the question of slavery alone, but, in the last analysis, the conditions of that choice reflect the very essence of civil society, which is inevitably organized around some transcendent political principles that are, in turn, reflected in some central political decisions and some immediate political institutions which give it shape. Whether they knew it or not, Americans in the middle of the nineteenth century were face-to-face with the fundamental questions that make civil societies of all but the most primitive political communities.

Most of those who espoused the cause of free soil perceived the real choice almost instinctively, though few would have been able to express it in so many words. Some of the men in their ranks, Abraham Lincoln among them, saw the choice for what it was from the first. In general, the men on the frontier who had to grapple with the decision saw it most clearly. Across the continent from Washington, the antislavery Californians expressed their opposition to the "peculiar institution," not because they feared that a slave labor system would dominate their new commonwealth, but because they were worried that even a temporary incursion of slaveholders would discourage a sober, industrious middle class of workers from coming to settle and establishing a better social pattern.

The slavery question in Texas and Oregon could still be treated without reaching the point of national disruption because geography and local custom dictated that one be slave and the other free. Although they each generated considerable heat in the political arena for nearly a decade, the solution was obvious before the problem was even considered in Congress; and the adoption of the obvious solution commended itself to that body because it would not only preserve the balance of forces in the Union, but would also allow the Unionists, North and South, to keep the entire issue hidden under the rug a bit longer. However, no sooner was that problem seemingly settled than the outbreak of war opened up the question of California and the Southwest which was not to be so easily resolved. Not enough Americans had settled in those areas to establish acceptable local customs and the geographic question (when considered in light of climate and topography) did not dictate any answer. Furthermore, national passions were already sufficiently aroused over the war itself, which much of the Yankee North had opposed as Southern-instigated adventurism designed to augment slave territories, to have eliminated the willingness on the part of both sides to compromise that had made the difference in the past.

The future of California was of particular concern. Stretching for close to a thousand miles along the coast from the latitude of Montgomery, Alabama, to that of Boston, it was open to settlement from both North and South and consequently offered an invitation to conflict between the potential settlers from each section. In the last analysis, the coming of the Mexican War, with all that it clearly meant in the way of territorial expansion, hardly could help but be the catalyst for placing the moral issue of slavery, with its economic and cultural overtones, squarely in the center of the political stage.

The slavery question was due to emerge in the political arena for yet another reason endemic to democracies. By 1846 it was already clear, to all who wished to see, that in a democracy few if any public institutions can remain nonpolitical ones, since, by the very nature of democratic government, politics is itself a public matter. The public character of politics is, indeed, one of the distinguishing characteristics of a democratic regime. (One need only compare the difference between the privatized politics of the

15

English ruling class before the seventeenth century to the public character of British politics since then to perceive the importance of this distinction.) Furthermore, in a democracy like the United States, which was founded on certain conceptions of transcendent morality as well as on the acceptance of popular government as a useful technique, questions of public morality are inevitably politicized. The history of the Civil War era is a testimonial to the strength of this principle, particularly since it involves the politization of an issue that statesmen consciously tried to exclude from the political realm because of its explosiveness.

Two generations earlier, the founders of the Republic, themselves revolutionaries who had introduced moral considerations into their revolution and their constitution-making, recognized the particularly explosive potentialities of moral issues in the politics of democratic republics. They attempted to create a constitution that would remove issues of morality from direct contact with the political realm by directing Americans to treat political questions as legal or procedural matters first and foremost. To a substantial degree they were successful in at least blunting the thrust of questions that took on moral overtones into the American political arena. Yet their policy reached its limits in relatively short order, foundering on the rock of slavery. The generation of the Civil War was to learn the limits of this policy through bitter experience and what the terrible consequences of transcending those limits would be. As a consequence of this experience, Americans were forced to reckon with the problem of handling moral issues in a democracy without disrupting the democratic system itself.

Men of goodwill and high moral character whose first moral commitment was to the maintenance of the Union recognized the dilemma being forced upon them. In October 1845, one of them wrote to a friend, "I hold it to be a paramount duty of us in the free states, due to the Union of the states, and perhaps to liberty itself (paradox though it may seem) to let the slavery of the other states alone; while, on the other hand, I hold it to be equally clear, that we should never knowingly lead ourselves directly or indirectly, to prevent that slavery from dying a natural death — to find new places of it to live in, when it can no longer exist in the old." Abraham Lincoln may have paused a moment before adding the next line, "Of course I am not now considering what would be our duty, in cases of insurrection among the slaves."

Bibliographic Notes — Chapter 1

The major works dealing with this period as a whole are Arthur C. Cole, *The Irrepressible Conflict* (1934); Avery Craven, *The Civil War in the Making, 1815-1860* (1959), *The Coming of the Civil War*, rev. ed. (1957), and *The Growth of Southern Nationalism, 1848-1861* (1953); Alan Nevins, *Ordeal of the Union*, 2 vols. (1947) and *The Emergence of Lincoln*, 2 vols. (1950); Roy F. Nichols, *The Destruction of American Democracy* (1948), and *The Stakes of Power, 1845-1877* (1961). See also James G. Randall, "Wandering Generation," *Mississippi Valley Historical Review* 27 (1940): 3. For more specialized studies, see Joel H. Silbey, *The Transformation of American Politics, 1840-1860* (1967); Henry H. Sims, *A Decade of International Controversy, 1851-1861* (1942); and Elbert B. Smith, *The Death of Slavery, 1837-1865* (1967).

For a general treatment of the themes discussed in Part One, see Ray A. Billington, *The Far Western Frontier: 1830-1860* (1956), and especially Bernard DeVoto, *Year of Decision* (1953). The congressional and political dimensions are well treated by Joel H. Silbey in his two books, *Shrine of the Party: Congressional Voting Behavior, 1841-1852* (1967), and *The Transformation of American Politics, 1840-1860* (1967); the latter is a collection of essays which he edited. The basic source of precise statistical, weather, and similar data for this period is Horace Greeley's *The Whig Almanac*, published annually throughout those years.

On the struggle for the annexation of Texas, see Kinley J. Brauer, *Cotton vs. Conscience: Massachusetts Whig Politics and Southwestern Expansion, 1843-1848* (1967), and Eugene C. Barker, "Annexation of Texas," *Southwestern Historical Quarterly* 50 (1946): 49. The Oregon question is treated in Frederick Merk, *Albert Gallatin and the Oregon Problem: A Study in Anglo-American Diplomacy* (1950) and *The Oregon Question: Essays in Anglo-American Diplomacy and Politics* (1967).

For the 29th Congress, see Charles A. McCoy, *Polk and the Presidency* (1960), and Leonard D. White, *The Jacksonians* (1954). In addition to the volume by McCoy, James Polk's presidency is discussed by Norman A. Graebner in "James Polk," a chapter in Morton Borden, ed., *America's Ten Greatest Presidents* (1961), and by James J. Horn in "Historical Interpretations: James K. Polk," *North Carolina Historical Review* 42 (1965): 454.

Memoirs of the leading members of Congress of this period are exceptionally rich. See, for example, Thomas Hart Benton, *Thirty Years' View*, 2 vols. (1845-1856); John C. Calhoun, *Works,* edited by R.K.

Cralle, 6 vols. (1853-1855, produced in 1968); Sam Houston's autobiography edited by Donald Day and Harry H. Ullom (1954); Daniel Webster, *Writings and Speeches*, edited by J.W. McIntyre, 18 vols. (1903); John Quincy Adams, *Memoirs*, edited by Charles Francis Adams, 12 vols. (1874-1877); and Stephen A. Douglas, *Letters*, edited by Robert W. Johannsen (1961).

For biographies of these figures, see Samuel F. Bemis' *John Quincy Adams*, 2 vols. (1949-1956); William N. Chambers, *Old Bullion Benton* (1956); Albert B. Smith, *Magnificent Missourian: Thomas Hart Benton* (1957); Margaret L. Coit, *John C. Calhoun* (1950); Charles M. Wiltse, *John C. Calhoun*, 3 vols. (1944-1951); Andrew C. McLaughlin, *Lewis Cass* (1899); Frank B. Witford, *Lewis Cass: The Last Jeffersonian* (1950); Albert D. Kirwan, *John J. Crittenden* (1962); Gerald M. Capers, *Stephen A. Douglas: Defender of the Union* (1959); Marquis James, *The Raven: A Biography of Sam Houston* (1929); M.K. Wisehart, *Sam Houston* (1962); Charles G. Sellers, Jr., *James K. Polk*, 2 vols. (1957-1966); Norman D. Brown, *Daniel Webster and the Politics of Availability* (1969); and Richard N. Current, *Daniel Webster* (1955). See also Peter J. Parish, "Daniel Webster, New England, and the West," *Journal of American Historians* 54 (1967): 524.

On the Wilmot Proviso, see Chaplain W. Morrison, *Democratic Politics in Sectionalism: The Wilmot Proviso Controversy* (1967); Joel H. Silbey, "The Slavery Extension Question and Illinois Congressmen, 1846-1850," *Illinois State Historical Journal* 58 (1965): 378; and R.R. Stenberg, "The Motivation of the Wilmot Proviso," *Mississippi Valley Historical Review* 18 (1932): 535. See also Charles B. Going, *David Wilmot — Free Soiler* (1924).

On the general question of the expansion of slavery into the territories, see Arthur C. Cole, *The Whig Party in the South* (1913), L.J. Calloway, *New Mexico and Sectional Controversy, 1846-1861* (1944); and C.W. Ramsdale, "The Natural Limits of Slavery Expansion," *Mississippi Valley Historical Review* 16 (1929): 151.

Democratization in the states is described in Chilton Williamson, *American Suffrage from Property to Democracy, 1760-1860* (1960) and Merrill D. Peterson, ed., *Democracy, Liberty and Property: State Constitutional Conventions in the 1820s* (1966).

On economic matters, see Douglass C. North, *Economic Growth in the United States, 1790-1860* (1966); and Peter Temin, *The Jacksonian Economy* (1969).

Other histories of this period worth consulting include Harold Bode, ed., *American Life in the 1840s* (1967); G. Sellers, Jr., *Jacksonian Democracy* (1968); Frederick Jackson Turner, *The United States, 1830-1850* (1965); and Charles N. Wiltse, *The New Nation, 1800-1845* (1961).

Reform Turns to the Slavery Question

On reform movements, see Charles C. Cole, Jr., *The Social Ideas of Northern Evangelists, 1826-1860* (1864); Henry Stuart Conover, *The Era of Reform, 1830-1860* (1960); David B. Davis, comp., *Ante-Bellum Reform* (1967); Clifford S. Griffin, *Their Brothers' Keepers: Moral Stewardship in the United States, 1800-1865* (1960); Robert E. Riegel, *Young America, 1830-1840* (1949), Arthur M. Schlesinger, *The American as Reformer* (1950); and Alice Felt Tyler, *Freedom's Ferment* (1944).

For a discussion of the party system, see Richard J. McCormick, *The Second American Party System: The Jacksonian Era* (1966); and Herbert Agar, *The Price of Union* (1950); Roy F. Nichols, *The Invention of the American Political Parties* (1967); Thomas A. Bailey, *Democrats vs. Republicans* (1968); Wilfred E. Binkley, *American Political Parties*, 4th ed. (1963); Hugh Bone, *Party Committees and National Politics* (1958); William N. Chambers and Walter Dean Burnham, eds., *American Party Systems* (1967); William N. Chambers, *The Democrats, 1789-1964* (1964); R.M. Goldman, *Democratic Party in American Politics* (1966); William Goodman, *Two-Party System in the United States*, 3rd ed. (1964); George H. Mayer, *Republican Party, 1854-1966*, 2nd ed., (1967); Malcolm C. Moos, *Republicans: A History of Their Party* (1956); Howard P. Nash, *Third Parties in American Politics* (1958); Roy F. Nichols, *Invention of the American Political Parties, 1800-1850* (1967).

Chapter 2

THE NATION TURNS TOWARD NEW FRONTIERS

A Congress in Chicago

While the slavery issue was moving toward the point where the American people would be forced to focus their attention upon it and face the dilemma of strict constitutionalism versus fundamental morality, political stirrings of an entirely different sort were also abroad in the land. The same Congress that had considered the Wilmot Proviso had earlier in its session passed the first omnibus rivers and harbors bill, a measure containing some forty projects, something for every state and section. If anything aside from the issue of free soil caused major dissatisfaction in the ranks of Northern congressmen in the session of 1846, it was President Polk's veto of that bill just five days before Mr. Wilmot's motion.

Polk, a strict constructionist of federal powers under the Constitution in the Jacksonian manner, outdid his mentor in rejecting the legitimacy of federal aid for internal improvements. Whereas Jackson refused to extend federal support to purely local road and canal projects while continuing aid to public improvements of an interstate character, Polk, using the same argument, refused to aid projects affecting navigation on the nation's natural waterways. Federal improvement of the great East Coast harbors and removal of obstructions to navigation on the major rivers of the eastern Mississippi Valley had been accepted as legitimate by all Polk's predecessors. Federal power in this field was at least implicitly sanctioned by specific constitutional provision.

The rise of the Northwest, however, brought new demands for the transformation of undeveloped anchorages on the Great Lakes and the upper Mississippi river system into improved harbors at federal expense. The Westerners argued that equity demanded a fair distribution of federal services in this regard. The president correctly perceived that acceptance of the principle of equity as advocated by the Northwesterners could only lead to a great expansion of federal activities and expenditures in the internal

21

improvement field. Believing such a trend to be detrimental to the perpetuation of the federal system, Polk was determined to do all in his power to prevent it. Consequently, when confronted by a measure which embodied that trend to the fullest, he acted fully in character.

Polk's veto was sustained by the Democratic-controlled Congress, but the Northern and Western publics were not convinced by his reasoning. Too much precedent for federal action in the internal improvement field existed for constitutional arguments to hold weight among people who felt an immediate interest in the proposed projects. Within the year, the partisans of internal improvements had called for a meeting of like-minded Americans from all sections, in Chicago, to make their feelings known. The Chicago River and Harbor Convention of July 5-7, 1847, though it advocated nothing revolutionary or unprecedented, was as much a landmark in the change of generations as the Wilmot Proviso. While primarily concerned with harbor and navigation improvements on the Great Lakes, the convention spoke for the new West of middle-class farmers and merchants who sought to combine agriculture and business for their mutual profit and also for the new urbanizing East of self-made capitalists who sought to exploit Western resources for industrial development. It effectively redefined the constitutional questions that dominated the discussion of internal improvement so as to justify federal aid for the improvement of the nation's interior as well as its seacoasts.

Delegates from nineteen of the thirty-one states and territories participated in the sessions. The bulk of them naturally came from the states bordering on the Great Lakes. Illinois, Indiana, Michigan, New York, Ohio, and Wisconsin were each represented by more than a hundred. The New England states, with the exception of Vermont, were all represented, and Massachusetts, whose commercial interests in the West were widespread, had twenty-eight in attendance. Only the South failed to participate in due proportion. Ten of the fifteen slave states sent no representatives. Of the other five, Missouri, which still prided itself as being the spokesman for the greater West, sent a full-blown delegation of forty-five and thus was the only one to send more than two delegates. In fact, Andrew Jackson's "united West" of a half generation earlier was already divided into North-West and South-West, even over erstwhile neutral issues.

The South's absence was, in truth, not just an extension of other conflicts into the realm of commerce. On the contrary, the convention itself revealed how the slavery issue was so greatly reinforced by new economic questions. In earlier days, the West had united in the face of the overriding commercial issue of how to export its surplus produce anywhere. By 1847, the question had become one of which way to export it. A conference meeting in Chicago, designed to agitate for the improvement of the Great Lakes, could only reflect the expansion of the commercial interests of the Northeast and the closer linkage of that section and the Northwest.

In this case, commerce followed population. For two decades, Yankees had been pouring into the Northwest states to settle, bringing with them not only Yankee notions but firm ties with the commercial interests back home. The South, which had heavily dominated Western settlement until the opening of the Erie Canal in 1825, even to the point of providing a majority of settlers in Ohio, Indiana, and Illinois (the three states formed north of the Ohio River before that event), found itself increasingly disadvantaged by this turn of events. Not only were the states of the Southeastern seaboard without adequate lines of communication to the West, but their commercial interests did not have the wherewithal to supply the capital necessary to forge those lines of communication or to finance Western development.

The conference met in a significant place at an historic time. Chicago in 1847 was less than twenty years old as a settlement, having been located by the commissioners for the Illinois and Michigan Canal (one of the federal-state cooperative enterprises authorized before the reaction against government participation of the 1840s) as the eastern terminus of that work in 1829 and platted on the section of land granted by Congress to the state of Illinois for that purpose. It was one of the first planned cities in the West, in the sense that its site was fixed by state officials in line with the canal that was to connect the Great Lakes with the Mississippi and its plat established a true north-south grid as the basis for its future development. Moreover, it was typical of the new West in its reliance on federal aid for its development. Incorporated as a city in 1837, the lusty ten year old had a population of 16,000 and stood at the threshold of a generation-long boom that would begin the following year with the opening of the canal and its first railroad.

Though the Missourians who attended the conference may not have realized it, Chicago was already challenging St. Louis for supremacy in the Mississippi Valley. Its victory over that city in securing this very conference was a sign of the times. The

Southern absence implicitly recognized this. A conference in St. Louis would have been bound to concern itself with the improvement of the country's interior river system which, through the Ohio, the Tennessee, the Cumberland, and the Mississippi itself, gave the South its only easy opening to the Middle West and which, through the Red, the Arkansas, and the Missouri, might possibly have extended that opening into the Far West. A conference in Chicago meant primary consideration of projects that would divert commerce from the Ohio-Mississippi system to a Great Lakes-Mississippi route. This, in itself, would have diverted commerce from St. Louis and the South to Chicago and the North. In fact, the coming of the railroads in the next decade was to strengthen lake traffic while undermining the use of the rivers for commerce and reinforcing the tendencies already apparent in 1847.

As the delegates to the congress assembled in the city's public square at the head of Michigan Avenue (part of a congressional land grant for park purposes), they could well have contemplated a different nation than the one viewed by David Wilmot and his colleagues eleven months earlier. By July 1847, the war had transformed anticipation of territorial gains into reality, waiting only for the conclusion of hostilities and formal ratification in the treaty of peace. California, which unbeknown to Congress had already been virtually conquered by American arms the previous August, was fully pacified by mid-January 1847. Independence Day of that year, celebrated with the pomp of a grand parade of the state delegations in Chicago, was observed in Los Angeles for the first time by the United States Army of Occupation with more limited but equally appropriate ceremonies. August 1846 also saw the conquest of Santa Fe and the establishment of a provisional government in New Mexico to cover the interior Southwest below the Arkansas River. The war had virtually ceased in northern Mexico after Zachary Taylor's victory at Buena Vista in February and General Scott was posed eighty miles from Mexico City awaiting reinforcements before launching his final offensive.

War and conquest may have dominated public attention in the intervening year, but, in light of the purposes of the conference, a number of other significant events had occurred. Iowa had taken her place in the Union as the first free state west of the Mississippi. The Mormons had begun the settlement of Utah. Railroad construction, which had slowed to a virtual standstill in the depression years of the early 1840s, was picking up again. Just days earlier, Congress had authorized the issuance of the first postage stamps, revolutionizing the nation's mail service. At the same time, that body had turned Samuel Morse's experimental telegraph line, built with federal funds, over to private enterprise in a policy decision of far-reaching consequences for the course of the industrial revolution in the United States and the struggle between Northern and Southern systems of economic organization.

Federal subsidies for transatlantic steamers were inaugurated so that regular steamship service across the ocean could begin at a time when the floodgates of Europe were ready to open. Although immigration had been climbing steadily since 1820, the number of new immigrants to reach the United States in one year passed the 150,000 mark for the first time in 1846. By the end of 1847, a new annual record of 234,968 would signify the arrival of the era of mass migration across the Atlantic.

The United States Supreme Court had held, in the License Cases, that the states had the power to levy a tax on interstate commerce for purposes of regulation (in this case, of liquor) altering numerous traditional doctrines in one fell swoop. The Court "clarified" John Marshall's great interstate commerce decisions to endorse the notion of state police powers as a counterbalance to federal power to regulate commerce. Going beyond Marshall, it magnified the rights of the states to regulate manufacturing within their boundaries, even if the product being regulated was manufactured elsewhere, and confirmed the power of the states to regulate for purposes of morality. This offered new incentives to utopian reformers with their various nostrums for human improvement to enter the political arena. One immediate consequence of this decision was the temporary spread of Prohibition legislation throughout New England and the Northwest — the first, albeit short-lived, triumph for one set of perfectionists.

McCormick reapers began finding their way westward to join the ever growing parade of agricultural machinery that enabled free labor to tame the prairies. The first reaper plant was opened in Chicago in 1847. Back east, that same year, the first steam power textile mills were opened in Salem and New Bedford, Massachusetts, ending industry's dependence on water power. Other new inventions patented or revealed during that year included the sewing machine and the rotary press. The doors of the Smithsonian Institution were opened, giving the federal government an instrument with which to keep pace with the accelerating advance of science.

At that moment of great change, the deliberations of the conference, even more than the remarks made in Congress, presented the Northern alternative to Calhoun's theory of the Constitution. This alternative was embodied in the conference's resolutions which, though directed specifically to the issue of harbor improvements, were couched in terms capable of the broadest construction:

> The Constitution of the United States framed by practical men, for practical purposes, declared in its preamble, "To provide for the common defence, to promote the general welfare, and to secure the blessings of liberty"; and was mainly designed to create a government whose functions should and would be adequate to the protection of all states, or of two or more of them, which could not be maintained by the action of the separated States.

Continuing to spell out the meaning of this in relation to internal improvements, the resolutions pointed out that, as the federal government had been endowed with what amounted to exclusive power to raise revenues from commerce, it was equally obligated to utilize those revenues for the benefit of the states which had surrendered their right to collect them. Citing the many examples of federal action in this field in the past, the conference concluded that, "by a series of acts which have received the sanction of the people of the United States, and of every department of the Federal Government, under all administrations, [the understanding that the Constitution includes this power] has become as much a part of that instrument as any one of its most explicit provisions."

Of special significance about the conference, however, was not its espousal of broad constructionist principles (which would not clearly become dominant for two more generations), but the advance of its participants, albeit informally, into the new world of the new technology. On the afternoon of July 7, after completing its deliberations on rivers and harbors, the conference formally adjourned and then immediately reconvened as a committee of the whole under the chairmanship of Horace Greeley. Greeley yielded the floor to William Mosely Hall of Buffalo, New York, the originator of the idea for the conference, who proceeded to lay before the delegates a grand scheme for the construction of a railroad from the Missouri River to the Pacific, from the westernmost limits of the states then constituted to the end of the newly acquired federal territory.

Hall's suggestion was not new, even in 1847. As he himself said, "The thought was the natural and inevitable sequence to the progress of steam...." His words were important, however, because he relied upon the technical information made available in the early 1840s by the army exploration parties sent westward. They were prophetic because he foresaw the commencement of operations at the Missouri, the ultimate utilization of South Pass in what is now Wyoming to cross the Rockies, the development of a great port at San Francisco, and the desire of Westerners to emancipate themselves economically from the East. There was no argument offered against the northern route he proposed, which, like everything else endorsed by the delegates, would serve to reinforce the North's ties with the greater West and its hegemony in the Union.

The terms of the conference's unhesitating endorsement of his proposal were also prophetic. Their tone transcended economic interest to express a larger goal more in keeping with the delegates' mood. The conference called for a nationally owned line to be constructed through the cooperative efforts of the federal and state governments, believing that a nationally owned line, properly administered "would perform the highest achievement of Republican philanthropy, by elevating labor to its true importance in the social scale" as well as stimulate an unprecedented expansion of commerce:

> The national plan...will guarantee the soil...and preserve it for the homestead of the settler; it will recognize its honorable workers as men and not as serfs; and it will pay them in honest coin and in unshackled land instead of round jackets, shoes, and "orders" upon huge corporation groceries. It will not establish monopolizing foundries to crush out the hopes of individual enterprise, nor will it condemn the land to waste through the continual transfers of infesting land-companies; but it will draw in upon the rich and yielding soil, thousands and tens of thousands of enterprising emigrants whose unfettered competitions will challenge its generous bosom to production, make solitude vocal with songs of contented labor, and confer upon the rising West a class of free, intelligent, and substantial husbandmen, who will be the chief pride and chief dependence of the country.

Adopting Hall's resolutions as its last act, the convention permanently disbanded. The majority of its proposals were to find their way into the Republican party platform eight years later.

The Technological Revolution and Its Yankee Progenitors

The men who led the Chicago conference — politicians, promoters, and entrepreneurs alike — knew that in earlier years the federal government had actively participated in the financing and construction of needed roads and canals and in the improvement of rivers and harbors and had been expanding the scope of its activity until Andrew Jackson was elevated to the presidency. Jackson, seeking only to impose some limits on the federal government's role by excluding direct federal action to purely local projects, had, intentionally or not, convinced his hard core supporters that any federal role was unconstitutional. The new Jacksonian orthodoxy was reinforced by the panic of 1837, the economic hard times which followed it, and the resulting collapse of so many overextended state banks and internal improvement projects. Money was tight, the federal surplus which offered the possibility for such aid disappeared, and the states lost what in a later age came to be called credibility.

With the disappearance of neomercantilism and the use of laissez-faire, the idea of intergovernmental sharing as normal gave way to a new doctrine of dual federalism whereby federal and state activities were viewed as moving most appropriately in separate orbits. Perhaps William Henry Harrison, who was elected to the presidency in 1840 as a Whig on a traditional Whig platform, would have changed course, but his death after one month in office and the accession of Vice President John Tyler, who was really a Democrat, ended that possibility. Between 1837 and 1846, the federal role in internal improvements had been diminished as old federal-aided projects were completed and no new starts were authorized.

As the federal role diminished, so did that of the states. This was partly because many of the same Jacksonians who felt federal aid was unconstitutional also supported the laissez-faire notion that even state activity should be kept to a minimum. While they would normally have been hard put to win support for that position, the panic of 1837 and the resultant depression made it difficult for states to undertake large scale projects of any sort. Indeed, most of the states had been caught financially overextended in the midst of grandiose internal improvement schemes when the panic struck and had yet to recover from the blow.

Paradoxically, while government activity in the realm of internal improvement was tapering off, the United States crossed the threshold of industrialization and irrevocably embarked on the long road toward the creation of an urban industrial society. By the time of Jackson's inauguration, lower New England had become an industrial center. During his administration, skilled Yankees were actively inventing the tools which would transform the nation's technology within a generation. Between 1816 and 1846, the beginnings of industrialization had been obscured by the rise of the West in national politics and the continued concern of the nation as a whole with the extension of American authority across the continent. It was not until after the Mexican War that settlement of the West would come to depend upon processes, techniques, and products of the new technology — especially rails, farm implements, and mining equipment — that accompanied industrialization. However, by the mid-1840s, the first of these were already becoming important as aids in taming the country.

Agriculture was the first to benefit from the new technology. The key to that new technology was a rapid advance in the invention and adoption of new farm implements. Scientific agriculture, which had been gaining momentum for some twenty years, began to extend its concern with better farming methods to include encouragement of better farm technology as well. In the two decades before the Civil War, agriculture was to advance farther than it had in six or eight millennia, just by changing its tools. The cast iron plow no sooner replaced the wooden moldboard plow (1825-1840) when it, in turn, was replaced by the steel plow. By 1845, the latter was standard equipment on the prairies. The mechanical reaper came into use in the East around 1846 and in the West about two years later. Within half a generation it would replace the cradle (which, in turn, had been introduced to replace the sickle as recently as 1820). A practical mowing machine was patented in 1844 and the binder was invented in 1850. The use of such machines as well as others for threshing and haying became widespread between 1845 and 1860.

The use of machinery greatly increased American agricultural production. Between 1850 and 1860, the number of bushels of wheat and corn produced in the old Northwest at least doubled, as did the number of bales of cotton produced in the South. Overseas markets became even more important as outlets for this torrent of produce. Grain handling procedures improved at the same time.

The first grain elevator was opened in Buffalo in 1844, and many others soon followed, to cope with the increases in yield and the continued expansion of land under cultivation. With all of agriculture's progress, the greatest benefits of the new technology were reserved for industry. By mid-century steam power was just coming into common use. This revolution in the energy source of both manufacturing and transportation led to a number of secondary revolutions. During the 1840s, power weaving replaced hand weaving in New England wool manufactures. Steam power was introduced in Massachusetts textile mills in 1847, ending the need to rely on water power. The iron industry was transformed in the same period, substituting coal for charcoal as its basic fuel, replacing the open forge with a revolutionary-type closed furnace, developing new methods for iron refining and rolling and the production of pig iron, and changing to steam power as an energy source. The vulcanization process for working with rubber, developed in 1838, was patented in 1844, the same year the first telegraph message was sent.

Mass production of machine shop products expanded radically in the 1840s, particularly in the farm implement field. Production of farm implements initiated the process of industrialization in the old Northwest. In the Northeast, the manufacture of home appliances such as sewing machines, stoves, and clocks became commonplace. The production of the rotary printing press, beginning in 1846, made the daily newspaper a household item in the newly industrializing cities. By the end of the decade, the manufacture of machine tools was emerging as a separate industry. At the same time, household manufacturing, which had reached a peak in 1830, began an accelerated decline after 1840.

The technological revolution was not confined to the means of production. In true American fashion, the fruits of the new technology were quickly applied to improving man's creature comforts. The first private bath was introduced in a New York hotel in 1844. Two years later, the Eastern Exchange Hotel of Boston became the first public building to be heated with steam. Chewing gum was first marketed commercially in 1848 and the safety pin was patented in 1849. Even a rudimentary air conditioning system was developed and installed in a Broadway theater in 1848.

By the late 1840s, railroads had ceased to be novelties and were rapidly becoming the cornerstones of the American transportation system. The early short line roads, most of which were severely hurt in the depression that followed the panic of 1837, began to link their tracks with one another and then to merge their operations as well. After a virtual moratorium on construction, track began to be laid with great rapidity, assisted in part by technological improvements in railroad construction. The first rolled iron track was produced in 1845. At that time, the United States had something less than 4,000 miles of railroad. In the next fifteen years, some 28,000 miles of track were added, a sevenfold increase. By 1853, the Atlantic coast was connected with Chicago by rail. A year later continuous track extended to the Mississippi River and by 1856 rails reached the Missouri.

Railroad construction both stimulated and profited from a financial revolution in the United States. The first railroad boom of the early 1830s had attracted many European investors. Its collapse in 1837 had burned them badly. They were slow to renew their interest and, by the time business conditions had improved sufficiently to attract them back, American capital was more readily available. The discovery of gold in California in 1848, followed as it was by fifty years of intensive exploitation of America's gold and silver resources, did its share to transform the United States from a "have not" to a "have" country. After 1848 America was far less dependent upon Europe for capital investment than heretofore, and although European capitalists supplied a respectable share of the funds for railroad building in the 1850s, the work was clearly an American enterprise.

The availability of American capital in large amounts signified the emergence of a new group of very rich families whose fortunes were built on the exploitation of the new technology rather than on trade or land in the old pattern. As a general rule, these families had yet to emerge as an upper class or to be admitted into existing socially prominent circles. Consequently, they had to use their wealth to advance their status aspirations in new ways. Within the next several decades, they were to promote the patterns of conspicuous consumption later associated with new wealth, in direct violation of earlier upper class mores. Their impact on American politics was to be a curious one.

The hand of the Yankee was as evident in the technological revolution as it was in the abolitionist movement. Virtually every major American invention of the 1830s, 1840s, and 1850s was a New England product or the brainchild of a displaced Yankee working elsewhere. The great new business and manufacturing corporations that translated those inventions into usable products were created and led by Yankees or descendants of Yankees in similar proportions. Other Yankees were actively creating a new national culture around Boston. Others were busy establishing a greater New England in the upper Mississippi Valley; still others were spreading the gospel of reform from state to state, while some were preaching new revelations from the Atlantic to the Rockies. All in all, it seemed as if the descendants of the Puritans were out to remake the whole United States in their image. In the face of this "aggression" (no less potent because it was often unwitting), the Southerners recoiled in fear and determined to hang on to their power in Washington at all costs — or dissolve the compact.

Enter the Age of Organizations

Much of the secret of the Yankees' growing power could be found in another aspect of their new technology, the technique of organization as a means of mobilizing and managing power. The emergence of organized abolitionism was no more than one reflection of the uses of this new technique. It marked the coming of a new age, an age in which society was to become infinitely more complex and in which men would have to form large organizations in order to achieve mastery over their environment. While the trend toward the organization society can be traced back to the previous century, it was not until the mid-1840s — when the environment began to demand that technique in earnest — that it accelerated sufficiently to form a pattern.

Private, voluntary associations are products of the modern world, possible only in societies in which men are free to combine as they will for their own purposes. In America, the first organizations other than those usually reckoned among the pillars of society — the church, the army, the university, and the state corporation — emerged in the last quarter of the eighteenth century. They were of two kinds. General interest associations such as the two political parties, a few college fraternities, and veterans' groups like the Society of Cincinnatus were the first to become national in scope while remaining quite rudimentary in structure. The special interest associations, on the other hand, developed more formally. The first of these were primarily local societies devoted to the arts and sciences, the promotion of culture, and the preservation of historical records. While many of these boasted impressive names implying broad constituencies — for example, the American Philosophical Society (Philadelphia) and the American

Academy of Arts and Sciences (Boston) — they remained primarily local institutions.

The first of the special interest organizations that were truly nationwide in character were the interdenominational religious societies developed between 1810 and 1824 to spread the gospel in a country that separated church and state while sending its people out to the farthest frontiers, away from the normal influences of organized religion. Organizations such as the American Bible Society (1816) and the American Sunday School Union (1824) were formed by the association of a number of local societies, either through merger or federation, to serve established and newly settled areas alike by mobilizing resources from all corners of the nation. These organizations devised the felicitous system of combining local groups into nationwide associations of every stripe in years to come, often by using the same federal principles applied in the governmental sphere.

While state and local religious organizations were joining together in national union, other state and local societies dedicated to the causes of reform were beginning to emerge, particularly in New England. As early as 1775, Benjamin Franklin, a transplanted Yankee, helped organize an abolitionist society in Philadelphia and, in 1789, 200 farmers of Litchfield, Connecticut, organized the nation's first temperance society. It was not until the second decade of the nineteenth century, however, that organized reform really began to take hold with the emergence of the Connecticut Moral Society (1810) which united the Protestant clergymen of the state in efforts to reform the "Sabbath-breakers, rumselling, tippling folk, infidels, and ruff-scrufs"; the Boston Society for Moral and Religious Instruction of the Poor (1815); and the Peace Society of Massachusetts (1816).

In its early days, the line between religious and reform organizations was thin indeed. One was considered a function of the other and men of the cloth were instrumental in founding both. Even later, when the religious aspects of reform were no longer quite as visible and their leadership drawn from other ranks, it was generally the religious impulse that stimulated even ostensibly secular reformers.

The first national reform organization was the American Temperance Society founded by a Baptist minister in 1826. By 1840, three more national reform organizations had been established: the American Peace Society (1828), the American Antislavery Society (1833), and the American Moral Reform Society

(c. 1837). Each of these represented a natural outgrowth of earlier trends brought about through federation of state and local societies to campaign for common ends throughout the nation.

Though the corporation was another form of organization produced by the modern world, until the Jacksonian era corporate organization in the United States remained quasi-governmental in the mercantilist tradition. The number of corporations was severely limited by the necessity for each to acquire a special government charter. Most of the corporations that were chartered were established to serve public purposes such as banking and the construction of canals and turnpikes. Many were joint stock companies involving partial government ownership. Each charter granted was, in effect, the extension of special privilege to a favored group.

The simultaneous rise of manufacturing and spread of laissez-faire ideas led to the rapid expansion of the number of enterprises seeking corporate charters from the states. This not only placed exorbitant demands on the time of legislatures but involved the granting of corporate status for radically new purposes. The new corporations were no longer created to specifically serve public purposes but were designed to compete with one another for public favor. Consequently, government grants of special privilege in this manner became highly discriminatory while the creation of corporations by the dozen made the public functions of the charter system meaningless.

The solution was to change the status of corporations in the law to more closely resemble their new status in society. From quasi-governments their status was slowly redefined as that of quasi-persons entitled to the same freedoms granted real persons in a free society. While two generations were required for the full development of this concept of the corporation as a person, one preliminary step could be — and had to be — taken immediately. Beginning with Connecticut in 1836, the states enacted general incorporation laws, establishing procedures whereby any group of qualified people could organize a corporation by complying with specified administrative procedures without requiring special legislative action. This was a major reform that immediately had profound effects on the American economic system. By the late 1840s, the reorganization of the American economy along corporate lines was virtually certain. The new corporations had already begun to grow in wealth and power. And because they were immortal, they could accumulate strength beyond the wildest dreams of any individuals.

While banking and manufacturing corporations were among the first to take advantage of the new laws, the first great corporate structures were those organized to construct and operate railroads. The earliest of these had been organized under special charters and with favored status prior to the enactment of general incorporation laws. Actually the railroads, because of their quasi-monopolistic character, were never entirely emancipated from their quasi-public obligations, nor were they ever fully denied a privileged position in the halls of government. Later the anomalous situation of the free incorporation of railroad companies in a field where the market was limited led to great struggles among the various companies for government favors and for the same markets, to bankruptcies resulting from wasteful competition, and, beyond that, to public demands for government regulation.

The years before 1846 were ones of experiment in the new world of railroading. The only one of the later railroad giants incorporated before 1846 was the Baltimore and Ohio, the recipient of a special charter from the Maryland legislature in 1828. Even so, its major construction efforts were to come after 1848. Many of the smaller railroads incorporated between 1826 and 1846 were to build short lines that would later be absorbed into larger systems, but the larger systems themselves did not emerge until after the Mexican War. Between 1846 and 1855, however, the Pennsylvania; Gulf, Mobile, and Ohio; Burlington; Missouri Pacific; Illinois Central; New York Central; Delaware, Lackawanna; Louisville and Nashville; Erie; and Rock Island railroads were created and all completed substantial sections of their routes.

In the 1840s, the organization of American society took a new turn with the emergence of state and national professional societies. This development was a reasonable consequence of the nation's growing complexity and its growing need for trained specialists in a variety of fields. Among the first to organize were representatives of older callings who were seeking to impose new standards of professional training and conduct upon those admitted to professional participation. The American Society of Dental Surgeons was the first, in 1840. The American Medical Association was organized in 1847 by representatives of all the national medical societies and schools. In 1852, the American Pharmaceutical Association and the American Society of

Engineers and Architects (now the American Society of Civil Engineers) were founded.

These transition years also witnessed the rapid growth of new professions whose members sought to combine for mutual support and encouragement. The first of these to organize was the Association of Medical Superintendents of American Institutes for the Insane (1844), later to become the more happily-named American Psychiatric Association. Within a decade the educators and librarians had organized in the states and nationally as well.

The 1840s witnessed a great expansion of organization among workingmen. Labor organizations became widespread at roughly the same time as the competitive corporations, though they were not to develop equal power for a century. Until the early 1840s, labor unions were generally considered unlawful combinations and illegal conspiracies under the common law. Under the influence of Chief Justice Lemuel Shaw, one of the nation's great jurists who was responsible for reshaping much of American law to meet new conditions during these transition years, the Massachusetts Supreme Court held trade unions to be legitimate means for workers to use in an effort to improve their lot, opening the doors to similar decisions in other states and to the rapid spread of unionization.

In the early Jacksonian period labor reformers had turned to the formation of labor parties in an effort to achieve their goals. Perhaps the opening of organizational opportunities helped move them away from that route in the 1840s. Perhaps it was a realization of the weaknesses of third party movements in the context of American politics. In any case, by 1845, organized labor in America had opted for the use of pressure techniques against the regular parties as a means of achieving their goals, rather than separate appeals to the electorate.

That same year, the first broad-gauged national labor and reform organization to survive beyond its birth was established. The Industrial Congress of the United States combined local congresses of labor, reform, and cooperative groups throughout the country. It was to survive for eleven years. By the early 1850s, local craft unions were uniting into national organizations such as the National Typographical Union (1852), the Hat Finishers (1854), the Journeyman Stone Cutters Association (1855), and the United Cigar Makers (1856). Only the stronger unions survived the panic of 1857, but the pattern of organization remained intact to be revived later on a larger scale.

The spread of the organization society was felt in every field of national endeavor. The American Association for the Advancement of Science was founded in 1846, the same year as the Smithsonian Institution. The two of them plus the revitalized United States Coast Survey (reorganized in 1842), the Naval Observatory, and the increasingly scientific-oriented Topographical Engineer Corps formed a new base of national support for organized scientific activity in cooperation with the universities and the emerging state scientific surveys. The nation's newspapers organized the Associated Press in 1848 to serve as a cooperative news gathering agency. The newly arrived German immigrants (who contributed greatly to the spread of organization in the United States) organized a national network of turnvereinen to provide organized sports and recreation activities.

Many of these "national" organizations were, in fact, Northern only, not by design, but because of the differences between the two sections and the growing gap between them. Nevertheless, even the Southerners, the Americans most resistant to the new organized life, felt compelled to organize the Southern Rights Association in 1850 to fight the abolitionist movement. Its existence added to the gap.

The political parties were among the first to embrace the new mechanisms and techniques of organization, first in the states, but increasingly in the national arena as well. Until the late 1820s, the American parties, like other institutions in American society, were built around traditional ties between persons and families. In the older parts of the country, these ties were based on the existence of elites well entrenched in their respective social systems. Along the frontier, then in the eastern Mississippi Valley, similar ties were being forged by an element attempting to establish the same kinds of social patterns in their respective states and communities.

The political system of Connecticut, for example, was dominated by an oligarchy of merchant aristocrats from old Puritan families tied together by personal friendship and family intermarriage among "social equals." Similarly, in Virginia, the masters of the great plantations and their relatives, men even more aristocratic in their self-perceptions, had forged a powerful ruling elite whose members were united or divided politically by bonds of family that could be traced back to the early eighteenth if not to the seventeenth century. In a new state like Mississippi where the frontier was being conquered by the plantation system highly conducive to the development of a ruling elite, a class of parvenu "aristocrats" was in the process of assuming similar powers. Even in a state like Illinois — a part of the new West of small landholders with no plantation system to support oligarchic government — one political faction, representing the largely Southern gentry who had obtained positions in the territorial government from the "Virginia Dynasty" entrenched in Washington before 1824, competed with another faction consisting of "new men" who did not have the proper family connections in Washington to see who would have the inside track in the creation of a new elite in the new land.

The coming of Jacksonian democracy with its expansion of the suffrage and of the basis of political participation was to put an end to these traditional modes of political power-holding in most states and in the nation as a whole and to replace them with new ones more suitable to mass democracy. It is now known that the real innovation of the Jacksonians was not so much the expansion of the franchise — the theoretical power to participate in public affairs — but the creation of mechanisms that allowed democratic participation on the part of an existing mass electorate. The foremost of these was the application of modern organizational techniques to the political process. Thus, the Jacksonian revolution, which was not the province of the supporters of Jackson alone, was really a revolution in organization.

It should not be surprising that the first successful application of new organizational principles to partisan politics came in New York State, already the center of the drive towards the organizational society. During the 1820s, politics in New York was increasingly removed from the hands of older gentry and placed into the hands of new managers — professional politicians who knew how to organize people for political purposes and how to control the organizations they created. In the 1840s, the New York approach, or some variation of it, spread to states and communities throughout the country.

Though not every state followed New York's lead, some states in every section embraced the new system. Least successful in the South where the socioeconomic system worked against removal of political power from the hands of the gentry except in the few urban centers, organized politics became the dominant form in the middle states from New York through Illinois. Professional politicians came to the fore in those states by the early 1840s, either driving out the gentry or co-opting them into the new politics. After

1848, "amateurs" had virtually disappeared from political office in those states.

New England, on the other hand, and to a lesser extent its western colonies, embraced the principles of party organization but insisted on maintaining descendants of the old elites in their former leadership capacities. By doing so, the door was left open to "amateur" participation and the new professionals had to share the stage and its rewards. Amateurs in greater New England were able to make the transition to organized politics because they were Yankees and sympathetic to the uses of organization. Still, after 1848, the political doors of old New England were also open, albeit unwillingly, to newcomers including the Irish who found the new political situation well suited to their taste.

From a strictly political perspective, these new-style parties were organized first in those states and localities where electoral competition was greatest and developed more slowly, if at all, where one party dominated the polls. But electoral competition itself was merely an expression of these other factors. The same states most affected by the urban industrial frontier also developed the most heterogeneous populations, generating the most in political competition and necessitating greater political organization. Where old elites were unchallenged, there was little need to change.

The transition in national politics from traditionalistic to organizational behavior was also apparent by 1848. Presidential elections through Andrew Jackson's first term were characterized by the nomination of candidates by small coteries of national leaders bound together by common service in Washington. By Jackson's second term, the national party convention had emerged and, though it was not to achieve its full flowering until 1840, presidential nominations were already being determined by the leaders of the state party organizations acting in concert.

Congress, which had served as a natural home for the gentry system, was reduced to virtual impotence as a body in the dictation of presidential nominees. Equally significant was the change in the selection of members of that body. Whereas in the first generation and a half of the republic men had been powerful at home because they served in Congress, now men went to Congress because they were powerful at home.

In 1848, the Democrats took the next step along the road toward the development of nationally organized parties by creating a national committee to function between conventions. This was the first such national political body and while its powers were severely limited, it did provide some means for the exchange of information among state Democratic organizations in an effort to better cope with the new mass electorate.

The Opening of the Urban Frontier

In the pre-Civil War period, the consequences of the organization society were yet to be widely felt outside of the political realm. It was a period of emergence and growth, even of promise, with impacts as yet unforeseen. Impacts were already being felt, however, in the patterns of American settlement.

The combination of technological advance into a period of industrialization and the expansion of organizational techniques was reflected in growing urbanization. Whereas the 1840 census indicated that it had required thirty years for the percentage of city dwellers in the United States to increase by one-half (from 7.3 percent to 10.8 percent), it took only ten more years for it to increase by one-half again (to 15.3 percent in 1850). In percentages, the increase between 1840 and 1850 was almost equal to the full increase between 1790 and 1840, and in absolute figures it was greater. Furthermore, whereas the average decennial increase in the percentage of urban population before 1840 was between one and two percent, the average since 1840 remained almost constant at five percent for the next century. By 1850, one-third of the nation's urbanized population lived in cities of 100,000 or more, as compared to one-sixth three decades earlier. The former figure is much closer to the two-fifths mark achieved a decade later which has held relatively steady for over a century.

By 1850, the nation had 236 urban places (population in excess of 2,500), which was an increase of over 100 from the previous decade and was nearly ten times the number in existence in 1790. Whereas there were only thirty-seven cities of more than 10,000 population in 1840, by 1850 there were sixty-two, six of which had over 100,000 people. New York, the nation's largest city, had a population of 515,547. The changing regional patterns of urbanization were even more revealing. Up through 1820, the North and the South each had approximately the same number of cities of over 10,000 population. By 1830, however, the North had twice as many as the South, a ratio which held for better than a decade. Between 1840 and 1850, the number grew to four and a half times as many.

In the latter year, five of the nine cities over 50,000 population were in the Northeast, two were Southern and two were in the West.

The rise of the Western city was an important phenomenon between 1840 and 1850. In 1840, there were only two Western cities of over 10,000 population. By 1850, there were ten. Urbanization was becoming something more than an Eastern phenomenon. After 1845, the West would be settled directly by urbanites as well as by farmers.

The years 1846 to 1848 fell right in the middle of the "heroic age" for the foundation of American cities. Thirty-nine of the fifty largest cities of today were incorporated in the two generations on either side of the watershed, fourteen within an eleven year span cutting across its heart. All told, twenty-seven of the fifty were incorporated after 1845, as well as the overwhelming majority of the nation's smaller cities. The links between the new industrial city and the new East that could only be tamed by its products were to be forged between 1846 and 1861 to the point where they could not be torn asunder by the constitutional theories or political predilections of any group.

Bibliographic Notes — Chapter 2

For the role of government in the economy, see Lance E. Davis and John Legler, "Government and the American Economy, 1815-1902," *General Economic History* 26 (1966): 514; Carter Goodrich, *Government Promotion of Canals and Railroads, 1800-1890* (1960); W.F. Gebhardt, *Transportation and Industrial Development in the Middle West* (1900); Forrest G. Hill, *Roads, Rails and Waterways: Army Engineers and Transportation* (1957).

For a description of the 1847 Chicago Rivers and Harbors Congress, see *Chicago Rivers and Harbors Congress of 1847* (1899).

The license cases are discussed by Felix Frankfurter in *The Commerce Clause under Marshall, Taney and Waite* (1937); Gerald Garbey, "The Constitutional Revolution of 1837 and the Myth of Marshall's Monolity," *Western Political Quarterly* 18 (1965): 27; R. Kent Newmyer, *The Supreme Court Under Marshall and Taney* (1968).

For a review of constitutional law and the courts in this period, see John H. Schmidthauser, "Judicial Behavior in the Sectional Crisis of 1837-1860," *Journal of Politics* 23 (1961): 615.

On technology and its impact, see Stuart Chase, *Men and Machines* (1929); Leo Marx, *The Machine in the Garden: Technology and the Pastoral Idea* (1964); Hugo M. Meier, "Technology and Democracy, 1800-1860," *Mississippi Valley Historical Review* 43 (1967): 618; and "Technology in the 19th Century World," *American Quarterly* 10 (1958): 116; John W. Oliver, *History of American Technology* (1956); Roger Burlingame, *March of the Iron Men* (1939); Grace R. Cooper, *The Invention of the Sewing Machine* (1968); James T. Flexner, *Steamboats Come True* (1944); I.B. McCallum and Frances T. McCallum, *The Wire that Fenced the West* (1965); Edward C. Kendall, *John Deere's Steel Plow* (1959); Hope W. Kohlmeyer and Floyd L. Herum, "Science in Engineering and Agriculture," *Technology and Culture* 2 (1961): 368; Alan G. Bogue, *From Prairie to Cornbelt: Farming on the Illinois and Iowa Prairies in the 19th Century* (1963).

On John Tyler, see Oliver P. Chitwood, *John Tyler* (1969); and Wyham G. Tyler, *Letters and Times of the Tylers*, 3 vols. (1884-1896).

The treatment of New Englanders and their descendants as a distinctive Yankee ethnic group is relatively new. The thesis is presented by Steward A. Holbrook in *Yankee Exodus*; Ellsworth Huntington in *Mainsprings of Civilization* (1972); and Daniel J. Elazar in *Cities of the Prairie*. It has subsequently been incorporated into the *Harvard Encyclopedia of American Ethnic Groups* (1982). Every one of the studies cited here offers evidence as to the accuracy of the thesis.

On the age of organization, see Murray M. Hausknecht, *A Study of*

The Nation Turns Toward New Frontiers

Voluntary Associations in the United States (1962); Arthur M. Schlesinger, "Biography of a Nation of Joiners," in *Paths to the Present* (1948); Anton-Hermann Chroust, *The Rise of the Legal Profession*, 2 vols. (1965); Charles Warren, *A History of the American Bar* (1911); Daniel H. Calhoun, *Professional Lives in America, 1750-1850* (1965); Kenneth S. Lynn, et al., eds., *The Professions in America* (1965).

The organization of science in this period is explored in Bernard I. Cohen, "Science in America during the Nineteenth Century," *National Academy of Sciences Proceedings* 45 (1959): 666; James B. Conant, "Knowledge in the Nineteenth Century," *Colorado Quarterly* 11 (1963): 229; E.S. Dana, *Century of Science in America* (1918); George H. Daniels, *American Science in the Age of Jackson* (1968); A. Hunter Dupree, *Science and the Emergence of Modern America, 1865-1916* (1963); Thomas C. Johnson, Jr., *Scientific Interests in the Old South* (1936); Nathan Reingold, ed., *Science in Nineteenth-Century America: Documentary* (1964); Dirk J. Struik, *Yankee Science in the Making*, rev. ed. (1962); David D. Van Tassel and Michael G. Hall, eds., *Science and Society in the United States* (1966); Ralph S. Bates, *Scientific Societies in the United States*, 3rd ed. (1965); Whitfield J. Bell, Jr., "American Philosophical Society as a National Academy of Sciences," *10th International Congress of Historical Sciences Proceedings* 1 (1964): 165; John K. Wright, *Geography in the Making: American Geographical Society, 1851-1951* (1952); Harry R. Skallerup, "Bibliography of the Histories of the American Academies of Science," *Kansas Academy of Science Transactions* 66 (1963): 274; Edwin G. Conglin, "History of the American Philosophical Society," *American Philosophical Society Yearbook* (1966): 37; A. Hunter Dupree, "The Founding of the National Academy of Sciences," *American Philosophical Society Proceedings* 101 (1957): 434; W.J. Reese, ed., *The Smithsonian Institution: Documents, 1835-1889* (1901); John K. Wright, *Geography in the Making: The American Geographical Society, 1851-1951* (1952).

On the medical profession, see James G. Burrow, *AMA: Voice of American Medicine* (1963); Joseph S. Kett, *Formation of the American Medical Profession: 1780-1860* (1968); Donald E. Konold, *History of American Medical Ethics, 1847-1912* (1962); and Richard H. Shryock, *Medical Licensing in America, 1650-1965* (1967). The engineering profession is treated in Daniel H. Calhoun, *The American Civil Engineer* (1960); Monte A. Calvert, *Mechanical Engineer in America, 1830-1910* (1967); Raymond H. Merritt, *Engineering in American Society, 1850-1875* (1969); Charles B. Stuart, *Lives and Works of Civil and Military Engineers of America* (1971); Leonard B. White, *The Jacksonians' Administrative History, 1829-1861* (1954); Glyndon G. Van Dusen, *The Jacksonian Era, 1828-1848* (1959). Unfortunately,

Building Toward Civil War

relatively little has been written about the development of the organizational society in the United States in this period; thus it is only possible to refer to general works or to studies of specific professions and societies, some of which are cited below. Bernard I. Cohen, "Science in America During the Nineteenth Century," *National Academy of Sciences Proceedings* 45 (1959): 666; James B. Conant, "Knowledge in the Nineteenth Century," *Colorado Quarterly* 11 (1963): 229; E.S. Dana, *Century of Science in America* (1918); George H. Daniels, *American Science in the Age of Jackson* (1968); A. Hunter Dupree, ed., *Science and the Emergence of Modern America, 1865-1916* (1963); Thomas C. Johnson, Jr. *Scientific Interests in the Old South* (1936); Nathan Reingold, ed., *Science in Nineteenth-Century America: Documentary* (1964); Dirk J. Struik, *Yankee Science in the Making*, rev. ed. (1962); David D. Van Tassel and Michael G. Hall, eds., *Science and Society in the United States* (1966); Ralph S. Bates, *Scientific Societies in the United States*, 3rd ed. (1965); Whitfield J. Bell, Jr., "American Philosophical Society as a National Academy of Sciences," *10th International Congress of Historical Sciences Proceedings* 1 (1964): 165; John K. Wright, *Geography in the Making: American Geographical Society, 1851-1951* (1952); Harry R. Skallerup, "Bibliography of the Histories of American Academies of Science," *Kansas Academy of Sciences Transactions* 66 (1963): 274; Daniel H. Calhoun, *The American Civil Engineer* (1960); Monte A. Calvert, *Mechanical Engineer in America, 1830-1910* (1967); Raymond H. Merritt, *Engineering in American Society, 1850-1875* (1969); Charles B. Stuart, *Lives and Works of Civil and Military Engineers of America* (1871).

For the development of the modern corporation, see C.C. Abbott, *The Rise of the Business Corporation* (1936); Edwin M. Dodd, *American Business Corporations Until 1860, with Special Reference to Massachusetts* (1954); George E. Evans, *Business and Corporations in the United States, 1800-1845* (1948); Oscar Handlin and Mary F. Handlin, "The Origins of the American Business Corporation," *Journal of Economic History* 5 (1945): 1; Alfred D. Chandler, Jr., *Strategy and Structure: Chapters in the History of Industrial Enterprise* (1962); Gail Hammond, *Banks and Politics in America from the Revolution to the Civil War* (1957); W.J. Schultz and M.R. Caine, *Financial Development of the United States* (1937); Davis R. Duey, *State Banking Before the Civil War* (1910); Frank C. James, *The Growth of Chicago Banks: 1816-1938*, 2 vols. (1938).

Organized labor in the period is treated in Mary Beard, *Short History of American Labor Movement* (1924); Thomas R. Brooks, *Toil and Trouble: A History of American Labor* (1964); John R. Commones, et al., *Documentary History of American Industrial Society*, 10 vols. (1910-1911) and *History of Labor in the United States*, 4 vols.

44

The Nation Turns Toward New Frontiers

(1918-1935); Philip S. Foner, *History of the Labor Movement in the United States*, 3 vols. (1947-1964); Selig Perlman, *A History of Trade Unionism in the United States* (1922); Philip Taft, *Organized Labor in American History* (1964); Walter E. Hugins, *Jacksonian Democracy and the Working Class: A Study of the New York Workingmen's Movement, 1829-1837* (1960); Edward Pessen, *Most Uncommon Jacksonians: The Radical Leaders of the Early Labor Movement* (1967); Norman J. Ware, *The Industrial Worker, 1840-1860: The Reaction of American Industrial Society to the Advance of the Industrial Revolution* (1924).

For studies of changes in the organization of transportation, see George R. Taylor, *The Transportation Revolution, 1815-1860* (1951); Horace B. Conklin and Margaret Conklin, *Butterfield Overland Mail, 1857-1869*, 3 vols. (1947); Edward Hungerford, *Wells Fargo* (1947); Alfred D. Chandler, ed., *The Railroads: Sources* (1965); John F. Stover, *American Railroads* (1961); George R. Taylor, *The Transportation Revolution, 1815-1860* (1951); L.H. Haney, *Congressional History of Railways*, 2 vols. (1908-1910); John B. Sanborn, *Congressional Grants of Land in Aid of Railways* (1899); Robert M. Sutton, "The Origins of American Land Grant Railroad Rates," *Business History Review* 40 (1966); Paul H. Cootner, "Railroads and Economic Growth," *Journal of Economic History* 23 (1966); Albert Fishlow, *American Railroads and the Transformation of the Ante-Bellum Economy* (1965); Robert W. Vogel, *Railroads and Economic Growth* (1964); Alfred D. Chandler, Jr., ed., *The Railroads: Sources and Readings* (1965); George P. Baker, *The Formation of the New England Railroad System: A Study of Railroad Combination in the Nineteenth Century* (1968); C.J. Corliss, *Main Line of Mid-America; The Story of the Illinois Central* (1950); D.M. Ellis, "New York Central and Erie Canal," *New York History* 29 (1948): 268; Edward Hungerford, *Baltimore and Ohio Railroad*, 2 vols. (1928), and *Men and Iron: The New York Central* (1938); E.H. Mott, *Between the Ocean and the Lakes: The Story of Erie* (1901); Harry H. Pierce, *Railroads of New York: Government Aid, 1826-1857* (1953); Merl E. Reed, *New Orleans and the Railroads 1830-1860* (1966); Frank W. Stevens, *Beginnings of the New York Central Railroad* (1926); Charles W. Turner, *Chessie's Road* (1956); Thomas Cochran, *Railroad Leaders, 1845-1890: The Business Mind in Action* (1953); Arthur M. Johnson and Barry E. Supple, *Boston Capitalists and Western Railroads: A Study in the Nineteenth-Century Railroad Investment Process* (1967); Paul H. Cootner, "Railroads in Economic Growth," *Journal of Economic History* 23 (1963): 477; Albert Fishlow, *American Railroads and the Transformation of the Ante-Bellum Economy* (1965).

On the opening of the urban frontier, see Alexander B. Callow, Jr., *American Urban History: An Interpretative Reader with*

Commentaries (1969); Charles N. Glaab, *The American City: Documentary History* (1963), and A. Theodore Brown, *History of Urban America* (1967); Constance M. Green, *American Cities in the Growth of the Nation* (1957), and *Rise of Urban America* (1965); Allan Pred, *Spatial Dynamics of U.S. Urban Growth, 1800-1914* (1970); Arthur M. Schlesinger, *Rise of the City* (1933); George R. Taylor, "American Urban Growth Preceding the Railway Age," *Journal of Economic History* 27 (1967): 309; Ernest S. Griffith, A *History of American City Government*, 3 vols. (1974).

Chapter 3

FROM RIGHTEOUSNESS TO POLITICS

Organizing the Politics of Morality

The increase in public attention and its transformation into political agitation reflected not only the ripeness of the hour but also the emergence of an organized antislavery movement. It was the existence of organizations that made it possible to transfer the inchoate, if willing, feelings of the public, both North and South, into meaningful political action. By 1846, the previously small and essentially nonpolitical abolitionist societies had taken some substantial steps into the political arena.

Organized abolitionism was itself a relatively new phenomenon. Just a decade earlier, the number of abolitionist societies had spurted from perhaps 150 (two-thirds of them in the South) to over 500 (328 new ones were founded between June 1835 and June 1836 alone), stimulated by and loosely held together within the American Antislavery Society (founded in 1833). By June 1837 there were over a thousand societies with approximately 100,000 members. Despite their reluctance to do so, these organizations began to play a political role from the first, just because they applied the kind of pressure that organizations are able to apply within a diffuse and individualized civil society.

The abolitionist movement became the first nationwide pressure group to apply the principles of organization to the advocacy of a cause and to demand public action on behalf of reform. By organizing the submission of petitions to Congress and the distribution of antislavery literature in the South, the organized abolitionists raised the slavery question before the nation's political leadership that was so anxious to avoid it, endowed it with a momentum that belied the essentially apathetic attitude of the general public (which considered abolitionists to be dangerous radicals), and forced both politicians and the public to come to grips with it.

In all this, the role of the Yankees — the New Englanders and their descendants in the new West — must be recognized. As a group they combined within themselves a susceptibility to reform movements with an inclination toward the new spirit of organization abroad in the land at midcentury. While some Yankees were winning fame as reformers, others had become the foremost pioneers of the newly emergent corporation as a device for organizing and managing growing business enterprises. Combining both devices, other Yankees were the first to organize "culture" and to combine for the advancement of science. And they were the first to organize reform.

At first, the Yankees who pioneered in abolitionist organizations were also among those who had least faith in the possibilities of political action to abolish slavery within the framework of the American Constitution. Before 1840, only the extreme radicals from that section of the country had embraced the cause of emancipation and they, like all of their type, had neither the faith nor the patience for sustained action in a political arena where negotiation and compromise were demanded. For them, the moral issue was too strong for such considerations.

By 1839, however, a sharp division appeared in abolitionist ranks between those who wished to continue their activities in a predominantly nonpolitical manner or were willing, at most, to function as a semipolitical pressure group and those who sought a more active political outlet. Though the latter had greater familiarity with the political process, they were hardly more practical than the former. Taking heart from the continued expansion of organized abolitionism (June 1840: approximately 2,000 societies with between 150,000 and 200,000 members), they decided to enter the 1840 presidential contest as a third party. On April 1 of that year, delegates from six states met in Albany, New York, and nominated James G. Birney — a Southern abolitionist of the old school, formerly of Kentucky and Alabama, who had moved northward just a few years earlier to avoid the intensified antiabolitionist pressures in his native section — for the presidency under the banner of the Liberty party.

This first essay into direct partisan action was poorly received. Only 121 people met at Albany and, of them, only 17 were not residents of New York. In the election Birney received 7,159 votes, about one-fourth of one percent of the 2,400,778 votes cast for president that year, even though the party was able to get on the ballot in every Northern state except Indiana.

The Liberty party did accomplish what the Southern efforts in congress could never do; it split the abolitionist movement. The American Antislavery Society divided into three groups, those who entered the Liberty party and advocated partisan action, those who followed William Lloyd Garrison and rejected any association with what they believed to be an immoral political system, and the great bulk in the middle who wished to continue their pressure group activities within the framework of the two party system. As a result of this schism, membership in the society and its affiliates fell from close to a quarter million to less than 60,000, substantially reducing the effectiveness of antislavery efforts in the nation. For a while it appeared that despite its organization, the abolitionists would follow in the footsteps of early abolitionist efforts into oblivion.

This time, however, the existence of the accoutrements of organization, rudimentary as they were, made the difference. Now there were people who devoted their full time to the maintenance of an abolitionist movement. There were chapters and clubs, newspapers and membership lists which they drew upon for support. Even the new party remained in existence despite its weak showing and, in 1844, again submitted Birney's name to the voters.

By that year, the agitation of the abolitionist organizers succeeded in driving a much larger number of abolitionists out of the regular parties. With both the Whigs and the Democrats nominating slaveholders in the persons of Henry Clay and James K. Polk, the hard core abolitionists had no other place to go. Birney received 62,263 votes in twelve states out of a total vote of 2,678,121.

While 2.25 percent of the national electorate still represented a very small minority, the locus of the Liberty party vote proved decisive in determining the outcome of the election. Birney's vote was enough to give the states of New York and Michigan to Polk and the election to the Democrats. Together, Clay and Birney outpolled Polk by over 23,000 votes. Birney polled more than five percent of the total presidential vote in New Hampshire, Vermont, Massachusetts, and Michigan — the Yankee heartland. While not yet even a sectional party but still the party of a cultural region within a section, the Liberty party demonstrated in 1844 that with the electorate so closely divided, even a small antislavery bloc was strong enough to influence even the most national of American elections.

Paradoxically, the very success of the Liberty party discouraged many sincere antislavery activists from taking the third party route to end slavery. Polk's victory led directly to the annexation of slaveholding Texas and to the Mexican War, actions opposed by both the abolitionists and the Whigs. Many thoughtful opponents of slavery were convinced that Henry Clay in office would have made policy decisions more favorable to the antislavery movement in both cases. As a result, they opted for pressure — on governments and within the major parties — rather than third party electoral politics on behalf of their cause, until they had a chance to enter the partisan arena under altered circumstances.

While one wing of the antislavery movement was making itself felt at the polls, to the short range detriment of its cause, the other was gaining a small but pregnant victory in Congress. In 1836, the nation's legislative assembly — still acting negatively — forbade local postmasters from interfering with the United States Mail. Eight years later, after the results of the 1844 election were in, doughty old John Quincy Adams was able to get the gag rule lifted and the full right of petition was restored. The era of negative attention was rapidly coming to an end.

The Moral Polarization of the Nation

The Thirtieth Congress, elected in the fall of 1846, met with its members cognizant of the developing Northern sentiment against the extension of slavery. Northern congressmen undoubtedly had it in mind when they supported the Wilmot Proviso. The Southerners also considered it in shaping their tactics.

Coming from a section where the way of life was as yet untouched by the social and economic changes that promoted organization in the North and the West, the Southerners had consistently misread the situation confronting them during the 1830s and early 1840s. Unable to understand the difference between the organized agitation of a still unpopular minority and earlier pressures against the slave system that drew support from many of the nation's leading figures, they miscalculated the strength of abolitionist activity and launched a massive response that could only heighten the power of Northern antislavery elements and weaken their own position by driving Northern moderates into the antislavery camp. The Nat Turner uprising of 1831 had its effect here, convincing many Southerners of the possibility that radical abolitionists could influence more slaves to rebel against their masters, with frightening and bloody consequences.

It would not be unfair to say that the most important success of organized abolitionism was to goad the South into a series of highly injudicious responses to the actually rather feeble pressures exerted by the antislavery forces. Southerners' efforts to stop the delivery of the mails and to interfere with the accepted right of petition only served, by broadening the issue beyond the slavery question itself, to attract attention in the North where public interest had previously been conspicuously lacking. This is not to say that the ultimate outcome of the slavery struggle would have been different had the South ignored the abolitionist plaints — the worldwide trend toward individual freedom was too powerful to be resisted very long by a nation moving toward world leadership — but the timing and manner of abolition could very likely have been quite different had the Southerners adopted different courses of action at certain critical junctures between 1830 and 1860.

By 1846, however, the Southerners had no other choice as long as they wished to see slavery justified and extended as well as maintained. Until the 1840s most Southerners were content to justify slavery as a necessity. They did not seek to elevate the slave system into a positive good. In the face of repeated attacks from the North, Southerners began to crystallize their own feelings in regard to their unique social institutions. Psychologists would undoubtedly label their response a natural one. Their reaction to the attacks of the abolitionists and the implicit criticism of their way of life by so many Northerners was to become more firmly committed to that way of life, less willing to yield on any point regarding its future, and anxious to demonstrate the validity of their choice by insisting that the slave system be allowed to spread to new territories as a matter of right.

Meanwhile, public reaction to the Wilmot Proviso was delayed in coming. In the fall campaign, the war itself and the tariff issue dominated the scene. The abolitionist movement had reached a low point in public appeal primarily because of the highly visible fanaticism of its adherents, throwing the entire antislavery movement into some disrepute. It was not until the third session of the Twenty-ninth Congress was concluded in the spring of 1847 that the public really took notice of the matter.

With the Mexican War fairly won and the prospect of acquiring the territory in question quite real, the implications of Wilmot's action and the Southern opposition to it became plain. Though nothing had been done to interfere with slavery in the states where it existed, American policy had consistently prevented the extension of slavery into previously free territories (the status of the old Southwest in this regard may be ambiguous but slavery was known there from its first settlement).

Congressional support for the Wilmot Proviso had been based on just this point, one which could unite abolitionists and nonabolitionists alike. Now the Northerners were asking, in effect, for the application of this policy in such a way as to prevent any further spread of slavery. The Southerners, in order to secure any advantage from the war, found themselves forced to ask for a reversal of the policy itself. As a final irony, it had been the Southerners who had led the way into war with Mexico over the opposition of many Northerners, particularly the Yankees. Now the latter stood to gather in the fruits of victory from a war they had opposed.

A measure embodying the Wilmot Proviso passed the House in the spring of 1847, only to fail in the Senate after an extensive and important debate. The debate in the Senate opened the door for aging John Calhoun to restate the Southern position on the slavery question in his four famous resolutions of February 19, 1847. Calhoun's restatement, like Wilmot's amendment, shifted the position of his section to the offensive and set the terms of the debate over slavery and sectionalism that was to occupy Congress in the 1850s. The basic premises of his argument were not new. He had enunciated them repeatedly in his years of public service, earlier applying them to issues ranging from national defense to internal improvement.

Calhoun asserted that all territories under federal control were the joint and common property of the states; that the federal government was merely acting as the agent of the states in their administration; that, as an agent, Congress had no right to deprive the citizens of any state of the same rights they possessed at home if they chose to enter into the territories; that enactment of any law interfering with slavery would be an unconstitutional infringement on the equality of the states within the Union; and that the settlers in any territory had a right to determine for themselves whether their future state would be slave or free since the only restriction imposed upon them by the Constitution was that their government be republican. In presenting these resolutions, Calhoun set out the new Southern line even more firmly, insisting that the federal government had a positive obligation to protect slavery throughout the national domain under the terms of the Constitution, reiterating that the slavery issue rested on that of states' rights because the Constitution was a compact among the several states; restating his theory that recognition of the sections through use of the concurrent majority principles was essential for the maintenance of the Union, particularly since the South was becoming the minority section; and attacking the "aggressive measures" of the North.

Wilmot, in the meantime, had set the terms for public response in his own discussion of the proposal:

> What do we ask?...That free territory shall remain free.... [T]he issue now presented is not whether slavery shall exist unmolested where it now is, but whether it shall be carried to new and distant regions where the footprint of the slave cannot be found....I ask not that slavery be abolished. I demand that this Government [sic] preserve the integrity of free territory [sic] against the aggressions of slavery....[T]he whole of Texas has been given up to slavery. The Democracy of the North, almost to a man, went for annexation....Shall further concessions be made by the North? Shall we give up free territory, the inheritance of free labor?...[W]e are told that the joint blood and treasure of the whole country being expended in this acquisition, therefore, it should be divided, and slavery allowed to take its share. Sir, the South has her share already; the installment for slavery was paid in advance. We are fighting this war for Texas and for the South....

The Northern public responded by recognizing this argument in a way that the abolitionist arguments could never be recognized by a Constitution-supporting populace. In the South, on the other hand, it was quickly recognized that, whatever the merits of the Northern claim, the concession that newly acquired free territory would be transformed into free states effectively ended any possibility for the future expansion of slavery and would ultimately destroy the balance between the North and South in Washington.

Though the proviso was submitted and debated again and again (Lincoln was to say that he voted for it at least forty times while a member of the Thirtieth Congress), the final legislative product, the Great Compromise of 1850, ostensibly left the door open to the extension of slavery throughout the Southwest by establishing the principle of "popular sovereignty," better termed local option, at the time of statehood. Since this principle implied that the first settlers to arrive would make the decision, it also transformed the policies of both sections from essentially defensive to actively offensive. The rest of the compromise legislation also encouraged the adoption of an offensive posture by the sections. The new fugitive slave laws, in particular, raised Southern hopes that their position would become politically dominant.

The upshot of it all was that throughout the North the view that status quo meant no further spread of slavery gained wider acceptance. The South, no longer content with holding the line against antislavery encroachments, began to demand protection for slavery even outside its geographic limits. Thus the two sections embarked on a road toward active antagonism and intensive polarization.

Constitutional Theories of Polarization

Myths about the pragmatic and atheoretical nature of American politics to the contrary, both the North and the South were quick to express this new polarization in theoretical terms. For Americans, theoretical discussions are traditionally of two kinds, theological and constitutional. Both theological and constitutional doctrines were invoked in the slavery controversy and were to leave their marks on American thought and action for years to come. This is not the place to go into the theological arguments as to the legitimacy or illegitimacy of slavery under God's law. Each side cited the Bible to prove its case; the South looking to the immediate meaning of the biblical text and the North looking to its larger and long range implications. The sociological consequences of those arguments were felt immediately with the division of the Methodist and Baptist churches into Northern and Southern bodies during the 1840s. This division, soon to spread to other churches as well, was no doubt inevitable in a society which took its religious morality seriously. In a curious way, it demonstrated the vitality of organized religion in the United States but it also meant that religious ties were to be a divisive rather than a unifying force for another century or more.

In the immediate political realm, spokesmen for both sections appealed to the Constitution as their authority. Future generations, viewing their actions through a veil imposed by the Civil War itself, were to be misled as to how they did so. While appeals to the Constitution in the pre-Civil War years required considerable elaboration of existing theories, they did not require the invention of new ones out of whole cloth or the abandonment of traditional ones for reasons of convenience.

The constitutional ideas of both sections were well within the framework of American political thought, sharing common seventeenth- and eighteenth-century roots. Both saw the Constitution as a grand compact. However, the interpretation dominant in the North, following that of the Puritans and Daniel Webster, accepted the Constitution as a solemn covenant in the biblical mode, involving the nation, the states, and the people — something more than a limited compact uniting sovereign states. Consequently, the Northerners viewed the Union as a vital entity in and of itself, whose dedication to the preservation of liberty (as Lincoln said) gave it a value beyond that coming to it as the sum of several separate sovereignties.

The dominant Southern interpretation, as stated so effectively by Calhoun, accepted a version of Lockean compact theory which made the Constitution no more than a limited businesslike contract between the states acting as independent parties who ultimately retained their freedom of action. In the Southern view, this arrangement endowed the Union with no more moral authority than that of a policeman charged with maintaining order for the sake of commerce and no more character than that of a broker seeking to balance interests.

Though each of these approaches came to be associated with different sections, in point of fact, there were many in each section who supported the theory identified with the other one. Nevertheless, through the elaboration of these diametrically opposed theories, Americans were able to conduct a great debate over the nature of the Union and, in the end, to endow their political actions as a nation with moral purpose. But, by relying too heavily on the immediate elaborations of their theories (developed hastily in response to immediate legislative pressures) for guidance in practical situations, they also moved dangerously close to ideological politics. This in turn meant that they reacted to their common problems without viewing those problems directly; rather they were seen through spectacles colored by previously concocted doctrine.

The intensification of this growing commitment to ideology would ultimately lead to a war to preserve the Union. A major political accomplishment of that war was the practical settlement of one aspect of this clash of theories, once and for all. At the same time, public reaction to the excesses of the war produced a reaction against the entire question of the moral implications of political ideas that was to bear fruit as well.

For Americans, constitutional principles are matters of morality, hence the break between the North and South over the meaning of the federal Constitution meant a moral rupture as great as slavery itself. By the close of 1848, the moral gap between the sections was complete. While it may still have been bridgeable at that time, none of the steps taken in the next half generation were able to bridge it. David Wilmot had given voice to the one sentiment that could unite a Northern majority against the South. While that sentiment alone was not enough to provoke secession and civil war, it could serve as a potent catalyst in a Pandora's box of sectional difficulties.

The "Four Freedoms" of 1848

Early in 1847, President Polk noted in his diary that "the slavery question is assuming a fearful and most important aspect. The movement [reintroducing the Wilmot Proviso]...if persevered in, will be attended with terrible consequence to the country, and cannot fail to destroy the Democratic party, if it does not threaten the Union itself." After the rejection of the Wilmot Proviso in the spring, events moved with increasing rapidity. By summer, the party conventions in the Southern states were indicating that they would support no candidate who did not repudiate the proviso and its principles. State legislatures below the Mason-Dixon line unanimously rejected the proviso while those in all but two of the free states endorsed it with equal fervor.

By the winter of that year, "the prince of the doughfaces," Lewis Cass, a Northern senator whose party regularity and moderate temperament were to lead him into an acceptance of Southern principles, had virtually secured the Democratic presidential nomination by his outright embrace of the Southern viewpoint. The leaders of the Democratic party had made their decision to "go south" rather than risk loss of their majority status. The free-soil Democrats were left with a Hobson's choice between taking a stand on the slavery issue as an overriding moral one and bolting their party or remaining loyal to the national ticket and abdicating what they believed to be their moral responsibility.

Those who determined to stay with their party sought refuge in the new constitutional theory, the doctrine of popular sovereignty, which was to play havoc with the nation's political stability six years hence. By claiming that Congress should not legislate for the territories on the slavery question but should let the actual settlers decide, the advocates of popular sovereignty put forward one of those pseudodemocratic ideas which often make headway in democratic societies until their specious character is revealed. The theory also made it possible for them to vote with the Southerners who claimed that Congress could not legislate in that area, thus temporarily covering the growing rift in Democratic ranks.

Other Democrats could not swallow this rationalization and began to look elsewhere. By the summer of 1848, some of them had made their choice and a real antislavery third party movement was under way. On August 9, 1848, 10,000 men (465 of them delegates) from all fifteen free states, plus representatives from Delaware, Maryland, Virginia, and the District of Columbia, assembled at Buffalo, New York — the geographic center of greater New England — to create a new antislavery party. Leading them was a strange alliance of some of the more radical free-soil advocates and the men of Martin Van Buren's New York "machine" in the process of following their leader into revolt against the regular Democratic organization. The fruits of the previous years were harvested as members of the original Liberty party, antislavery Democrats, and the so-called "Conscience Whigs" of New England, who could not accept slave-owning Zachary Taylor as their candidate, combined to nominate Martin Van Buren for the presidency. The Free-Soil party, as the new association was called, numbered among its charter members many of those who were to become the prominent Northern revolutionaries of the Civil War, among them Benjamin Butler, Charles Sumner, and Charles Francis Adams of Massachusetts, David Wilmot of Pennsylvania, and Salmon P. Chase of Ohio.

While the new party's battle cry, "Free soil, free speech, free labor, and free men" presaged a broader program than simple opposition to the extension of slavery, most of its active adherents in Buffalo were either single-minded abolitionists or political opportunists seeking a new platform from which to launch an assault on the bastions of national power. Both of these groups could unite in viewing Southern control of national politics as a conspiracy of the "slave power." Accordingly, the party orators condemned slavery generally but directed their strongest attacks against the aggressiveness of the Southern slave power.

The party's platform, written in the main by Chase, was more of a forecast of things to come. It reaffirmed the principles of the Wilmot Proviso and called for federal intervention against slavery wherever constitutionally possible, carefully adding that it did not advocate federal intervention within established slave states. Beyond that, it called for lower postage rates, extensive river and harbor improvements, and free land for settlers through a homestead act. Thus it foreshadowed the Republican coalition that was to emerge, partly from Free-Soil ranks, within six years.

In its attacks on conservative Southern power in Washington and its combination of three of the programmatic pillars upon which the Republican party would later ride to power (only the protective tariff was omitted), the Free-Soil party was the first to enunciate the demands of the new generation just beginning in 1848. Yet its appeal remained limited and many free-soil Whigs — Daniel Webster, Horace Greeley, and Abraham Lincoln among them — refused to risk the election of Democrat Cass or the division of the nation into sectional voting blocs by voting a third party ticket.

In the fall presidential elections, the first to be held in every state but Maine and Vermont on a uniform date set by Act of Congress, the Free-Soil party won 291,263 votes out of a total of 2,878,023, better than ten percent of the total. While it did not carry any states, it did win thirty-one counties; three in New England, seven in New York, and twenty-one in the Old Northwest (Illinois, nine; Ohio and Wisconsin, six each). Its diversion of votes from the regular parties determined the outcome of the election but, unlike the Liberty party in 1844, this time it took more votes from the Democrats, enabling the Whigs to elect Zachary Taylor with less than a national majority. Furthermore, when the Thirty-first Congress assembled in December of 1849, two Free-Soilers sat in the Senate and thirteen sat in the House, including Chase, Wilmot, George W. Julian, and Preston King. These thirteen held the balance of power in a chamber divided 112 Democrats to 105 Whigs and it was their decision that gave the latter party control of the House machinery. The off-year elections in 1850 were to bring the Free-Soilers another senator, Charles Sumner of Massachusetts, and four more representatives.

The relative success of the Free-Soil party in denting the two party system was something less than a triumph of unadulterated idealism. It was made possible by a convergence of antislavery feeling, dominant among New Englanders; interest in expanded federal aid on the frontier, dominant among Westerners; and an intraparty fight among New York Democrats. The latter was especially significant since nearly half of the party's total vote came in New York where the Van Buren organization followed their leader into the new party. Indeed, the core of the party's organizational strength came from that intraparty division that had led

Van Buren to bolt the Democracy. When Van Buren returned to his regular allegiance, the Free-Soil party was doomed.

By 1848 it was apparent that both major parties were dependent for victory on the shifts among third party movements whose existence stemmed from the slavery controversy. At the same time, the antislavery forces with political sense had come to realize that to achieve real success they had to capture one of the major parties — or replace one of them with a party of their own. They were beginning to learn that this could only be done by abandoning single interest politics and developing a broad-based program capable of riding the entire crest of the revolutionary wave beginning to engulf the nation. Such a program could appeal to all those made dissatisfied with the status quo by the impact of the new age. It was their hope that these disaffected groups would rally under a single banner, one that could be used to drive the Southerners and their allies out of power in Washington.

Within eight years they were to forge just such a coalition and become the nation's second party. Within half a generation they would become its first. Paradoxically enough, conditions generated by the wave of revolution (and therefore beyond their control) were to make them the precursors of two generations of active third party movements in which the major parties would only be able to elect minority presidents and would be forced, time and again, to co-opt revolutionary ideas from those third parties in order to steal their thunder.

Beginning an Age of Revolution

If a new era of third parties and minority presidents had come to the United States by 1848, it was only a reflection of the passing of an older era and the arrival of new times and new problems. Eighteen forty-eight was a year of revolutions in Europe where new forces were at work. The age of reactionary absolutism that followed the Napoleonic Wars was being brought to a thundering close by revolutions from the Seine to the Vistula. Though most of the revolutions were aborted, democratic institutions took another step forward over much of that continent. As in North America, a technological revolution was sweeping over the Old World, though in Europe even the new technology was frequently forced to accommodate itself to long established social and political patterns.

The less encumbered New World did not lean toward political

revolution even though Horace Greeley, in a moment of excitement following the presidential victory of his new Whig hero, Zachary Taylor — the first such Whig victory in eight years — attempted to draw a comparison between that victory and events in Europe. Taylor's victory was a fluke, a public's reward for a military hero, and his popularity did not extend to his congressional compatriots. The Whig program remained unimplemented and, indeed, the national government embarked upon a decade of "donothing" politics. It was to be the last national Whig victory of any sort. Two presidential elections later, the party ceased to exist.

In the United States, the years between 1846 and 1848 marked the beginning of a generation that was to experience revolution in due course, once the forces of economic, technological and social change intensified to the point where the political order was forced to respond to them. The Civil War came in the midst of that revolution and was, in large part, a product of it. As a cataclysmic event of major proportions, the war was bound to influence the revolution's course in many ways. Yet the revolution was inevitable even before the war became likely and the direction of the forces which unleashed it was already substantially determined by 1861. In certain very important respects even the means that were used to deal with the revolution had been devised by the time of the war's outbreak. Any judgment about the impact of the Civil War on American life and politics must be made in the context of this larger picture of a new generation and a new age.

The introduction of the Wilmot Proviso, the meeting of the National River and Harbor Convention, and even the establishment of the Free-Soil party were not, in and of themselves, revolutionary actions. On the contrary, all three represented continuing trends in American political life well rooted in established precedent. Yet when viewed together and in connection with other events of those years, they can be seen to have marked a crossroads — if an unperceived one — in the history of American government, a turning point which led in the immediate future to a decade of intersectional conflict culminating in the Civil War with its disarrangement of the American political system and, at longer range, to a rearrangement of certain political institutions and patterns of political behavior so as to enable a reconstituted political system to better serve the needs of a reconstructed social and economic order.

The three political events considered here were especially important because they united the issues of slavery, sectionalism, territorial expansion, and constitutional interpretation with the emerging needs of commerce in an industrializing society and with the demands of the new technology. By playing this role, they sharpened the divisions between the North and the South. The former section avidly embraced the new technology and fostered its growth even at the expense of established traditions; accepted the pursuit of social justice as a reasonable element in the social order; and favored a broader construction of the Constitution where necessary to meet the demands of innovation. The latter, on the other hand, increasingly sought refuge from the perils of social change in a rejection of the new age with its new technology and new pursuit of social justice which its leaders viewed as a menace to that section's established institutions, through a strict construction of the constitutional compact.

The personal alignments formed around the three events were to shape a new generation of political life, raise a new generation of political leaders, and lead to the creation of a new political party and national party realignment. The issues raised by the measures would come to the center of the political stage to form the basis for the politics of the new generation. The men who voted with David Wilmot on the evening of August 8, 1846; those who marched in the grand procession in Chicago the following July 5; and those who met in Buffalo on August 9, 1848, were voting and marching America into a period of intense political reconstitution which, unlike the Reconstruction of twenty years later, was to affect the whole nation, not just the South. Abraham Lincoln, speaking in Peoria, Illinois, several years later, summed the matter up most succinctly in a reference to David Wilmot's motion: "It created a great flutter; but it stuck like wax."

Bibliographic Notes — Chapter 3

On abolitionism, see John Jeffery Auer, ed., *Antislavery and Disunion, 1858-1861* (1963); Gilbert H. Barnes, *Anti-Slavery Impulse* (1933); Dwight L. Dumond, *Antislavery: The Crusade for Freedom in America* (1961); idem, *Antislavery Origins of the Civil War in the United States* (1939); Louis Filler, *The Crusade Against Slavery, 1830-1860* (1960); Arthur Y. Lloyd, *The Slavery Controversy, 1831-1860* (1939); Gerald Sorin, *New York Abolitionists: Case Study of Political Radicalism* (1971).

On abolitionist thought, see Richard O. Curry, ed., *Abolitionists* (1965); John Demos, "Antislavery Movement and the Problem of Violent 'Means'," *New England Quarterly* 37 (1964): 501; Betty Fladeland, "Who Were the Abolitionists?" *Journal of Negro History* 49 (1964): 99; Staughton Lynd, *Intellectual Origins of American Radicalism* (1968); Roman J. Zorn, "New England Anti-Slavery Society: Pioneer Abolition Organization," *Journal of Negro History* 42 (1957): 157.

On specific abolitionists, see Irving H. Barlett, "Wendell Phillips and the Eloquence of Abuse," *American Quarterly* 11 (1959): 509; Francis E. Kearns, "Margaret Fuller and the Abolition Movement," *Journal of the History of Ideas* 25 (1964): 120; Perry Miller, "Theodore Parker," *Harvard Theological Review* 54 (1961): 275; Bertram Wyatt-Brown, "William Lloyd Garrison and Antislavery Unity," *Civil War History* 1 (1967): 5.

On religion and abolitionism, see John R. Bodo, *Protestant Clergy and Public Issues, 1812-1845* (1954); Charles C. Cole, Jr., *Social Ideas and Northern Evangelists, 1826-1860* (1954); T.E. Drake, *Quakers and Slavery* (1950); Donald G. Mathews, *Slavery and Methodism: A Chapter in American Morality, 1780-1845* (1965); Madeline H. Rice, *American Catholic Opinion in the Slavery Controversy* (1944).

On the Wilmot Proviso, see Chaplain W. Morrison, *Democratic Politics and Sectionalism: The Wilmot Proviso Controversy* (1967).

On the election of 1848, see Holman Hamilton, "Election of 1848," in Arthur M. Schlesinger Jr. and Fred L. Israel, eds., *History of American Presidential Elections, 1789-1968*, vol. 2 (1971); Joseph G. Rayback, *Free-Soil: Elections of 1848* (1971).

On the revolutions of 1848 and their American impact, see Horace Greeley's *Whig Almanac* for the years 1846-1850 and Daniel J. Elazar, ed., *Horace Greeley's History of the Mexican War*, an edited compilation in which he advances the thesis that the Mexican war was part of the revolutionary ferment that swept the world at that time.

PART TWO:

GOVERNMENT AND SOCIETY IN THE 1850s

Chapter 4

THE FEDERAL SYSTEM ON THE EVE OF THE WAR

In 1842, Alexander Dallas Bache, scion of a politically prominent Philadelphia family, descendant of Benjamin Franklin,
and one of America's leading scientists, was appointed director of
the United States Coast Survey. An intelligent and politically as-
tute public servant, Bache spent the next twenty-five years as one
of the few "career experts" in government of his time. His political
know-how enabled him to get more money for scientific endeavors from a niggardly Congress than ever before and to build the
first federal scientific empire.

Bache was the leading scientific organizer of his day and,
with Louis Agassiz of Harvard, dominated the American scientific "establishment" until his death in 1867 by using his position
in Washington to best advantage. Consequently, he was in constant contact with the nation's intellectual and political elites. Yet,
until the winter of 1860-1861, Bache was apparently so involved in
"business as usual" that he paid no public heed to the impending
crisis. His voluminous correspondence contains discussions of
numerous matters of political concern but always concern with the
day-to-day operations of the Coast Survey or the destiny of the scientific community that he dominated.

Although he was politically aware and adept in every other respect, Bache was not driven to consider the possibilities of disunion because his business was Union-wide in character and took
the bulk of his time up to the very eve of the war itself. Dealing
primarily with those undramatic activities that bound the states
and sections together, he was so involved with them as to make
disunion appear to be unnatural and, consequently, not really
possible. Aware of the nationwide scope of the business of government, he was so immersed in the routine execution of his mission,
from north to south and from coast to coast, that he had come to accept its continuance as a matter of course. In this respect, he — a
strong Unionist who was to render signal service to the Union
cause — like Jefferson Davis appears to be highly inconsistent if
not patently misled.

Bache's view of the world around him during the 1850s, if limited by the perspective of the federal bureaucracy, was no less accurate than that of John Brown, who, in the limited world of Kansas, saw civil conflict all around him. This persistence of civilian routine in the shadow of armed conflict may be a curiosity of cold war but it also reflects normal human behavior. The persistence of normal governmental activities until the spring of 1861 was quite a reality. It was to be an important element in the later resumption of political life in reunification.

In Bache's world, "business as usual" meant a great deal of business indeed. The attention-getting disruptions attendant upon the Civil War have obscured the real character of the American political system in the years before the conflict in several ways. First of all, there is considerable confusion as to the actual role of government in American society in the mid-nineteenth century. There is equally great confusion as to the relations between governments — especially between the federal and state governments — in that period. There is also a general misunderstanding of the character of political organization in the nation and of the politicians who manned the political organizations. Finally, there is almost no appreciation of the tremendous continuity of normal *governmental* activity up until the outbreak of actual hostilities in 1861, even as the political bonds that held the Union together were breaking, one by one.

Briefly put, American government on all planes in the years before the Civil War, while a far cry from the activist government of the next century, was still a potent force on the American scene, engaged in active collaboration with private and public nongovernmental bodies to promote the general welfare in the same spirit of partnership and within the same framework of a mixed economy that was not to be publicly labeled as such for many years. Moreover, after 1848, government on all planes began to expand at an accelerating rate as American society changed from an agrarian to an industrial one.

The American Partnership

By 1848, the American system of government had long since become an intricate mechanism of delicately interrelated parts. Following the federal principle, these interrelationships were delicately structured around the formal divisions of power among the federal, state, and local governments and between the legislative, executive, and judicial branches in each arena. The interrelationships of arenas, jurisdictions, and departments in the American system was not a mechanistic one in the Newtonian sense whereby each part was assigned its own sphere, worked within it, and touched the others only at specified points like a set of interlocking gears. Rather, it was an active interrelationship that had early produced a high level of immediate interdependence.

As a system of government it was not a piece of cold machinery, but was, after all, clothed with the flesh and blood of human beings; and these human beings found it desirable, advisable, and useful to actively cooperate with one another to achieve common ends even to the point where their cooperation would transcend and somewhat erase the formal divisions of jurisdiction that separated them. Furthermore, the system of intergovernmental collaboration had long since been extended to include the private sphere as well, so that the same blurring of lines was commonplace between public and private bodies as well as between federal and state agencies.

By the mid-nineteenth century, for example, it was possible to find an army engineer trained in railroad construction work on leave from his position in the Engineer Corps and assigned at the request of a state government to cooperate with a semiprivate railroad company in laying out a new railroad line. The observer looking at such a figure could well question whether he was a federal employee on detached service, a temporary servant of the state on loan to a local enterprise, or an employee of a private company recruited from the only available pool of railroad construction engineers then available. Or, one might ride a stagecoach across some region of the United States side by side with sacks of United States mail and reasonably wonder whether the stagecoach was not really able to operate only by virtue of the profit from its federal mail contract and if it carried passengers solely for additional revenue. The traveler's wonderment might well have been increased after stopping in town after town at a post office-cum-tavern-cum-inn and observing how the local postmaster also presided over his community's social and commercial life by virtue of his custody of the local post office.

Entering a bank in Indiana or Alabama or Ohio or any one of several other states during this period, the depositor could well ask whether he was in a state bank that also allowed private investors or a private bank supported by the state, or whether the bank would be in existence at all except for the federal funds on deposit that formed the bulk of its reserve. The road, railroad or canal over which one traveled was very likely the product of a cooperative effort involving all levels of government and usually private funds as well. If a person resided in one of the states carved out of the public domain, it was likely the schools his children attended had been founded with the assistance of funds gained from a federal land grant and were still supported in part by the income from the permanent fund created with the proceeds from the sale of the lands. If any member of his family used one of the relatively few social welfare institutions of his state, the chances were that federal funds had gone into creating it, that a state board was charged with its arrangement, and that a nationwide exchange of information among the professional social welfare workers was helping to raise the standards of care it provided.

The American federal system had been one of intricate partnership virtually since its inception. Indeed, the roots of that partnership go back to the very formation of the American nation in the years before 1776. By 1850, it would have been well nigh impossible to alter it. Even as the nation was being polarized by state and section in the decade before the war, it was simultaneously embarking on new cooperative ventures. As the compromise of 1850 was being ratified in Congress, to the dissatisfaction of Yankee Free-Soilers and Southern expansionists, the same Congress was voting to grant thousands of acres of land to the states of Illinois, Mississippi, and Alabama for the cooperative construction of a railroad to connect Chicago and northern Illinois with the Gulf of Mexico — the heartland of greater New England with the heartland of the aggressive new South. The product of that effort, the Illinois Central Railroad, is still one of the most important transportation links between Chicago and the Gulf.

The Illinois Central was simply one product of the spate of federal grants. Between 1850 and 1871, during the heart of the Civil War era, states of the North, South and West allocated more than 130 million acres, obtained from the federal government, for railroad construction. These grants, whose total cash value was to approximate $472 million by the end of the century, directly benefited about two-thirds of the states in each section.

As the cold war in Kansas was beginning to turn hot in the mid-1850s, Congress was inaugurating a major program of river and harbor improvements along the Atlantic, Gulf, and Pacific coasts, the Great Lakes, and the great interior rivers under the aegis of the United States Corps of Engineers that would cost over $110 million in federal funds over the next generation. The program they began is with us still, in proportions hardly foreseen a century ago.

As John B. Floyd of Virginia, President Buchanan's secessionist Secretary of War, was endeavoring to ship federal arms to Southern arsenals to the later advantage of his section, men like James B. Powell of Alabama and companies like the Butterfield Overland Mail (the darling of Jefferson Davis) were avidly competing for federal mail contracts that would provide them with enough funds to establish lines and increase their profits. In fact, the mail contract often meant the difference between profit and loss in even the most successful transportation operations (which could no more operate without a federal subsidy in 1860 than in 1960). Indeed, after the states of the lower South seceded, neither Union nor Confederate officials did anything to interfere with the maintenance of United States mail service and the mails continued to go through until late spring 1861 — Union officials because, as a matter of policy, they refused to recognize secession and Confederate officials because, as a matter of expediency, they wanted the mail delivered.

Even as the Union was falling apart, and South Carolina was demanding the evacuation of Fort Sumter in Charleston Harbor, William Porcher Miles, an arch secessionist congressman from that state, was begging Bache as the head of the United States Coast Survey to keep up his bureau's survey work in that harbor. Throughout January 1861, Stephen R. Mallory, then a United States senator from Florida and soon to be the Confederate states' Secretary of the Navy, importuned Bache to dispatch the scheduled survey party to continue work off Florida's coast, writing to him that "Florida does not war upon Triangulators, hydrographers nor plane table people," and later: "It [the Coast Survey] is a civil service, and so long as it confined itself to its legitimate duties, I doubt not it would meet with no interruption...."

The extent to which the several states were bound together into a common union through federal services is at least partly indicated by the figures. Between 1789 and 1860, federal expenditures for light houses, fortifications, internal improvements, navy yards, marine hospitals, and veterans' pensions were divided among the slave states and the free states in reasonable proportion to their respective populations, with the former receiving some $55 million and the latter some $81 million. In the last decade before the war, the free states received the benefit of some $24 million in federal expenditures and the slave states, some $18 million. The situation with regard to federal land grants was approximately the same. Between 1802 and 1857, the free states received 111 million acres in grants for universities, common schools, deaf and dumb asylums, government buildings, veterans pensions; river and harbor improvements; road, canal, and railroad construction; and salt springs, while the slave states received 77 million acres.

Yet judging from the comments of the leaders of the day, there was a serious blindness to the existence of sharing. On the eve of the Civil War, many talked of the American federal system in highly Newtonian terms. The year after the *Dred Scott* decision, Roger B. Taney, Chief Justice of the United States Supreme Court, summed up the prevalent view in *Abelman v. Booth*: "The powers of the general government and of the state, although both exist and are exercised within the same territorial limits, are yet separate and distinct sovereignties, acting separately and independently of each other, within their respective spheres." The prevalent doctrine, subsequently labeled "dual federalism," was expounded with exceptional force in the years immediately preceding the war because it offered a powerful argument for those advocating the states' rights heresy in defense of slavery and in opposition to abolitionist demands for federal intervention to limit the rights of slaveholders.

Advocacy of the principle of dual federalism was no more inconsistent with the Southerners' repeated requests for increased federal enforcement of the Fugitive Slave Act than it was in the face of repeated and routinized cooperative activities that infused the basic operations of government in the North, South, and West in the same period. Still, preservation of the argument, which was so very public, coupled with neglect of the real situation, was later to help foster the myth that the Civil War had transformed the American governmental system into one in which the role of the national government was substantially enhanced at the expense of state and local government.

The system of cooperative federalism did indeed undergo certain changes in the Civil War generation, changes that began at the very beginning of that generation in the years immediately following 1848. During the first two generations of the republic, when the Union was composed primarily of states whose origins antedated the establishment of the federal union, the development of specific cooperative programs was generally ad hoc. Moreover, the development of administrative techniques of intergovernmental collaboration and, indeed, a rudimentary institutional network through which to apply them, were paralleled by their emergence as such.

Nevertheless, the range of cooperative activities was great and their impact was vital. During the first two generations, the major vehicles of both intergovernmental and public-private partnership were the joint stock company (in which federal, state and local governments as well as private parties joined to invest in corporations established to undertake specific projects, usually in the realm of internal improvements and banking) and the cooperative survey (in which the federal government would send or lend army engineers to the states to survey and plan internal improvement projects). Secondary cooperative devices included land grants, generally for education, social welfare, and veterans' pensions, and periodic distribution of surplus revenues from higher levels of government to lower ones for the same kinds of service.

The major continuing programmatic concerns of American government had emerged and Americans already accepted government commitment to the extension of internal improvements, maintenance of sound fiscal systems, and the establishment of appropriate educational facilities. Less well accepted, but increasingly so, was government's responsibility for the provision of necessary public welfare aids. Finally, day-to-day collaboration existed in myriad little ways, based on common professional interests of officials at all levels of government.

What changed after 1848 was not the fact of intergovernment cooperation but the forms through which such cooperation was predominantly effectuated. The key word in the change was routinization. By 1850, a majority of the states in the Union were creatures of the Union rather than its creators — a real distinction, though not a constitutional one — and forty percent were public-land states as well. This meant that without engaging in constitutional controversies over the legitimacy of federal aid, Congress could utilize the land grant as the keystone of a policy of collaboration that extended to embrace private enterprise as well. The territorial experience of most of the new states had left them with links to the federal government. However strongly they reacted to the federal domination of territorial days, particularly political domination (and frequently the reactions were strong — in a true anticolonialist spirit), they had become accustomed to receiving federal funds for their governmental activities. Routinization of cooperative activities was a product of the twin forces of constitutionalism and organization and a response to the twin challenges of the older land frontier and the newly emerging urban-industrial frontier. By 1850 constitutionalism had determined the forms of cooperation. Among them were: (1) the existence of a dual governmental structure — federal and state, together serving a growing multitude of local communities which were, in turn, composed of public agencies and private associations closely intertwined in the pursuit of community goals; and (2) a federalist theory of government that, though still insufficient to describe the partnership, did embody the basic federal principles that made partnership the norm rather than unilateral local action or centralization.

In a real sense, the existence of a constitutional relationship meant that all parties to the constitutional compact had the right to be involved in actions taken in the name of the compact. This was true whether one held the Southern view or believed that the federal government served an indivisible nation composed of states that were part and parcel of it.

The new notions of organization that were emerging in the country at large stimulated the development of cooperation through more sophisticated programs such as railroad construction and revised land grant programs for support of public education, and through new administrative techniques. In an organized society ad hoc arrangements tend to be reduced to an interstitial role. As American society became more organized, the major cooperative programs acquired a new formality and a consistency in application that would reflect the increasing organization of American society. By the same token, ad hoc administrative techniques were also increasingly routinized.

The programs and processes of cooperation had to be adapted to serve the new challenges of industrialization, which not only affected the growth of urban areas around the country, but also affected the manner in which the remaining land frontier was tamed. In the years following 1848, as in the years preceding it, problems of internal improvement, fiscal organization, education, and public welfare were the dominant continuing concerns of government on all planes. Increasingly, these problems were met through the use of land grants.

Land grant programs actually dated to the very beginnings of the republic. The first federal grant programs were established under the terms of the Northwest Ordinances of 1785 and 1787, though actual transfers of granted lands did not begin until 1802 when Ohio, the first of the public-land states, achieved statehood. Before 1848, land grant programs had been instituted for public education at the elementary school and university levels; for internal improvements, particularly construction of canals and wagon roads; for public buildings and welfare institutions; and for small reclamation projects. All these programs were expanded after the mid-century point and, in addition, great new internal improvement and education programs were inaugurated. The railroad land grant program has already been mentioned. In 1849 and 1850, the federal government created the swamp land grant program which ultimately transferred hundreds of thousands of acres of land to the states for reclamation purposes and to support needed internal improvements.

Administrative and programmatic cooperation increased as the problems of administering the huge grant programs became more complex. The federal Department of the Interior, through its General Land Office, was responsible for the supervision of these programs while in the states, officials of every stripe were involved in handling them. The most striking fact that emerged from an analysis of the development of sharing in this period is the sheer weight of political time devoted to intergovernmental cooperation. Not only were the administrators in every arena heavily involved in cooperative activities, but the partnerships that were most highly developed as shared partnerships also preempted the bulk of the policy-makers' time. The president and Congress, state governors and legislatures, and executive departments in both arenas were all preoccupied with cooperative partnerships during the entire period. Their concern was not over the general theory of collaboration, but with the procedural aspects of the various partnerships.

Collaboration itself seems to have been taken for granted since, as a general phenomenon, it escaped public notice, attracting attention only in specific cases. Not only did active officials ratify the system by their very day-to-day actions, but competing interests sought aid from federal, state, and local governments acting in partnership, thus providing their tacit ratification as well. Legal ratification of a sort did not lag behind. Not only did state and federal law enforcement officers indicate their tacit approval of the constitutionality of such partnerships but the courts of the land, while never ruling directly on the constitutionality of the cooperative partnerships as such, sustained the specifics of the cooperative arrangement in case after case, thus developing a body of precedents that effectively overruled the *obiter dicta* of men like Taney such as that quoted earlier. This implicit political and legal ratification of the partnership system was all the more impressive because it was implicit.

Throughout the 1850s, and until the very beginning of hostilities in 1861, the cooperative system remained remarkably stable. While the nation seemed to be falling apart at its seams and hostilities grew in every other field, the administrators of the daily affairs of government faithfully continued to exercise their trusts in partnership with each other and with the relevant private concerns until the war itself put a stop to their activities. In sum, even as the Union was being disrupted, the cooperative system was serving to maintain relations between Northerners and Southerners that would leave a residue of common interests and identities that could be pulled together once again after the failure of the Confederacy.

The Changing Concerns of Government

In certain respects the stability displayed by the cooperative system deserved to be taken for granted in 1861. Partnerships between peoples with common interests are not unusual in a world where competing interests often lead to violence. Participants in a later cold war know that it is possible to cooperate with even potential enemies to achieve common ends when it is convenient for both parties to do so. What made American cooperative relationships into something of a different magnitude in 1861 was their pervasiveness, vitality, and importance to the very maintenance of civil society. By the third generation of independence, virtually every activity of government was a shared activity, and cooperation was as pervasive as federalism itself. Though it was not realized at the time, partnership in day-to-day activities had become an important element in the translation of federal principles into a meaningful system of free government.

Still, if the system of cooperation was not changing in its essence, the concerns of government were. Indeed, the role of government had been undergoing change since the adoption of the

Constitution. After 1848, however, the change was to become even more apparent, reflecting a change in the very interests that American governments, particularly the national governments, were serving. This shift in the interests to which government would be responsive was becoming apparent in the 1850s. Since it was a shift away from the interests of the South towards those of the most powerful elements in the North, it contributed in no small measure to the alienation of Southerners from the American polity. Sensing that the change meant the end of their great influence in national councils, they turned to more extreme measures.

The change was, in part, built on economics. After 1848, the American turn inward, which had started in the aftermath of the War of 1812, became even more drastic, especially in the North. Less and less concerned with the affairs of the Old World, after the failures of the 1848 revolutions to bring about change even in a commercial way, they were preoccupied with achieving success within the vast empire that had become the United States of America. Southerners, whose economic interests were perforce, outwardly directed, found their whole world view at variance with the new trend. Exporters of cotton to Europe, seekers of new slave territories in the Caribbean and Central America, they could not afford to become isolationist in their orientation.

The North, on the other hand, thrived by virtue of its attention to industrialization and exploitation of the land frontier now reserved as free soil. Both of these activities tended to encourage isolationist or, perhaps more appropriately, continentalist attitudes. The new industrialists demanded protection from the outside world for their growing enterprises and the new frontiersmen were far too preoccupied with conquering a hostile interior land basin to concern themselves with foreign affairs, except insofar as they needed occasional foreign markets for their produce. Northern continentalism of the post-1848 years was to survive as the dominant posture in American life for three generations, just as Southern internationalism would be reinforced to survive as the dominant posture of that section for the same period. While the Civil War would reinforce these tendencies in each section, they are still to be viewed more as causes of sectional conflict than as consequences.

The character of the post-1848 frontier also contributed to the changing interests of the national government. In the first place, the frontier became two-pronged. The forces of industrialization produced a new technology, transformed old societies and created a new kind of frontier in the urban areas that were generally confined to the North. This urban-industrial frontier was to become the equal of the agricultural land frontier in another generation and then supplant it as the dominant source of frontier dynamism and change in the United States.

In the Civil War generation, however, it was in the West that the frontier retained its magical meaning for the American people. Indeed, between 1848 and 1876, the hope of the American people lay in the West as never before or since. The West, whatever it may have been in reality, became the shiny haven of the American dream. It was in this period that the idea of the frontier was refined and added to the American mystique, just as it was in the West that the American partnership flourished and matured during those years.

The West of the 1850s, though, was one that by its very nature discouraged the Southern way of life. It was a haven for free people, not slave owners; for people who rejected traditional patterns, not those who sought to perpetuate them; for people who were neglectful if not openly contemptuous of narrow constitutional forms in their battle against a hostile environment, not strict constructionists who sought safety in a compact left virtually unaltered. None of this had been true of the pre-1848 West that had been just as hospitable to Southern ideas as well as to Northern ones. It was no accident that Southerners had outstripped Northerners in their march westward between 1780 and 1850. Thus, by 1848, Southerners were settling central Texas while Yankees were still confined to the southern corners of Wisconsin and the west bank of the Mississippi River in Iowa and southeastern Minnesota.

The land and the climate of the pre-1848 West was just as conducive to the slave system as to the system of free-soil farming, if not more so. Wherever rainfall exceeded forty-five inches annually, Southerners could establish the plantation system and could hope to replicate the society they had established along the Atlantic coast, in general social structure if not in specific detail. By 1848, the nation had advanced to the limits of the "45-inch line." Across it slavery was at a disadvantage. While Southern adaptations of the slave system for urban pursuits were already being developed and, conceivably, cattle ranching could have been based on slavery, conditions in the West generally favored the free. Thus Southerners had no place else to go with their peculiar institutions while Northerners now could see all the way to the Pacific. Most

Southern leaders understood this well, which is why many sought to expand the United States into southern Mexico and the Caribbean, to territories more promising to the slave system that could be admitted as slave states in the future to maintain the balance of power in the federal Senate.

The West would not again become an attraction for Southerners until the Civil War itself intervened. After the war had dislocated Southern society and its economy and many Southern whites sought new opportunities because their old ones had been destroyed, the West became, once again, a place for their visions. By that time, however, they were forced to fill in the interstices of a society organized along essentially Northern lines.

The increase in railroad mileage was a prime indicator of the new direction of the nation's growth after 1848. In that year there were 5,598 miles of track in the country as a whole, up from 3,535 miles in 1842. By 1860, however, track mileage had quintupled to 28,789 miles. In 1848, there were 1,810 miles of track in the slave states as against 3,788 miles in the free states, with Georgia and Virginia among the top five states in total mileage (Pennsylvania, New York, and Massachusetts were the nation's leaders). Of the seven states that had no railroad track in service, four were Southern and three Northern. By 1860, track mileage in the slave states had risen to 9,754 while in the free states the total mileage had reached 19,035, with the former actually gaining proportionately on the latter to a small degree. By then, however, the states with the greatest mileage were all in the North and had far outdistanced the leaders in the South even though the states of Dixie embraced more territory.

In the half generation before the war, Southern power in national councils reached its peak and began to decline. The shift of power from the South to the North and West was caused in the main by the changing long-range trends in American life described earlier in these pages. The progress of these trends can be seen by examining the statistics of American demography for the first half of the nineteenth century (Table 4-1).

The 1820 census showed that the population of the slave states exceeded that of the free states for the first and only time in American history. Between 1820 and 1850, however, there was a drastic shift in population balance. The population of the free states tripled, rising from 4,152,635 to 13,521,220, while that of the slave states hardly doubled from 4,485,818 to 9,664,656.

Table 4-1

RELATIVE POPULATIONS, FREE AND SLAVE STATES: 1790-1890

	1790	1800	1810	1820	1830	1840
N.	1,968,040	2,686,582	3,758,999	4,152,635	7,012,399	9,728,922
S.	1,961,174	2,621,901	3,480,882	4,485,818	5,848,303	7,334,431

Five Largest States (in rank order):

1790	1800	1810	1820	1830	1840
Virginia	Virginia	Virginia	New York	New York	New York
Massachusetts	Pennsylvania	New York	Virginia	Pennsylvania	Pennsylvania
Pennsylvania	New York	Pennsylvania	Pennsylvania	Virginia	Ohio
North Carolina	Massachusetts	Massachusetts	North Carolina	Ohio	Virginia
New York	North Carolina	North Carolina	Ohio	North Carolina	Tennessee

	1850	1860	1870	1880	1890
N.	13,521,220	19,127,948	24,549,056	31,470,835	40,239,470
S.	9,664,656	12,315,373	14,009,315	18,684,918	22,707,244

1850	1860	1870	1880	1890
New York	New York	New York	New York	New York
Pennsylvania	Pennsylvania	Pennsylvania	Pennsylvania	Pennsylvania
Ohio	Ohio	Ohio	Ohio	Illinois
Virginia	Illinois	Illinois	Illinois	Ohio
Tennessee	Virginia	Missouri	Missouri	Missouri

During the period in which the population of the sections was fairly well divided, Southern influence nationally was at its peak and, indeed, the South was the section that spoke for American nationalism. Fatefully, at the same time that the strength of the South reached its peak and began to decline, the opening of the political conflict over slavery and the initiation of serious industrialization in the North began to sharpen the differences between the sections. After 1820, Southern influence, while remaining strong, veered from a strongly nationalistic orientation to take on an increasingly sectional bias. Until 1848 the Southern leaders were able to combine sectionalism and nationalism into a single package, thus enabling the South to retain its position of influence virtually unimpaired.

Even though the proportionate differences in population established by 1850 were to remain fairly constant over the next generation, during that generation the political system had to be adjusted to reflect the changes of the preceding one. That adjustment shifted the balance of political power to the North and drove Southern sectionalism into a position ultimately incompatible with the nationalistic outlook.

The Southerners' consciousness in the 1850s of the relative decline in demographic strength of their section could not be predicated on the knowledge of later generations that the trend fixed by that decade was to remain fairly constant for nearly a century. They could only see an expanding North whose growth appeared endless and a changing national government that increasingly reflected the shift in relative population.

The new trend was reflected in the changing apportionment of Congress. The equal balance in the Senate, established in 1820 as part of the Missouri Compromise and so much a concern to the South in the antebellum period, remained stable until 1850 when the admission of California as a free state inevitably shifted it away from the South. By the end of the decade, the free states held thirty-six of the sixty-six Senate seats.

The change in the House was even more drastic. In 1790 the slave states elected forty-six percent of its members, 48 out of 105, a percentage that declined steadily thereafter. Under the 1850 apportionment, the eighty-eight slave state congressmen comprised less than thirty-nine percent of the House total. Before 1850, only three of the nation's twelve presidents had been born in the North. By 1852, even the Southerners recognized the new conditions and acquiesced in the nomination of Northern men (albeit of Southern sympathies until 1860).

After 1848 and until 1948, no president was elected from any of the former slave states. Of the five Southern-born presidents since the Mexican War, three were first elevated to that office from the vice-presidency through the unexpected death of the incumbent president and a fourth (Woodrow Wilson) had clearly established his residence outside of the South. Only in 1976 was a Southerner, Jimmy Carter, elected to the presidency directly. The total cabinet membership before 1849 was divided as evenly as possible, fifty-seven Southerners and fifty-eight from the rest of the country. The only department generally controlled by Northerners in those years was the Treasury (Southerners would no doubt have seen a significance in that). Through 1848, twelve of the nineteen Secretaries of State had been Southerners. Except for two from Delaware, a border state, there were to be no more until the New Deal.

Only in the cabinet did Southerners remain strongly entrenched during the 1850s, partly because Northern Democrats hesitated to become identified with the pro-slavery administrations in power during those years. There seems to have been something more than that, however. Those vital departments whose management was crucial to a section fighting for safety within the nation — or, alternatively, preparing for a free exit from it — were swamped by Southerners, even though all three had been under Northern leadership more often than not before 1849. Of the twenty-five Southerners holding cabinet positions between the administration of Zachary Taylor and the inauguration of Abraham Lincoln, twelve headed the Treasury, War and Navy Departments. From 1853 until secession, the Treasury was in Southern hands, as was the War Department from 1849. The Navy Department was in Southern hands (with two interruptions) from 1841 to 1857.

The South remained strongest in the federal judiciary, the least popular branch of government. The chief justice was a slaveholder from Maryland. Canute-like, he tried to use the United States Supreme Court to save the South from the consequences of the aforementioned changes. His failure only helped to precipitate the war itself.

Northerners may not have been a triumphantly advancing political horde in the 1850s, often feeling themselves stymied and frustrated by Southern power, as in tariff questions and social welfare policy. Nevertheless, the substantial diminution of over-all Southern influence in Washington and its transformation into essentially a negative power of veto over actions on the part of the federal government deemed hostile to the South, so noticeable in the postbellum period, really began in the years immediately after 1848. At the same time, in a last-ditch effort, Southerners were able to obtain control of three key departments that at least some of them used to prepare their section for a revolution they had come to believe was well-nigh inevitable. In this respect, the 1850s, then, were prologue; 1860 was the crunch. If even then the South could have bargained powerfully in Congress, had the Southern states chosen to stay in the Union, the fact that they did not can also be seen as an extension of the events and perceptions of events of the years since 1846.

Bibliographic Notes — Chapter 4

On science and federal government in the period, see A. Hunter Dupree, *Science in the Federal Government: A History of Policies and Activities to 1940* (1957); Patricia Jahns, *Matthew Fontaine Maury and Joseph Henry: Scientists of the Civil War* (1961).

On the second Bank of the United States, see Bray Hammond, *Banks and Politics in America from the Revolution to the Civil War* (1967).

For general reference, see Thomas B. Alexander, *Sectional Stress and Party Strength* (1967); Arthur C. Cole, *Irrepressible Conflict* (1934); Avery O. Craven, *Civil War in the Making, 1815-1860* (1959), *The Coming of the Civil War*, rev. ed. (1957), and *Growth of Southern Nationalism, 1848-1861* (1953); Donald Fehrenbacher, *Prelude to Greatness: Lincoln in the Fifties* (1962); Allan Nevins, *Emergence of Lincoln*, 2 vols. (1950), and *Ordeal of the Union*, 2 vols. (1947); Roy F. Nichols, *Disruption of American Democracy* (1948), and *Stakes of Power, 1845-1877* (1961); Thomas H. O'Connor, *Lords of the Loom: Cotton Whigs and the Coming of War* (1968); James G. Randall, "Blundering Generation," *Mississippi Valley Historical Review*, 27 (1940): 3; David Donald, *Civil War and Reconstruction*, 2nd ed. (1969); Joel H. Silbey, *Transformation of American Politics, 1840-1860* (1967); Henry H. Simms, *Decade of Sectional Controversy, 1851-1861* (1942); Elbert B. Smith, *Death of Slavery, 1837-1865* (1967).

Economic policies are discussed in Carter Goodrich, *Government Promotion of Canals and Railroads 1800-1900* (1960), and "The

Virginia System of Mixed Enterprise," *Political Science Quarterly* 64 (1949): 355; Oscar Handlin and Mary F. Handlin, *Commonwealth: A Study of the Role of Government in the American Economy — Massachusetts, 1774-1861*, rev. ed. (1969); Louis Hartz, *Economic Policy and Democratic Thought*, rev. ed. (1968); R.G. Wellington, *Political and National Influence of Public Lands 1826-1842* (1914).

On the public domain and land disposal, see J.H. Anderson, "Jurisdiction over Federal Lands within the States," *North Carolina Law Review* 7 (1929): 299; Vernon R. Carstensen, *Farms or Forests: Land Policy for Northern Wisconsin, 1850-1932* (1958), and *The Public Lands* (1963); Everett Dick, *The Lure of the Land: A Social History of the Public Lands from the Articles of Confederation to the New Deal* (1970); Thomas Donaldson, *Public Domain* (1884); H.H. Dunham, "Crucial Years of the General Land Office," *Agricultural History* 11 (1937): 117.

For information on the Taney Court, see Felix Frankfurter, *Commerce Clause under Marshall, Taney, and Waite* (1937); Robert J. Harris, "Chief Justice Taney: Prophet of Reform and Reaction," *Vanderbilt Law Review* 10 (1957): 227; R. Kent Newmyer, *The Supreme Court under Marshall and Taney* (1968); John R. Schmidhauser, "Judicial Behavior and the Sectional Crisis of 1837-1860," *Journal of Politics* 23 (1961): 615.

See also Daniel J. Elazar, "The Civil War and the Preservation of American Federalism," *Publius* 1:1 (1971): 39-58.

Chapter 5

NEW GOVERNMENT, NEW POLITICS

The Expanding Role of Government

Southern influence declined just as the government began to expand drastically. The transition from the quasi-mercantilism of the first generation of the American republic to the laissez-faire of the third had brought a temporary decrease in the prominence of government's role in American life. The role of Jacksonian democracy reflected this change which was further reinforced by the disastrous experience of the states in the panic of 1837. Policy decisions on the federal plane during the 1830s reduced the role of all governments in such fields as banking and regulation of business while the schemes of most states to foster the construction of roads, canals, and railroads on their own resources alone collapsed in the depression that followed the great panic. Ideas of laissez-faire, which first attained status at the very beginning of the second generation, were strongly encouraged by events to become dominant by the end of the 1840s.

Perhaps the high point of actual government withdrawal came with Polk's veto of the River and Harbor Act in 1846. From then on, despite the increasing prestige of theories of government non-intervention, the actual role of government on all planes began to increase. A series of important acts marked the turning point in the federal arena. State and territorial organization of the Pacific Coast and the upper Mississippi Valley put new demands on government to manage such far-flung territories, requiring a quantitative increase in government services provided by established agencies such as the army and the post office and leading to a qualitative increase in private pressures on government for new kinds of services as well. The abandonment of direct government banking activities, the expansion of trade, and the radical increase in the production of gold after the California Gold Rush began led to the creation of new federal financial institutions. The independent treasury system was reestablished to guard and disburse funds on deposit. The warehouse system was instituted to handle imported goods coming through customs. New gold coins were issued and in the next few years, new mints and federal assay offices in the West were established to handle the increased flow of gold.

The Department of the Interior was established in 1849 to handle the bulk of the federal government's domestic activities. Transferred to it were such important bureaus as the census office (which would be redesigned to conduct the first really professional census in 1850), the patent office (whose business was increasing geometrically in the wake of the technological explosion of the new generation, yet it remained responsible for the small amount of federal aid to agriculture), the pension office (soon to get an infusion of business from Mexican War veterans as well as aging veterans of the War of 1812), the Indian office (which would be confronted with a serious Indian problem for the first time since the 1830s as settlement moved into the trans-Mississippi West), and the General Land Office (which had inherited a vast new domain and was well on its way to becoming the leading agent of formal federal-state cooperation).

The changing impact of the federal government can be seen through the overall increase in federal expenditures and employees in the years following 1846. Looking at total federal expenditures (including cash and land grants at their cash equivalent) between 1789 and 1861, the pattern of increase becomes clear (Table 5-1). The increase of federal expenditures was steady but came in steps, each of which represented the kind of substantial increment that reflected a significant expansion of activity. Until the War of 1812 there was a gradual increase that more than doubled the nation's first budgets with the highest point coming during the years of America's heaviest external involvement, from the beginning of an undeclared war with France (1798) to the completion of the acquisition of Louisiana.

The War of 1812 brought a substantial step upward to unprecedented heights; after the war the budget remained at a new plateau. The Jacksonians were unable to do more than hold federal expenditure within the range established at the beginning of that period and even they had to give way before the demands of the second generation after 1835. Because of the Jacksonian response, in 1836 the expenditure pattern shifted upward to a new plateau without a major war though strenuous efforts by Jackson's successors restricted the increase far more than "Old Hickory" himself attempted to do.

84

Table 5-1

GROSS FEDERAL CASH EXPENDITURES: 1789-1861
(By Period – in $000s)

Period	Lowest Year	Highest Year	Total
1789-1811	$4,269 (1789-91)	$10,786 (1800)	$170,193
1812-1835	14,883 (1823)	34,721 (1814)	497,888
1836-1846	11,858 (1843)	37,243 (1837)	306,427
1847-1861	45,377 (1848)	108,794 (1850)	994,898

Source: U.S. Census Bureau, *Historical Statistics of the United States*

In 1847, the impact of the Mexican War broke all previous barriers to inaugurate a decade of great increases. The most striking thing about the pattern of expenditures in the half generation before the Civil War was that the federal outlays increased far beyond the highest ones brought about by the Mexican conflict. In fact, the lowest year of the period was 1848, at the height of the war. The neo-Jacksonian presidents of that period, who opposed these increasing expenditures, were powerless in the face of the coalition of Congress and the leaders of the executive departments, a coalition that was simply responding to the most pressing public demands. Even their response was often begrudging, as the next decade would show.

The growth of the federal government's role in society is even better illustrated if all federal expenditures related to war are excluded from consideration. The remainder of the federal civil expenditures follow a pattern very similar to that of the gross expenditures, but show an even greater increase after 1848. From less than $7 million in 1848, federal civil expenditures shot up to over $25 million the next year. A new floor of $30 million was established in 1853, to last for a decade until the great expansion of federal programs during the Civil War that would thrust federal expenditures to new heights.

Even more significant, the average annual share of the total federal budget devoted to civil expenditures rose from about one-third to nearly one-half after 1848. The nation's borders secured, the federal government could devote more of its resources to domestic affairs rather than to defense. While some of this growth could be explained by population increase, that alone is far from a sufficient explanation. The population of the United States in 1848 was approximately 20 million (23,171,876 by the 1850 census). By 1853 it may have reached 25 million and by 1860 stood at 31,443,321. Thus the population increased by some fifty percent in the intervening twelve years while expenditures increased more than fourfold almost at the outset of the period.

The pattern of federal expansion is even more clearly reflected in the growth of its per capita expenditures for civil functions, adjusted for fluctuations in the purchasing power of the dollar (Table 5-2). Increasing at nearly a constant rate of fifty percent from 1789 through Jackson's administration, subsequent Jacksonians were able to hold it steady for a decade, though even they were unable to reduce it despite their ideology. Then, in the half generation after 1848, it soared as old federal services were improved and new ones initiated to confirm what later generations would know as a truism, that industrializing societies must spend more for government than agrarian ones, ideological predispositions notwithstanding.

Table 5-2

AVERAGE FEDERAL CIVIL EXPENDITURES: 1789-1861

Period	Average Annual Expenditures in Thousands	Adjusted Percent Increase Over Previous Period	Average Per Capita Expenditures	Adjusted Percent Increase Over Previous Period
1789–1801	$ 937	—	$ .20	—
1802–1815	2,292	108%	.33	+45%
1816–1828	4,358	125%	.42	+50%
1829–1838	7,556	100%	.53	+50%
1839–1848	8,732	30%	.45	no change
1849–1861	37,403	300%	1.36	+175%

The growth of the federal establishment followed the same general patterns. While the total number of federal civilian employees grew steadily from decade to decade, much of that growth reflected the normal expansion of the country, particularly in the establishment of new post offices as settlement moved westward. In the 1830s, however, the federal departments in Washington began to expand as did the number of federal employees (other than those in the postal service) in the states (Table 5-3). The federal establishment as a whole doubled in size between 1841 and 1861, as did its Washington staff (Table 5-4).

Table 5-3

FEDERAL CIVILIAN EMPLOYMENT BY CATEGORY:
1816-1861 (Selected Years)

Year	War and Navy Departments	Post Office	Other Executive	Judicial
1816	190	3,341	948	115
1821	161	4,766	1,599	136
1831	377	8,764	1,926	135
1841	598	14,290	2,662	156
1851	403	21,391	3,919	177
1861	946	30,269	4,891	173

While comparable fiscal data for the states are difficult to secure, such information as is available indicates that much the same kind of progression took place at that level. Table 5-5 shows the growth of state expenditures in eight states selected from sections of the country. In the older states of the Northeast, the turn to laissez-faire policies and consequent abandonment of an activist role in economic life led to a drastic reduction in state expenditures in the 1840s. By the late 1850s, however, this brief period of retrenchment had come to an end and state expenditures were spiralling upward. The states of the South and the West show a constant increase, reflecting, in the case of the former, a less drastic change in their economic policies and, in the case of the latter, the

Table 5-4

FEDERAL CIVILIAN EMPLOYMENT BY LOCATION:
1816-1861 (Selected Years)

Year	Located in Washington, D.C.	Located in Rest of U.S.	Total
1816	535	4,302	4,837
1821	603	6,311	6,914
1831	666	10,825	11,491
1841	1,014	17,024	18,038
1851	1,533	24,741	26,038
1861	2,199	34,473	36,672

accelerating demands of the frontier such as continuous population growth.

Almost without exception, the new activities of government after the year 1848 were of greater benefit to the states of the North and the Northwest. In some cases, this was consciously designed to be so and in others, circumstances made it so. In either case, Southerners, who already felt discriminated against in the matter of federal support for their legal claims, now began to feel that the federal government was discriminating against them in formal aid programs as well.

One or two examples should suffice. The independent subtreasury system established in the late 1840s was designed to overcome the problem of security for federal funds created by the demise of government-sponsored central banks and the proliferation of private banks seeking federal deposits. However, the proliferation of private banks was peculiar to the North, particularly to the Northeast. In the South, state-sponsored banking continued to be widespread until the Civil War under conditions not substantially different from those which prevailed nationally in the early part of the nineteenth century. Thus, the Southern states, which could have responded quite adequately to a continuation or

Table 5-5

GROWTH OF STATE EXPENDITURES: 1800-1860
(Selected States)

Year	Calif.	Ky.	Me.	Mass.	N.Y.	Ohio	Tex.	Wis.
1790	—	—	—	(1794–$215)	$143	—	—	—
1800	—	$53	—	—	316	(1803–c.$26)	—	—
1810	—	(1815–$138)	—	—	606	(1813–c.$39)	—	—
1820	—	159	38	302	1,202	—	—	—
1830	—	146	189	330	1,969	92	—	—
1840	—	287	1,340	416	1,608	223	—	—
1845	—	—	—	416	1,809	201	(1847–$128)	—
1850	348	523	552	566	807	393	148	63
1855	1,337	—	636	1,411	1,754	442	269	342
1860	1,166	1,402	566	1,194	3,103	664	829	594

restoration of the old cooperative federal deposit system and thereby gained the revenue and income that came from having their banks serve as federal depositories, were forced out of the depository service because of the needs of the Northeast, where such a system was no longer adequate and was, in light of the proliferation of unsecured institutions seeking deposits, positively harmful.

It should be noted that originally the independent treasury system, a Democratic favorite, had strong Southern support at the time of its establishment, led by none other than Calhoun, who "seems to have reasoned that withdrawal of the federal funds from the banks would hamper the North, where most of the banks were and most of the funds, and be consequently to the South's advantage."* But these expectations were not fulfilled; the Northeastern interests learned how to master the new system while the Southerners lost as, judging by results, became apparent to them by the late 1850s. This is another example of how an erroneous theory — in this case as to whether dual or cooperative federalism would best serve Southern interests — leads to undesired practical consequences.

The creation of the Department of the Interior in 1849 was of direct benefit to the public-land states and the new territories of the trans-Mississippi West. And, of the twenty public-land states and territories that existed before the 1861 disruption, only six were slave territory. As the balance in the West turned against slavery, the new federal department became, for all intents and purposes, an agent of Northern interests.

The two-to-one edge of free commonwealths over slave in the public domain meant that the land grant programs, even when distributed equitably, ultimately favored the North at the expense of the South. Consequently, the great expansion of land grant programs after 1850 simply increased federal support of the farmer's interests. Also, the free states carved from the public domain were in the aggregate larger in territory than the slave states, so even though all six slave states received railroad land grants between 1850 and 1857, while only five of the free states did, some 15 million acres of land were granted to the latter as opposed to some 10 million granted to the former.

Still, the northward tendency of federal interest and support remained only a tendency through the 1850s. Southerners in

---

* Bray Hammond, *Banks and Politics in America* (Princeton: Princeton University Press, 1957), p. 542.

national office were able to maintain the previously established high levels of support for federal functions in Southern states throughout the decade, even increasing their share somewhat over previous years, but the tendency itself pointed to new possibilities in the future. If the South were ever to lose its influence in Washington even for a brief period of time, the tendency might become a real shift indeed.

Professionalized Politics and Governmental Leadership

If one were to seek the agent through which the various planes of government in the United States were brought together in cooperative action, the institution responsible for shepherding government into new channels in response to the changing environment, one would look no further than the political parties. By 1848, American politics was clearly national. Even the most local contests tended to reflect national party issues and divisions. Whatever theories of separation of political questions by arena may have been entertained by the founders of the Republic, they had been set aside by the reality of a national society functioning within a nationwide economic system. The new national politics was characterized by an important intermixture of concerns; while state and local elections were fought on national issues, national politics were just as frequently influenced by intrastate or local political interests and rivalries. Thus a fight between rival personalities in a state could determine the outcome of a presidential election, while a decision at the White House could make or break a mayor. This intermixture was enhanced by the fact that the national parties were no more than loose confederations of state parties.

By 1848, the political parties were busily adapting themselves to the new organizational society. During the 1850s, a subtle but important change took place in the structure of party organizations. Where professional politicians had developed and come into their own in the past, they had usually done so as open political figures, office-seekers and officeholders in their own right. Thus, Martin Van Buren in New York, Henry Clay in Kentucky, and Ninian Edwards in Illinois represented a type of leader who ruled with an iron hand, was professionally committed to political life, yet was also available to the public for all to inspect. The new generation of political leaders was as likely to operate from behind the scenes as on the open stage. The visible party leader frequently gave way to the invisible behind-the-scenes boss, a man whose role in party affairs might not be publicly known even if he were an acknowledged leader or even a person who might not be known to the public at all.

The leaders of the new state and local political organizations still tended to seek public office more often than not, and the Congress of the United States, which had traditionally offered such men a base of operations to complement their base of power, became even more attractive. Many senators and congressmen of the 1850s — Stephen A. Douglas of Illinois is a prime example — were as busy managing affairs back home as they were tending to the nation's business.

Political recruitment was more open after 1848 and indeed, by the mid-1850s, new immigrants were trying their luck in the political arena, particularly in the nation's larger cities. The old style of family-based politics whereby certain individuals had better access to public office by virtue of their publicly recognized lineage clearly declined. Family ties as a means of entering politics took on a new content, now functioning below the surface, though still evident to those who cared to look beneath the surface.

The trend toward mass-based party organizations continued unabated during the 1850s. By the eve of the Civil War, political patronage had reached a new level of importance, though that level would soon be overshadowed by Republican efforts to use the patronage system to build themselves into the nation's majority party.

Right up until the eve of the war, the loose nationwide confederacies of political party organizations represented the foremost effort at nationwide mass organization that the country knew. While the churches had been nationally organized at least in name even earlier, the North-South schisms of the 1840s had divided the nation's leading denominations — the Baptists and the Methodists — into sectional bodies. In any case, all the church organizations except those of the Catholics and the Episcopalians were noncentralized with a vengeance, with congregational organization predominating to the point where even state religious societies operated as conventions more than as organizations.

The new professional associations that had arisen in the 1840s, while on their way to becoming national in scope, were still in their formative stages. Much the same could be said of the few interstate business corporations that emerged after 1848. The nation's longest railroad barely served three states. On the frontier, large enterprises in the form of fur trading corporations did transact business that cut across state and territorial lines, but with minimal impact on the organization of society. While corporations were proliferating and were already beginning to concentrate capital in the Northeast, holding corporations were substantially unknown. The only nationwide organization to rival the political parties was the federal government itself.

With all the new activity in the realms of economics and government in the immediate antebellum period, political leadership — state and national — sank to its lowest ebb. Through the political breakdown of earlier compromises, through the industrial transformation of the face of the North and the Northwest, through the continued advance of settlement westward, through the decline of Southern power in national councils, those responsible for the government of the United States refused to fully accept that responsibility. They persisted in subscribing to the then current belief that government was to be passive, no more than a policeman responsible for keeping order, but not responsible for preventing disorder. This was particularly true among those entrusted with executive leadership — the presidents and governors of the nation and its states.

It has been mistakenly held that the failure to exert executive leadership lies with the individuals selected for those offices. The truth of the matter is that, after 1844, it was by design that only men who could not or would not take an active executive role were picked for office by party managers and public alike. Notions of democracy rampant in the country after 1830 denigrated the importance of such leadership and even held it to be undemocratic.

Public desires for limiting the power of their governors — executive, legislative, and judicial — were expressed in the introduction of detailed and highly restrictive state constitutions accompanied by the direct election of as many public officials as possible. In this the public was encouraged by professional politicians whose growing power was based on their ability to bring some order to the confusion that ensued from the long ballot and to secure some action from a government well-nigh paralyzed by constitutional restrictions. Political leaders used the party as a means of bringing a degree of order and limited energy to the tasks of government and, in return, exacted their price — power, prestige, or wealth, or some combination of all three.

This system grew and flowered most successfully in the populous middle states. There the political culture was conducive to the spread of the idea that politics as a profession was simply another form of business in which politicians could expect to make profits in return for services rendered. It was considerably less widespread in either the far North or the deep South where older patterns were better able to persist even in the face of the new pressures.

The condition of government on the federal plane was typical of the situation nationwide. In the thirty-two years between the election of Andrew Jackson and Abraham Lincoln, Democrats occupied the White House slightly less than twenty-eight years. Though "Old Hickory" himself had not hesitated to use the powers of his office aggressively when he felt it necessary to do so, his successors, who called themselves Jacksonians, assumed a defensive position. Even James K. Polk, who earned the sobriquet "Young Hickory" for being the most aggressive chief executive between Jackson and Lincoln, subscribed wholeheartedly to the theories of limited government of the strictest Democrats (as did Jackson, in words) and showed executive energy only because his nature got the better of his doctrine.

After Polk, the decline of public leadership set in with a vengeance. While federal activities and expenditures were growing at an unprecedented pace and the difficulties of sectional politics afforded endless opportunities for imaginative and creative leadership, both the entrepreneurial and the legislative branches of the national government were dominated by those who preferred to abdicate power rather than exercise it.

The men who occupied high office in this period were less Jacksonian than neo-Jacksonians in the sense that, while taking their cues from "Old Hickory," they distorted his ideas into a new ideology. While Jackson was for limiting the federal government because he believed it to be the servant of privilege, they were for limiting all government for any reason. While Jackson advocated the replacement of confirmed anti-Democratic partisans holding positions in the federal service so that his program would not be hampered, they embraced the principle of rotation in office to the point where each new president was entitled to the spoils of office for his own followers even at the expense of others from the same political party. While Jackson believed that the elimination of mercantilism was necessary in order to provide equal opportunity for the many up and coming small entrepreneurs, they believed that any government intervention in the economy against private businesses of any size was wrong in principle.

Thus no president after Polk had a legislative program to present to Congress, and Congress was not sufficiently organized internally to develop a program of its own. The level of administrative expertise in all areas of government was extremely low. The occasional cabinet member who, like Jefferson Davis, had prior experience in the field of his responsibilities stood out as a leader because of his exceptional qualifications.

The federal government had no more than a handful of career civil servants at the higher echelons and they were concentrated in the specialized branches of government — the Coast Survey, the Naval Observatory, the Topographical Engineers. These professionals were usually men with military training if not members of the armed services and their work was generally confined to their own areas of interest exclusively. They were not presidential advisors. There were no such advisors in government. The "kitchen cabinets" of the presidents were comprised of politicians whose concerns were entirely political — usually in the most conniving sense of the term. In short, the antebellum decade was one in which national politics sank as low as it would in the postbellum "Gilded Age" without the redeeming features of the morally proper Ohio Republican presidents of the later period. Under such a system, no government could live up to its potential and handle the problems of a cold war.

Lincoln and the Government of His Age

In a very real sense, Abraham Lincoln's own life and political career in the years before his nomination for the presidency illustrate the true state of the political system he was destined to save. Born into a family that followed the frontier, Lincoln's first contacts with government were typical of his time and place — a continuing, if intermittent, contact with the federal government through its local officials who handled the mails and managed the public domain; an irregular contact with local government when drawing upon its few services; and a continuous contact with state government primarily in the realm of partisan and electoral politics.

Lincoln's first sense of the presence of government appears to have come at the age of eight when his family moved to Indiana. There, in the wilderness of a state just one year old, his father purchased 160 acres of federal lands at two dollars an acre for a farm, making part of the down payment of $80 on October 15, 1817, at the United States Land Office in Vincennes and the rest of it ($64) two months later. While county government nominally existed in south central Indiana in Lincoln's childhood years, there were no public schools and no towns in an area that hardly boasted one person per square mile so that, in reality, the Lincolns lived unencumbered or sustained by local governmental institutions. Yet, for the next ten years, the presence of federal authority was always with them in the form of a debt for the impossible sum of $240 owed on the remaining farm acreage. This debt proved so burdensome to a backwoods family that by Lincoln's nineteenth year, his father was able to complete payments on only eighty acres and decided to relinquish the rest to the United States once again. Three years later, the remainder of the farm was sold at a loss and the Lincolns moved to Illinois, to repeat the process in another United States Land District.

The little formal schooling Lincoln obtained was offered by itinerant private teachers since Indiana was not to have a public school system for another generation. There is no record of Thomas Lincoln's participation in politics, even to the extent of voting. His son did not cast his first vote until August 1831 when he had already moved to New Salem. This was very likely his second (or third, considering the repetition of filing on public land) direct experience with government. A year later he was to be a candidate for the Illinois legislature from Sangamon County.

Perhaps because he deeply felt the lack of essential governmental services available to him as a child, Lincoln was a believer in active government from the first day he ventured into politics, espousing Henry Clay's "American System" and adopting the Kentuckian as his special hero. Lincoln's first platform outlined his view of the positive role of government in an expanding state, calling for extensive state-sponsored internal improvements, including roads for the New Salem area and improvement of the Sangamon River to connect the interior of Illinois with the nation's major lines of communication; better facilities for public education; and a law to limit the rates of interest charged by the few possessors of capital for its use by the common farmers and small businessmen of the frontier. It was a platform that expressed his firm belief in a certain kind of activist government, one active in promoting the public welfare and in fostering common enterprises on behalf of the common man.

Many years later, he was to sum up his governmental philosophy in a now-famous and often misinterpreted aphorism:

The legitimate object of government is "to do for the people what needs to be done, but which they can not, by individual effort, do at all, or do so well, for themselves."

This was his philosophy from first to last and he interpreted it broadly.

When Lincoln entered the legislative lists in 1832, party lines in Illinois were still relatively fluid. The divisions between the supporters of Andrew Jackson, who were to become the Democrats, and his opponents were just beginning to take form in the state. Those soon to be identified as Whigs leaned toward Henry Clay in Washington and Ninian Edwards in Vandalia (then the capital of Illinois). The first was Lincoln's idol and the second his patron.

While personal and family alignments were crucial in determining the leanings of most politically active people locally, the more thoughtful among them recognized doctrinal differences in the emerging parties. In a generation in which the nation's socio-economic character was changing from that of a mercantilist system dominated by the gentry to that of a free capitalist system dominated by entrepreneurs, both parties identified with the ideas of laissez-faire and social democracy to a greater extent than the previous generation. The Jacksonians, however, were already moving toward the notions (accepted in theory, if not always implemented in practice) of complete government abstention from interference in the economy, except for minimal police functions, and democratization of the political process to the point of constant rotation of officeholders and perennial election of policy-makers. Only the presence of Andrew Jackson in the White House held back the third pillar of what was rapidly becoming the Democratic creed — the restriction of governmental energy in the name of maximum private freedom.

The Whigs, on the other hand, had developed new notions of government's role in an entrepreneurial capitalist system. Best formulated by Henry Clay as "the American system," these notions involved the use of governmental powers to determine the direction of entrepreneurial capitalism through tariff and banking policies that would encourage internal self-sufficiency and to provide the entrepreneurial elements with the support they needed to flourish through support for internal improvement and basic public services. More communitarian than egalitarian, the Whig view looked toward the improvement of communities as well as individuals and, hence, accepted the notion of social distinctions as useful to assure proper leadership in a society which was influenced by energetic government.

Lincoln, a believer in Henry Clay and the "aristocracy of talents" as befitted a man socially "on the make," was drawn instinctively toward the Edwards faction, which offered him acceptable doctrines and the companionship of those who were considered the best element in the state. His platform in that 1832 campaign reflected principles that were to remain basic to him all his life and which would strongly influence his domestic program after 1861. Though he was defeated in that race by candidates better known outside of New Salem, he would go on to become an architect of an internal improvement program for Illinois before the decade was out.

In the meantime, out of a job and searching for a permanent career, Lincoln took a time-honored way to gain time. He joined the state militia for the Black Hawk War. Elected captain of his local militia company, he marched the unit off to join the state troops and be sworn into United States military service. For eighty days he was on the federal payroll, earning the largest sum he had yet seen in his life, $125, paid him by the army paymaster who went from town to town disbursing funds, thereby raising the amount of ready cash available on the Illinois frontier manyfold.

Lincoln's pay evaporated in an unsuccessful venture as a storekeeper, but the magnitude of that little sum from Washington is better understood when it is recalled that Lincoln's debts from the store came to $1,100, a crushing burden that was not entirely paid off for years. Out of a job within eight months of his return from the wars, he again turned to federal patronage for support, this time securing appointment as United States Postmaster for New Salem. Only the fluidity of the party situation made it possible for him, an incipient but still undeclared Whig, to gain this appointment from the Jacksonians.

Lincoln earned his livelihood as postmaster until the post office he served was moved to Petersburg in 1836, earning about $55 annually from fees based on receipts plus perquisites of free mailing and, as a federal employee, exemption from such state mandated tasks as militia service and jury duty. His annual income from the post office being insufficient, Lincoln maintained himself by doing odd jobs as well. He could usually raise his income by five percent each year by serving as an election clerk.

During this period, Lincoln also accepted the first of two local government offices he was to hold — the post of Deputy County Surveyor for the northwest part of Sangamon (now Menard) County. He held that position for three years coincident with his tenure as postmaster and was also paid on a fee basis. Several of the roads he surveyed are still in use and towns that grew from his town site surveys are still the leading communities in that area. The latter two positions put Lincoln in technical violation of the constitutional prohibition against holding federal and state office simultaneously though it is unlikely that the residents of New Salem viewed it as such since, in their eyes, all three offices were considered "local ones." The complications of Lincoln's career in government reached a high point in 1834. Elected to the state legislature that year, Lincoln became a living link between the three arenas of government in America by serving simultaneously as postmaster, legislator, and county surveyor.

Lincoln's election as a Whig at the height of Jacksonian power was in large measure the result of a conflict over the best means to implement one of the most important federal-state cooperative programs of the age, the construction of the Illinois and Michigan Canal to connect the Erie Canal-Great Lakes waterway system with the Mississippi River and its numerous tributaries. This enterprise, for Illinois and the West comparable in importance to the construction of the Erie Canal, was the beneficiary of an 1827 federal land grant of alternate sections along its proposed right of way which could be used to finance construction of a canal or a railroad as the states would choose. It was soon discovered that the grant would not become valuable until the canal was built to open that part of the state to intensive settlement. While it would ultimately bring in sufficient revenue to cover the entire cost of the canal's construction, the state had first to arrange for the financing of construction through the issuance of bonds and then repay the borrowed funds later. Lincoln and the Whigs backed immediate construction of the canal and swept into office on that issue.

Vandalia, which years before had been strategically located on the National Road build by the federal government to connect the Atlantic Coast with the Mississippi River, gave Lincoln his first contact with an arena of government organization that transcended, however minutely, the overwhelmingly casual and personal government of his earlier experience. The ramshackle village of less than a thousand inhabitants was dominated by the state government and its meagre institutions. The sixteen year old state of Illinois with its 200,000 people was already closely connected to the mainstream of American politics. Still, the legislature's local tasks were limited to the enactment of a few general laws and the authorization of local roads and bridges to be laid out or constructed locally. Much of its time was spent discussing the great national issues of the day such as the proper fate of the United States Bank — the greatest of the federally-sponsored joint stock companies then under Jacksonian attack.

The great preoccupations of that legislative session served to introduce the young Illinoisian to the problems of intergovernmental collaboration and government participation in the economy. Fully one-fourth of the session was devoted to considering and taking action toward the construction of the Illinois and Michigan Canal. Another was devoted to the question of establishing a state bank, a Whig measure designed to provide an alternate system of government fiscal control in the face of the pending demise of the United States Bank. Lincoln supported the successful measures that led to state action in both cases.

Lincoln was to serve for eight years in the Illinois General Assembly, rising to a position of leadership in that body and constantly active in promoting internal improvements. A decade later he served a brief two years in the Congress of the United States. In both bodies, his platforms would invariably advocate full suffrage for all whites paying taxes or bearing arms, federal distribution of the proceeds of public land sales to the states for internal improvements, support for the state-owned Bank of Illinois, and similar measures that reflected an Illinois version of idol Henry Clay's American System locally while he supported the original nationally.

When not engaged in legislative duties, Lincoln was active in local and national politics, participating in campaigns for county judge or congressman with equal vigor. He served as town trustee of Springfield, his new home city which he helped to put on the map by making it capitol of Illinois; practiced law in the state and federal courts impartially; and promoted railroads in central Illinois as a private person with political connections. During his brief tenure in Washington, he not only did his congressional chores but also argued a case before the United States Supreme

Court, obtained a patent on a device to aid boats navigating shallow rivers, and persistently concerned himself with federal patronage in Illinois. In the years of Lincoln's forced retirement from active politics, he performed yet another major role in the development of the new cooperative railroad construction program, serving both the Illinois Central and the Rock Island line as lawyer and promoter.

His pattern of political thought established by the beginning of the Civil War generation, Lincoln's theoretical position had been hardened by practical experience in all the various corners of the American partnership. As his biographer, Benjamin P. Thomas, put it:

> Lincoln's conception of the government's relation to the economic welfare of the people went beyond (the Jacksonians') laissez-faire philosophy; he favored direct government expenditures for public improvements, as well as grants in aid to states, and help to private enterprise.

Unlike others of his generation, Lincoln had penetrated to the essence of the American system in both understanding and action. The consequences of his perceptions were to become apparent after 1861.

Bibliographic Notes — Chapter 5

On politics in the post-1848 period, see Thomas A. Bailey, *Democrats vs. Republicans* (1968); William N. Chambers, *The Democrats, 1789-1964* (1964); George H. Mayer, *Republican Party, 1854-1966*, 2nd ed. (1967); Malcolm C. Moos, *Republicans: A History of Their Party* (1956); William S. Myers, *Republican Party: A History* (1928); Howard P. Nash, Jr., *Third Parties in American Politics* (1958).

On presidential conventions and elections, see Herbert Agar, *People's Choice, From Washington to Harding* (1933); Richard C. Bain, *Convention Decisions and Voting Records* (1960); William B. Brown, *People's Choice: Presidential Image in Campaign Biography* (1960); Walter Dean Burnham, *Presidential Ballots, 1836-1892* (1955); Paul T. David, Ralph M. Goldman, and Richard C. Bain, *Politics of National Party Conventions* (1960); Kirk H. Porter and Donald B. Johnson, comps., *National Party Platforms, 1840-1964*, 3rd ed. (1966); Eugene

H. Roseboom, *History of Presidential Elections*, 2nd ed. (1964); Richard M. Scammon, ed., *America at the Polls: Handbook of Presidential Election Statistics* (1965); Arthur M. Schlesinger, Jr., and Fred I. Israel, eds., *History of American Presidential Elections, 1789-1968*, 4 vols. (1971).

On state and regional politics, see Royce D. Delmatier, et al., eds., *The Rumble of California Politics; 1848-1970* (1970); Walter K. Ferguson, *Geology and Politics in Frontier Texas, 1845-1909* (1969); Richard P. McCormick, *History of Voting in New Jersey: 1664-1911* (1953); Dorothy Riker and Gayle Thornbrough, comps., *Indiana Election Returns, 1816-1851* (1960); Charles P. Smith, *New Jersey Political Reminiscences, 1828-1882*, ed. Hermann K. Platt (1965).

On government and the economy, see Lance E. Davis and John Legler, "Government in the American Economy, 1815-1902," *Journal of Economic History* 26 (1966): 514; Carter Goodrich, *Government Promotion of Canals and Railroads, 1800-1890* (1960); Oscar Handlin and Mary F. Handlin, *Commonwealth: A Study of the Role of Government in the American Economy: Massachusetts, 1774-1861*, rev. ed. (1969); Louis Hartz, *Economic Policy and Democratic Thought: Pennsylvania, 1776-1860* (1948); Milton S. Heath, *Constructive Liberalism: The Role of the State in Economic Development in Georgia to 1860* (1954); Gerald D. Nash, *State Government and Economic Development, 1849-1933* (1964); James N. Primm, *Economic Policy in the Development of a Western State: Missouri, 1820-1860* (1954).

On Lincoln, see William E. Baringer, C. Percy Powell, and Earl S. Miers, eds., *Lincoln Day by Day*, 3 vols. (1960); Albert J. Beveridge, *Abraham Lincoln, 1809-1858*, 2 vols. (1928); John J. Duff, *A. Lincoln: Prairie Lawyer* (1960); Don E. Fehrenbacher, *Prelude to Greatness: Lincoln in the 1850s* (1962); John P. Frank, *Lincoln as a Lawyer* (1961); *Abraham Lincoln, Collected Works*, ed. Roy P. Basler, 9 vols. (1953-1955); *Abraham Lincoln, Political Thought*, ed. Richard N. Current (1967); Allan Nevins, *Emergence of Lincoln* (1950); John G. Nicolay and John Hay, *Abraham Lincoln, A History*, 10 vols. (1890); Donald W. Riddle, *Congressman Abraham Lincoln* (1957), and *Lincoln Runs for Congress* (1948); Carl Sandburg, *Abraham Lincoln*, 6 vols. (1926-1936).

PART THREE:

THE POLITICS OF REVOLUTION

Chapter 6

THE POLARIZATION OF POLITICS

The Critical 1850s

In 1847, an authentic hero of the Mexican War, who had used his West Point training to good stead as a colonel in a volunteer regiment in the Battle of Buena Vista, entered the United States Senate. For four years, he stood for strengthening the Union through territorial expansion while safeguarding the interests of his section in the new territory annexed from Mexico. He left the Senate to run for governor in his home state as a Unionist Democrat and, after he lost to an even stronger Unionist, went into brief retirement. Recalled to national prominence as Secretary of War, one of his first acts was to launch surveys of the various possible routes for a railroad to the Pacific, which he supported because of its potential value in holding the Pacific slope for the Union while improving the position of his section. As an active and progressive manager of the nation's military affairs, he tried to maintain sectional impartiality in the assignment of officers and political impartiality in the staffing of his department.

Returning to the Senate, he became one of that chamber's legislative leaders. He championed federal action to enforce the fugitive slave laws and to prevent abolitionist raids like that of John Brown, on Southern states, arguing the preeminent right of the federal government to enforce its laws even in the face of strong state and local interposition. He led the fight for the adoption of resolutions to that effect and secured formal Senate condemnation of state laws in conflict with the Constitution as null and void and official rejection of the nullification doctrine.

In a speech made less than a year before the outbreak of the war, he said:

> Our principles are national; they belong to every State of the Union; and though elections may be lost by their assertion, they constitute the only foundation on which we can maintain power....Our flag bears no new device. Upon its folds our principles are written in living light; all proclaiming the constitutional Union, justice, equality, and fraternity of our ocean-bound domain, for a limitless future.

105

Eight months later, after a career that illustrated the interlocking character of the federal system no less than that of Abraham Lincoln, he reluctantly bade farewell to the Senate and followed his state out of the Union. The following month Jefferson Davis became president of the Confederate States of America.

Fighting for the South, Senator Davis had espoused the cause of the Union to the fullest. Eager to maintain the rights of his state, he had advocated virtually unprecedented levels of federal intervention in other states, albeit only in the very special circumstances involving the interstate flight of slaves. Proclaiming the virtues of Calhoun's concurrent majority idea, he denied the rights of the Northern states to nullify federal fugitive slave laws. Afraid that the slave states were doomed to minority status because the Far West was unsuited to slavery, he tried to promote a Pacific railroad to assure that region's continued connection to the Union. Davis was neither hypocritical nor stupid in his stands. Rather, his public career in the half generation between 1847 and 1861 displayed all the contradictory characteristics of those years, contradictions which have greatly confused subsequent generations in their efforts to understand the nature of the American Union before the Civil War.

This last antebellum period has been rightly described as one of cold war by several eminent historians. Cold war it was, with all the apparent absurdities and inconsistencies of policy and action the term implies. On one hand, the normal and little-noted processes and programs of government continued apparently undisturbed. Men from all sections competed for public office and the rewards of public office as before. Interest groups competed for governmental benefits as always. In the offices of government, it was "business as usual," in some cases well into May 1861.

In the realm of public politics, on the other hand, crisis after crisis deepened intersectional misunderstanding and mutual suspicion, even within the club-like United States Senate. Misconception piled upon misunderstanding to divorce the two sections and incident piled upon incident to promote civil conflict. The course of the cold war is clearly outlined in the sequences of landmark events between 1850 and 1861. Parallel to those events were developments that marked the emergence of the new age that was to dominate even the Civil War. Together, the cold war and the new age would create the postwar era.

From Hot Peace to Cold War

The Compromise of 1850 marked the last successful effort to avert an open break because leaders of the already passing generation of Northerners and Southerners who put the integrity of the Union above the slavery issue were able to apply the old methods of political give and take for one last time to put together a package minimally satisfactory to both sections. Even so, only two of the four great Unionists who had dominated national affairs for a generation — Henry Clay and Daniel Webster — united behind it; and the compromise itself was the work of one of the "new" breed of politicians, Stephen A. Douglas of Illinois, who shared the unionist goals of the older generation and who was to pay for being out of step with the times during the course of the new decade. Their two great compatriots — Thomas Hart Benton and John C. Calhoun — stood against them. Both had already come reluctantly to the conclusion that the old politics were inadequate and that the Union could be preserved only by taking a stand one way or the other and making it stick.

For all four, this was to be their last appearance on the scene. The stand of the younger men who were to become the leaders of the 1850s and 1860s was more portentous of the future. Three of the future war leaders, Senators William H. Seward of New York, Salmon P. Chase of Ohio, and Jefferson Davis united in opposing the compromise, like Benton and Calhoun, as strange bedfellows. They, too, had settled on the slavery issue as the essential one. The former two opposed any extension of slavery under any circumstances and the latter just as firmly resisted any limitations of any kind on slavery. Senator Lewis Cass of Michigan joined Douglas to support the compromise fully. Heirs apparent to the Clay-Webster position, they were to fall into political quicksand before the decade was out in their efforts to apply the normal techniques of politics after the moral gap had become too great to be compromised.

The two great points of contention in 1850 were matters that hinged upon questions of federalism. There was the question of the organization of new territories which would ultimately be admitted to the Union as states. This was of crucial importance because each territory would attract slaveowners and their supporters or Free-Soilers, depending on congressional delineation of its character, and thus would take its stand with the North or the South upon achievement of statehood to affect the sectional balance of the Union. There was also the question of enforcement of the fugitive slave laws against Northern state opposition to them, whether active or tacit. This was of crucial importance because of a change in the ostensibly private activities of the opponents of slavery during the 1840s. The commitment of additional participants in the Underground Railway made it easier for slaves to escape and less likely for them to be recovered without extensive government policing, thus threatening the whole structure of slavery in the South. If the state governments of the North were to throw their weight against the apprehension of fugitive slaves, or even remain neutral, the task of policing would become virtually impossible. This proved to be the case despite the series of United States Supreme Court decisions designed to strengthen federal enforcement powers.

In the midst of the congressional debate over the compromise measures, representatives of nine Southern states met at Nashville to consider a common course of action. The Nashville convention encompassed Southerners of three political persuasions. Urging the states on to secession were the states' rights fireeaters — the Rhetts and the Yanceys — men who placed their chief loyalties with their states even as they sought South-wide secession and opposed what they believed to be the centralizing tendencies of the federal government as well as the antislavery elements in the compromise package. These were young men distinguished for their power of logic and their firm rejection of the "illogic" of party activity that might lead to compromise of the secessionist movement. Opposing them were the Unionists who, though supporters of Southern rights, were also committed with equal fervor to the maintenance of the Union. Most of them were older, really members of the preceding generation, with one last battle for preservation of the Union left in them. Between the two extremes stood the new Southern nationalists who were young like the first group and, like the second, predisposed to maintaining the Union; or, if not, to forming a Southern version of it without an overwhelming regard for their ties to the individual states.

Only the belief of Southern moderates that the South could dominate the national government if the Southern states acted in concert deflected precipitous action on behalf of secession. The moderate victory was bought at the price of laying the groundwork for a secessionist conspiracy. Southern radicals of the first group learned that sectionwide action was needed if secession were to become a reality, but that sectionwide conventions worked against secession by giving the Unionists time to take preventative measures. They recognized that they would have to confront the South with a fait accompli in a few states, thereby forcing the Southern nationalists into their camp if they were to get the whole South to secede. The Southern decision for Union in 1850 had the real effect of transforming a potential "war between the states" into what would really be "when it came" a "war between the sections," because it made clear that the South would only leave the Union as a section even if the formal work of seceding would be, perforce, left to the states.

During the decade following the Compromise of 1850, the five measures which comprised it were successfully implemented or ignored, depending on how well they favored the North:

(1) California's admission as a free state was quickly accomplished and, while Southerners who settled there struggled for control of the state's affairs until the war was well underway, the fate of the Pacific Coast as part of the North's west was decided by that act.

(2) The creation of New Mexico territory was theoretically without prejudice against the extension of slavery, but, in fact, the requirement that Texas abandon her territorial claims west of that state's present borders actually reduced the territory open to the extension of the slave system. The Mexican-Americans of New Mexico had not seen slavery within their limits since Mexican abolition of the institution. Moreover, they associated slavery with the positively hated and feared "Texicans" and would have no part of it. To them, "free soil" was to be a bulwark against Texas expansionist tendencies.

(3) Creation of a territorial government for Mormon Utah also allowed slavery to spread in theory only. The Mormons were predominantly Yankees with a social system complete in and of itself. Neither their cultural heritage nor their religiously-organized social structure was likely to encourage slavery.

(4) Abolition of the slave trade in the District of Columbia was a clear Northern victory.

(5) The main hope for Southern satisfaction with the compromise lay in the enforcement of the strengthened fugitive

slave act. The interposition of "personal liberty" laws by the Yankee-dominated Northern states, beginning with Vermont the very same year, and the acceleration of popular resistance to the enforcement of the federal law meant that even this hope was to be a forlorn one.

When achieved, the compromise was a great hope for many. It was endorsed by both parties in 1852. To the perceptive observer, however, the ultimate failure of the compromise was foreordained before the year was out. As early as October 1850, the extremists among the Southerners, predicting that the Northern states would not encourage the return of fugitive slaves, organized the Southern Rights Association to serve as an organized vehicle for the coordination of Southern defense against antislavery onslaughts. On February 15, 1851, Shadrach, the first slave to be apprehended under the strengthened Fugitive Slave Act, was rescued by a black mob and shipped to safety in Canada, elevating the spokesmen of the Southern Rights Association to prophets among their Southern brethren. With each new incident, Southerners became further alienated from the American political system which appeared to be unable to guarantee their agreed upon rights.

The Politics of Polarization

The temporary character of the settlement of 1850 became evident when Stephen A. Douglas, in his own mind seeking to extend the principles of that settlement, championed the Kansas-Nebraska Act in 1854, effectively repealing the Missouri Compromise in the name of popular sovereignty. Regardless of his personal motivations in reopening the issue, which are still a matter of debate, the immediate consequences of his action were to destroy the one remaining political institution supporting national unity — the Democratic party — and to begin the extension of the cold war in revolutionary directions.

Within a year after opening the territorial questions under these conditions, the Whig party, already in great difficulty after 1852, was in ruins; the Democratic party was badly split into factions, and two new parties — the Republican and American (Know-Nothing) — were competing for the bodies of dissidents from both. In the midst of all this, there was the culmination of the trend begun by the Liberty party in 1840 (Table 6-1). After 1836, American national elections had been contested by parties that

Table 6-1

PRESIDENTIAL ELECTIONS: 1840 – 1860

Year	Winning Party	States Carried (Electoral Vote)	Popular Vote	Losing Parties	States Carried (Electoral Vote)	Popular Vote
1840	Whig	11F,8S (234)	1,275,612	Democratic Liberty	2F,5S (60) —	1,130,033 7,053
1844	Democratic	7F,8S (170)	1,339,368	Whig Liberty	6F,5S (105) —	1,300,687 62,197
1848	Whig	7F,8S (163)	1,362,101	Democratic Free Soil	8F,7S (127) —	1,222,674 291,616
1852	Democratic	14F,13S (254)	1,609,038	Whig Free Soil	2F,2S (42) —	1,386,629 156,297
1856	Democratic	5F,14S (174)	1,839,237	Republican American Whig	11F (114) 1S (8)	1,341,028 849,872
1860	Republican	18F (180)	1,867,198	Democratic Southern Democratic Constitutional Union	1S (12) 11S (72) 3S (39)	1,379,434 854,248 591,658

F = Free states   S = Slave states

111

sought to avoid all programs. In the aftermath of Jacksonianism, this had been sufficient for the Democrats, who could live off the capital of a past that rested on the principles of Jefferson, Madison, and the Jacksonians. The Whig party, however, had developed, survived, and occasionally won elections by avoiding serious commitments to any major principles and had finally reached a point of emptiness that even pragmatic Americans could not tolerate.

The Democratic strategy in the 1852 presidential election of selecting a Yankee with Southern principles and a Southern Unionist to head their ticket in the name of the compromise of 1850, which was fully consistent with the party's traditional aspiration to speak for a united nation, had given them decisive victories at the polls and the most decisive victory in the electoral college since the election of James Monroe. The Whigs, who adopted a similarly conciliatory strategy, could not beat the Democrats at their own game. The antislavery wing of the party was alienated while many Unionist Whigs in the South, reacting to the experiences of the previous two years, defected to the Democrats as the best hope for preserving the Union. Most Northern antislavery Democrats, equally anxious to prevent further steps toward disunity, returned to their party. The Free-Soil party, without Van Buren's machine to deliver forty percent of their vote as in 1848, held its hard-core abolitionist support, but no more. Never were the Democrats truer to their basic instincts as national unifiers than in 1852. Combining unionism with laissez-faire, they seemed to come extraordinarily close to reflecting a true national consensus.

The Democratic-forged consensus was an illusion. Events of the next four years only served to further polarize the nation. In fact, that election inaugurated the "Solid South" in national politics (Table 6-2). Until then, the Southern states were as internally divided in politics as their Northern sisters. The change in county voting patterns is sharply revealing (Table 6-3). Before the election of that year, almost every Southern state was not only sufficiently divided in party ties that it could be carried by either major party based on the issues at hand in specific elections, but the Southern counties were similarly divided as well. After 1852, over eighty percent of the counties in the states of the deep South were carried by the Democratic party in presidential elections, and most of those that were not were traditionally anti-Democratic strongholds that persisted in voting Whig or voted for the

112

Table 6-2

STATE PRESIDENTIAL VOTING PATTERNS: 1840-1860

	1840	1844	1848	1852	1856	1860
Ala.	D	D	D	D	D	SD
Ark.	D	D	D	D	D	SD
Del.	W	W	W	D	D	SD
Fla.	—	—	W	D	D	SD
Ga.	W	D	W	D	D	SD
Ky.	W	W	W	W	D	CU
La.	W	D	W	D	D	SD
Md.	W	W	W	D	A	SD
Miss.	W	D	D	D	D	SD
Mo.	D	D	D	D	D	D
N.C.	W	W	W	D	D	SD
S.C.	D	D	D	D	D	SD
Tenn.	W	W	W	W	D	CU
Tex.	—	—	D	D	D	SD
Va.	D	D	D	D	D	CU
Calif.	—	—	—	D	D	R
Conn.	W	W	W	D	R	R
Ill.	D	D	D	D	D	R
Ind.	W	D	D	D	D	R
Ia.	—	—	D	D	R	R
Me.	W	D	D	D	R	R
Mass.	W	W	W	W	R	R
Mich.	W	D	D	D	R	R
Minn.	—	—	—	—	—	R
N.H.	D	D	D	D	R	R
N.J.	W	W	W	D	D	4R,3D
N.Y.	W	D	W	D	R	R
Ohio	W	W	D	D	R	R
Ore.	—	—	—	—	—	R
Pa.	W	D	W	D	D	R
R.I.	W	W	W	D	R	R
Vt.	W	W	W	W	R	R
Wisc.	—	—	D	D	R	R

Table 6-3

COUNTY VOTING ALIGNMENTS BY STATE: 1840-1860

Slave States

	Ala.	Ark.	Del.	Fla.	Ga.	Ky.	La.	Md.	Miss.	Mo.	N.C.	S.C.	Tenn.	Tex.	Va.
1840															
Dem.	25	25	—	—	37	16	8	3	26	45	20	D	29	—	52
Whig	24	13	3	—	55	74	24	18	29	17	46	—	37	—	61
D-W	—	—	—	—	1	—	1	—	1	—	—	—	—	—	—
1844															
Dem.	32	33	1	—	49	42	25	3	43	56	27	D	38	—	73
Whig	19	5	2	—	44	56	20	18	15	21	43	—	35	—	56
1848															
Dem.	22	33	1	10	40	28	23	4	34	69	24	D	33	71	70
Whig	30	11	2	15	53	68	24	17	25	24	49	—	40	3	67
D-W	—	1	—	—	—	—	—	—	—	—	—	—	—	—	—

1852															
Dem.	42	50	1	22	76	50	31	12	51	83	30	D	42	86	17
Whig	8	2	2	4	5	50	17	10	9	19	41	—	37	0	17
X	2	—	—	—	17	—	—	—	—	—	—	—	—	—	—
D-W	—	—	—	1	—	—	—	—	—	2	1	—	—	—	—
1856															
Dem.	44	49	3	22	89	57	34	7	45	80	51	D	49	101	121
Rep.	—	1	0	—	—	—	14	—	—	—	—	—	—	—	—
X	8	—	0	8	28	38	—	15	14	27	32	—	32	8	27
D-X	—	—	—	—	1	—	—	—	—	—	—	—	—	—	—
1860															
SD	42	47	3	29	85	43	36	6	49	21	41	SD	38	117	74
CU	5	7	—	7	40	60	9	16	11	45	41	—	40	3	75
ND	5	—	—	—	6	7	3	—	—	44	—	—	1	—	4
SD-CU	—	—	—	—	1	—	—	—	—	—	—	—	—	—	1
Rep.	—	—	—	—	—	—	—	—	—	2	—	—	—	—	—

Key:

D-W	Democrat and Whig
X	Know-Nothing
D-X	Democrat and Know-Nothing
SD	Southern Democrat
CU	Constitutional Union
ND	Northern Democrat
SD-CU	Southern Democrat and Constitutional Union

Free States

	Calif.	Conn.	Ill.	Ind.	Iowa	Me.	Mass.	Mich.	Minn.	N.H.	N.J.	N.Y.	Ohio	Ore.	Pa.	R.I.	Vt.	Wis.
1840																		
Dem.	—	—	38	24	—	7	5	10	—	8	5	26	26	—	35	—	—	—
Whig	—	8	49	63	—	6	9	20	—	2	13	32	52	—	20	5	14	—
D-W	—	—	—	—	—	—	—	—	—	—	—	—	—	—	—	—	—	—
1844																		
Dem.	—	1	72	50	—	11	3	22	—	9	6	35	34	—	42	—	2	—
Whig	—	7	27	40	—	2	11	9	—	1	13	23	45	—	16	5	12	—
1848																		
Dem.	—	1	51	55	22	9	—	29	—	10	6	2	49	—	38	—	1	12
Whig	—	7	38	35	6	4	13	3	—	13	47	30	—	22	5	11	6	6
X	—	—	9	—	—	—	1	—	—	—	—	9	6	—	—	—	2	—
D-W	—	—	—	—	1	—	—	—	—	—	—	—	—	—	—	—	—	—
1852																		
Dem.	23	8	70	69	32	10	3	29	—	10	12	44	53	—	47	2	—	26
Whig	0	—	29	22	15	3	11	5	—	—	8	15	31	—	16	3	13	3
X	—	—	—	—	1	—	—	—	—	—	—	—	4	—	—	—	1	2
D-W	—	—	—	—	1	—	—	—	—	—	—	—	—	—	—	—	—	—

1856																		
Dem.	37	—	60	58	23	—	—	4	—	3	16	12	43	—	47	—	—	11
Rep.	2	8	35	33	54	15	14	35	—	7	1	44	45	—	16	5	14	35
X	3	—	5	—	1	—	—	—	—	—	3	4	—	—	1	—	—	—
1860																		
SD	19	—	—	1	—	—	—	—	—	—	—	—	—	8	12	—	—	—
U	—	—	—	—	—	—	—	—	—	—	—	—	—	—	—	—	—	—
ND	16	—	57	32	24	—	—	7	5	—	11	14	29	1	—	—	—	11
Rep.	9	8	45	59	72	16	14	44	37	10	10	46	59	8	53	5	14	45
ND-R	—	—	—	—	1	—	—	—	—	—	—	—	—	—	—	—	—	—

American (Know-Nothing) candidates during a transition period before going over to the Democracy (Figure 6-1). A key element in this shift was the presence of the antislavery Northern Whigs such as William Seward of New York who tore apart their party over the slavery issue and virtually drove the Southerners out of it. Most Southerners could not abide Winfield Scott. They distrusted him and his backers, many of whom failed to endorse the Compromise of 1850 in the 1852 Whig convention.

After 1852, only the four border slave states of Kentucky, Tennessee, Maryland, and Virginia departed from the pattern of solid Southern Democracy. The first two, which had stayed Whig in 1852, supported the Constitutional Union party in 1860. It took the war itself to finally polarize them internally and externally. The latter two each made one attempt to avoid being forced southward politically. Even of the four, three had previously been solidly Whig. On the other hand, three slave states formerly Whig and two formerly possessing a competitive two-party system entered the Democratic column "for good" in 1852. All five supported the Southern Democratic ticket in 1860. Thus, for the South, the 1852 election established a pattern of solidarity that would last — except for the Reconstruction period — for exactly 100 years until Dwight D. Eisenhower cut into it in 1952.

While the 1852 election briefly delayed polarization in the North, the issues of 1854 ended the twelve-year "honeymoon" of cross-sectional electoral balance and replaced it with a clearly sectional division. The Republican party, created in the old Northwest that same year, offered a home not only to those opposed to the extension of slavery, but also to those seeking government support for the new economic developments sweeping the Northwest leaning West. It also restored a programmatic concern to American politics.

The impact of the new party was first felt in the states. By the time of the 1856 presidential campaigns, Republican governors had been elected in six states, the GOP controlled the legislatures of several more, and the new party controlled the House of Representatives with a plurality. The new party never had a chance in the South. It was not even to be on the ballot of any of the slave states until 1864. Its very existence was anathema to Southerners, sectionalists and Unionists alike.

The catastrophe of the Kansas-Nebraska Act was to take on immense proportions because of the deterioration in the nation's psychological climate by 1854. Though formal antislavery

Figure 6-1

THE POLARIZATION OF ELECTORAL POLITICS
IN THE STATES: 1840-1860

A¹ Whig Consistently to Republican
Connecticut
Massachusetts
Rhode Island
Vermont

Whig to Democratic to Republican
Indiana
Maine
Michigan

C¹ Democratic Consistently to
Republican
California
Illinois
Iowa
New Hampshire
Wisconsin

B¹ Whig Consistently to Democratic
to Divided
New Jersey

A³ Entered Republican
Minnesota
Oregon

C³ Consistently Divided
to Republican
New York
Ohio
Pennsylvania

(left margin, upper section) Greater Polarization Northward

B² Dem. Consistently to Douglas
Dem. or Const. Union
Missouri
Virginia

C² Whig to Democratic to
So. Dem.
Delaware
Maryland
North Carolina

A² Democratic Consistently to
So. Dem.
Alabama
Arkansas
Mississippi
South Carolina
Texas

B³ Whig Consistently
to Const. Union
Kentucky
Tennessee

C⁴ Divided to Dem.
to So. Dem.
Florida
Georgia
Louisiana

(left margin, lower section) Greater Polarization Southward

agitation had declined somewhat after 1850, other efforts to undermine national unity, all the more sinister for having been made by people not known as radicals yet acting from sincere motives, had done their work to poison the atmosphere to the point where men would turn to violence for the highest of motives.

Uncle Tom's Cabin, the best example of this kind of psychological polarization that was the hallmark of the decade, was published in 1852 after serialization in the press the year before. One million two hundred thousand copies were sold in little more than a year (one for every four families in the country or one for every two families in the North). It was first dramatized that same year. In dramatic form, its antislavery message, distorted far more than in the book, reached millions more. In a few years, embryonic Northern stereotypes of Southerners as Simon Legree emerged fully formed, affecting even those who had no desire to force the South to abandon slavery. Southerners, in turn, ceased to have any faith in a North that could believe such things about them.

The problem was as much in Southern misreading of *Uncle Tom* as in its spread in the North. Both indicated how far the psychological climate had deteriorated by 1852. Stowe bent over backwards to be generous to Southerners as individuals. She let the adorable (in nineteenth-century literary terms, however problematic she is in our generation) Little Eva speak for the Southern system in terms of love. The villain, Simon Legree, was a Vermonter. The author even lampooned Yankee women abolitionists in the form of Aunt Ophelia, who preaches antislavery but is personally a bigot. In fact, Mrs. Stowe was stunned by the passions and hatred she stirred in the South.

The impact of *Uncle Tom's Cabin* and abolitionist propaganda generally was no better illustrated than in the post-1852 decline of the "Young America" movement. Young America had originated in the 1840s as a vague antidote to increasing sectional polarization and as a means for coming to grips with the new trends that its spokesmen sensed were transforming the nation. Liberal and nationalistic, it attempted to divert Americans' attention from the slavery issue to a renewed concern with their nation's "manifest destiny" to expand territorially in the New World, promote democracy in the Old, and foster increased interaction between both through free trade.

Proposed by members of the younger generation of Southerners, it was opposed by the older leaders of that section who saw that its platform, if implemented, would radically expand the power of the federal government. After 1848, the movement became increasingly identified with the middle states of the new West. The "frontiersmen" of Illinois and Kentucky, Ohio and Tennessee, and even California contributed heavily to the strength of Young America, combining their growing interest in overseas markets for their agricultural products with the sense of national mission most frequently found on the frontier and a desire to lessen the sectional conflict that left them caught in the middle under growing pressure from both sides. By 1852, its chief political spokesman was Stephen A. Douglas. The Illinoisian, himself a member of the rising new generation, was interested in the movement for the foregoing reasons but also saw it as a means to lessen the influence of the "Old Fogies" — the leaders of the Democratic party held over from the previous generation who dominated the party's national power structure.

In Douglas' view, these "Old Fogies" were unable to respond adequately to the new problems facing the country which he, as a much abler, as well as younger, man easily foresaw. Giving form to their program, Douglas was, in effect, proposing a new alternative to the rapidly obsolescing Jacksonian persuasion which still dominated his party. He and his faction were temporarily encouraged by the outcome of the election of 1852 since Franklin Pierce was sympathetic to Young America ideas. Unfortunately for the movement, Douglas, and the Democratic party itself, the old guard remained strong so that the new generation had to continue to fight them throughout the 1850s, exacerbating the party's problems already made difficult by the slavery issue.

Young America as a movement declined rapidly after 1852. Seeking to remain unconcerned with the slavery issue at a time when it was becoming paramount, identified as an internationalist movement when America was turning inward, and vociferous as a low tariff movement at a time when the North wanted more protection for its new industry, the movement reached its greatest strength with the election of Pierce and then virtually came to an end. It was to be replaced by movements devoted to emphasizing the things that divided Americans at the expense of those that united them — the evils of slavery, the rights of immigrants, and sectional differences.

In the election of 1856, the Democrats tried the same technique that worked so well for them four years before, nominating James Buchanan of Pennsylvania, a Northerner with Southern sympathies, for president and John C. Breckinridge of Kentucky, a border state Unionist, for his running mate. Buchanan was an old-time politician from Pennsylvania who was an earlier embodiment of the "new style" politics from a state which was one of the first to move in that direction. He cared little for the great issues of the day, but sought the rewards of politics as high as the presidency.

In fact, however, the candidates selected masked a growing conflict between the party's new generation and its old guard that would soon come out into the open. Despite the intraparty struggle between the "doughfaces" (Northerners with Southern sympathies) and Douglas, who honestly sought a reasonable compromise even as he opposed the extension of slavery, they did pull out a victory, though the GOP took every Northern state that did not have a substantial Southern-born population or border on the South, and some that did.

There is good evidence that the Democrats won the 1856 election by corruption, which was apparently decisive in a presidential contest for the first time in American history. New York business interests sent money into Pennsylvania to save Buchanan's home state for the Democratic party. Heavy expenditures were matched by the voting of aliens and outright fraud in Indiana and Illinois as well. Nevertheless, the 1856 election demonstrated that the Republicans could win the presidency with Northern votes alone. At the same time, the Southerners, including arch-secessionists like Edmund Ruffin who knew of the Democrats' resort to corruption, had their basic presuppositions as to the greater virtue of their civilization reinforced, even as they recognized that only corruption had enabled them to keep their hold on Washington.

All in all, the election of 1856 was a critical one for the North and for the nation, one that saw the shift of major blocs of voters into new alignments that would survive and set the voting pattern for the next generation. The Republicans had found the right combination of issues to bring enough Whigs, Free-Soilers, and Northern Democrats together into a viable coalition. All they needed after 1856 was a leader.

As in all such critical turning points, it was not so much the shifting of the allegiances of old voters which made the difference. It was the attraction of new voters to parties and individuals who appeared to offer better responses to the new problems of a new generation, as a result of which new allegiances were forged. Those new allegiances were to last well into the next century.

Bibliographic Notes — Chapter 6

On Jefferson Davis, see *Jefferson Davis, Constitutionalist, His Letters, Papers, and Speechs,* ed. Dunbar Rowland, 10 vols. (1923); *Jefferson Davis, Private Letters, 1823-1889,* ed. Hudson Strode (1966); Hudson Strode, *Jefferson Davis,* 3 vols. (1955-1964).

On the Compromise of 1850, see Herbert V. Ames, "Calhoun and Secession 1850," *American Antiquities Society, Proceedings* 28 (1918): 19; Herbert J. Doherty, Jr., "Florida and the Crisis of 1850," *Journal of Southern History* 19 (1953): 32; Holman Hamilton, *Prologue to Conflict: The Compromise of 1850* (1964); G.D. Harmon, "Douglas and the Compromise of 1850," *Illinois State Historical Society Journal* 21 (1929): 453; Joseph H. Parks, "John Bell and the Compromise of 1850," *Journal of Southern History* 9 (1943): 328; Morton M. Rosenberg, "Iowa Politics and the Compromise of 1850," *Iowa Journal of History* 56 (1958): 193; Robert R. Russel, "The Compromise of 1850," *Journal of Southern History* 22 (1956): 292; R.H. Shryock, *Georgia and Union in 1850* (1926); St. George L. Sioussat, "Tennessee, the Compromise of 1850, and the Nashville Convention," *Mississippi Valley Historical Review* 2 (1915): 313; N.W. Stephenson, "Southern Nationalism in South Carolina in 1851," *American Historical Review* 36 (1931): 314.

See also the biographies and writings of Thomas Hart Benton, 1782-1858; John C. Calhoun, 1782-1850; Lewis Cass, 1782-1866; Henry Clay, 1777-1852; Jefferson Davis, 1808-1889; Stephen A. Douglas, 1813-1861; Millard Fillmore, 1800-1874; William H. Seward, 1801-1872; Alexander H. Stephens, 1812-1883; Charles Sumner, 1811-1874; Zachary Taylor, 1784-1850; Robert Toombs, 1810-1885; and Daniel Webster, 1782-1852.

On the election of 1852 and the Pierce Administration, see Roy F. Nichols, *The Democratic Machine 1850-1854* (1923), and Jeannette Nichols, "The Election of 1852," in Arthur M. Schlesinger, Jr. and Fred L. Israel, eds., *History of American Presidential Elections, 1789-1968,* Vol. 2 (1971).

For examinations of the fugitive slave controversy, see Stanley W. Campbell, *Slave Catchers; Enforcement of the Fugitive Slave Law, 1850-1860* (1970); Allen Johnson, "Constitutionality of Fugitive Slave Acts," *Yale Law Journal* 31 (1921): 161; Jerome Nadelhaft, "The

Building Toward Civil War

Somerset Case and Slavery," *Journal of Negro History* 51 (1966): 193; Robert R. Russel, "Constitutional Doctrines with Regard to Slavery in the Territories," *Journal of Southern History* 32 (1966): 466. The Kansas-Nebraska Act is treated in Frank H. Hodder, "Genesis of the Kansas-Nebraska Act," *Wisconsin Historical Society Proceedings* (1912): 69, and "Railroad Background of the Kansas-Nebraska Act," *Mississippi Valley Historical Review* 12 (1925): 3; Robert W. Johannsen, "The Kansas-Nebraska Act and the Pacific Northwest Frontier," *Pacific Historical Review* 22 (1953): 129; Roy F. Nichols, "The Kansas-Nebraska Act," *Mississippi Valley Historical Review* 43 (1956): 187; James C. Malin, "Motives of Douglas in the Organization of the Nebraska Territory," *Kansas Historical Quarterly* 19 (1951): 321, and *The Nebraska Question, 1852-1854* (1953); Joseph H. Parks, "Tennessee Whigs and the Kansas-Nebraska Bill," *Journal of Southern History* 10 (1944): 308; P.O. Ray, *Repeal of the Missouri Compromise* (1909); Robert R. Russel, "The Kansas-Nebraska Bill, 1854," *Journal of Southern History* 29 (1963): 187.

On the election of 1856, see Murat Halstead, *Trimmers, Trucklers, and Temporizers: Notes from Political Conventions of 1856*, ed. William B. Hesseltine and Trex G. Fisher (1961); Roy F. Nichols and Philip S. Klein, "Election of 1856," in Arthur M. Schlesinger, Jr. and Fred L. Israel, eds., *History of American Presidential Elections, 1789-1968*, Vol. 2 (1971).

On the last years of the Whig Party, see Arthur C. Cole, *The Whig Party in the South* (1913); Norman A. Graebner, "1848: Southern Politics," *Historian* 25 (1962): 14; Fletcher M. Green, *Constitutional Development in the South Atlantic States, 1776-1860* (1930); Charles G. Sellers, Jr., "Who were the Southern Whigs?" *American Historical Review* 59 (1954); Ralph A. Wooster, *People in Power: Courthouse and Statehouse in the Lower South, 1850-1860* (1969).

On state studies of the Whig Party, see Thomas B. Alexander, et al., "The Alabama Whigs," *Alabama Review* 16 (1963): 5, and "The Basis of Alabama's Ante-Bellum Two-Party System," *Alabama Review* 19 (1966): 243; Charles H. Ambler, *Sectionalism in Virginia, 1776-1861* (1910); Mary E.R. Campbell, *Attitude of Tennesseans toward the Union, 1847-1861*; William S. Hoffman, "Willie P. Mangum and the Whig Revival of the Doctrine of Instructions," *Journal of Southern History* 22 (1956): 338; Eric R. Lacy, *Vanquished Volunteers: East Tennessee Sectionalism from Statehood to Secession* (1965); Lynn L. Marshall, "The Whig Party," *American Historical Review* 72 (1967): 445; Malcolm C. McMillan, *Constitutional Development in Alabama, 1789-1901* (1955); Grady McWhiney, "Were the Whigs a Class Party in Alabama?" *Journal of Southern History* 23 (1957): 510; John V. Mering, *The Whig Party in Missouri* (1967); Horace Montgomery, *Cracker Parties* (1950); Powell Moore, "The Revolt Against Jackson

The Polarization of Politics

in Tennessee, 1835-1836," *Journal of Southern History* 2 (1936): 335; H.R. Mueller, *The Whig Party in Pennsylvania* (1922); Paul Murray, *The Whig Party in Georgia, 1825-1853* (1948); G.R. Poage, *Clay and the Whig Party* (1936); Percy L. Rainwater, *Mississippi: Storm Center of Secession, 1856-1861* (1938); William A. Schaper, *Sectionalism and Representation in South Carolina* (1901); Harold S. Schultz, *Nationalism and Sectionalism in South Carolina, 1852-1860* (1950); Charles G. Seller, Jr., "Who were the Southern Whigs?" *American Historical Review* 59 (1954): 335; Henry T. Shanks, *The Secession Movement in Virginia, 1847-1861* (1934).

On the rise of the Republican party, see Andrew W. Crandall, *Early History of the Republican Party* (1930); Eric Foner, *Free Soil, Free Labor, Free Men: Ideology of the Republican Party before the Civil War* (1970); F. H. Harrington, "Fremont and North Americans," *American Historical Review* 44 (1939): 842; Jeter A. Isely, *Greeley and the Republican Party* (1947); George H. Mayer, *The Republican Party, 1854-1964* (1964); David S. Sparks, "Birth of the Republican Party in Iowa, 1854-1856," *Iowa History* 54 (1956): 1; Roger H. Van Bolt, "The Rise of the Republican Party in Indiana, 1855-1856," *Indiana Magazine of History* 51 (1955): 185.

Chapter 7

THE POLARIZATION OF CULTURE AND IDEOLOGY

The Clash of Stream and Section

By 1855, the Northern and Southern extremities of the nation had clearly lost meaningful contact with one another. While their representatives stood face to face in Washington, they talked at, rather than to, each other and their words heightened tensions rather than diminishing them. Though Winston Churchill's maxim, "It is better to jaw, jaw, than to war, war," may be applicable in most situations, there comes a point where talking exacerbates conflicts instead of ameliorating them, where the massive involvement of different cultures with one another leads to hatred rather than affection, and where understanding leads to disgust rather than respect.

While the immediate bone of contention dividing the two extremities of the nation was the slavery issue, the roots of their mutual antagonism lay much deeper, embedded in major cultural differences between the Yankees in greater New England (which by the mid-1850s extended through the Great Lakes states across the upper Mississippi Valley to the Pacific Northwest), on one hand, and the self-proclaimed cavaliers of the plantation South, on the other. The fact that these cultural differences were manifested within a common American civilization only served to deepen the intensity with which they clashed.

American civilization in its northern, southern and middle states components, and their eastern and western modifications, was held together from the first by a common tradition that emphasized certain fundamental principles, values, and visions which could be shared by all Americans. At the same time, the specific interpretation of those principles, values, and visions, particularly in their most practical manifestations, could vary greatly among individuals and particularly among the several states and sections that formed the building blocks of the Union.

So long as the varying interpretations were not solely products of different sectional groupings in the country, it was possible to

127

maintain a dialogue between the different interpreters. As the nineteenth century advanced, however, there was a progressive polarization of the accepted interpretation of the nation's principles, values, and visions along geographic lines, particularly in the northern and southern extremities of the country.

In the 1850s, Americans, North and South, continued to share a basically agrarian image of the United States. That is to say, they shared a vision of a nation of rural households, each rooted in its own land, possessing property through private ownership, yet cooperating to achieve both private and public good within a marketplace economy. Among the Yankees this agrarianism was increasingly expressed in a practical concern for the development of yeomen farmers and small to middling entrepreneurs whose stake in society would be relatively equal to that of their neighbors and who used their property as a means to foster enterprise and competition. The new Southern ideology, on the other hand, saw the essence of agrarianism in the plantation system where the cultivation of large landholdings under a slave system led to the development of a leisure class that served as society's elite and who, while participating by necessity in the marketplace for economic reasons, rejected marketplace values for their own society.

Similarly, although federalism permeated the way of life of the nation as a whole, Yankees and Southerners had developed divergent views as to the meaning of the federal constitution. In the first place, while Southerners sought to restrict the definition of the compact to that of a contract between the states and to limit its application to white men only, the Yankees wished to understand it as a perpetual covenant that embraced, at least in some measure, all Americans, white or black, and to interpret the terms of the covenant in such a way that it could be used as a vehicle for moral progress. The Southerners' efforts to construe the constitution as a legal contract were intended to limit the operation of the federal government except insofar as it supported the member states in their rights; while Yankee efforts to construe the covenant broadly were leading them to advocate an energetic national government that would assist in the development of the country.

Finally, the messianic vision that animated all Americans was increasingly interpreted by Southerners to involve the extension of the "white man's burden" through imperialistic adventures outside the boundaries of the United States where they would be able to impose their patterns of culture upon non-Americans.

The Yankees, on the other hand, were progressively reinterpreting the messianic view to concentrate on man's burden as an internal reformer responsible for correcting the evils of American society. For a growing number of Yankees this included the "white man's burden" to emancipate and uplift the blacks.

After two centuries and more of historical development starting from separate points in Virginia and Massachusetts, spreading latitudinally along the coast, and then longitudinally across the mountains, the cultural differences between Yankees and Southerners had become pronounced in many spheres including differences in political attitudes and expectations. Their differences were equally pronounced in matters of everyday political life. So, for example, the perceptive observer who understood American political life in general could not fail to note intersectional differences in the sets of perceptions about the nature of politics and expectations from government that predominated in greater New England and the South. He would be struck by the differences in the kinds of people who became active in government and politics — as holders of elective offices, as public officials, and as political workers — and by the actual way in which the arts of politics and government were practiced by citizens, politicians, and public officials in light of their perceptions in the two sections.

The observer would note that within the general framework of the marketplace outlook dominant north of the Mason-Dixon line, Yankees saw the purposes of politics to be the development of the good commonwealth, expected their politicians to be primarily concerned with public service, and accepted the idea that all citizens have the responsibility of participating widely in the political process, viewing such participation as part of the achievement of the good political order. Southerners, on the other hand, believed the central purpose of politics to be the preservation of the existing social order. They generally accepted and enjoyed rule by a political elite — that portion of the population with the necessary leisure to cultivate the political arts and at the same time best articulated the traditions which Southern politics was designed to preserve. The average Southerner, white as well as black, was not expected to participate in politics unless he had ties to the political elites.

There were pockets within the South that had been settled by people who rejected the section's dominant political culture. During the eighteenth century they had fought against it with tenacity.

By the 1850s, however, they had either been coopted into the dominant culture or had retreated into the hills where they were isolated from the mainstream of Southern life.

The obvious differences between the Yankee broad-based, future-oriented political culture and the Southern elitist political culture oriented to the past did more to aggravate relations between the two sections as they deepened through the normal passage of time. The fact that in both cultures the political leaders essentially viewed their role in moral terms, as one of serving their communities rather than enriching themselves from that service, only served to provide leaders who were capable of taking extreme positions regarding the other section's set of values.

The coming of industrialization and the emergence of free enterprise capitalism as a manifestation of Yankee commercial attitudes further exacerbated the differences between the two subcultures. Not only was reform a future-centered idea characteristic of the moralistic political culture of greater New England — a matter that bred apprehensiveness in the South — but industrialization offered possibilities for inducing unwanted changes that were less amenable to control than political action. And the Yankees were the great industrializers just as the Southerners were the least oriented toward change.

The cultural bases of the North-South division were of the utmost importance because they reflected the deep-seated and fundamental values of the people. Each subculture presented, in effect, a particular coalition of human traits and attitudes that were transmitted from generation to generation through ethnic and religious ties, particularly the later. Moreover, in the mid-nineteenth century, each was intensified through its sectional location, which cultivated certain patterned responses to continuing economic and political concerns characteristic of whole sections. Finally, the demands of the frontier, which under other circumstances could have worked to reduce the cultural differences, operated to strengthen them since the forces it generated had a direct bearing on the very problems that lay at the root of the cultural differences in the first place.

Polarization and the Vital Center

All that remained to hold the American political system together was the vital center — the people who had as yet refused to take a position on either extreme but, with their eyes on other questions, stood willing to live with both sides without rocking the boat. Such people were scattered throughout the Union and, in a quantitative sense, probably formed the majority based on sheer numbers without regard for energy expended and one based upon effort as well as quantity. Even in a democracy, those who take an active role in public life effectively acquire more than one vote per man in the making of public decisions. Thus, the committed people on both sides were earning a majority status that might otherwise have been denied them. The difference between quantitative and working majorities was already apparent in the extreme Northern and Southern states, but in the middle states, above and below the Mason-Dixon line, both majorities continued to support Union through compromise.

The middle states remained strongholds of the vital center in the typical pattern of American sectionalism — through a geographic expression of basic socio-economic interests. Three such interests influenced them. Their location "in the middle," where they were subject to pressure from both sides to make choices they did not wish to have forced upon them, was enough to force a mediating role upon their political leaders. Location also contributed much to their commercial interest in union. As the section that dominated American commercial life, its people had a stake in retaining a system that made possible the nearly continent-wide free flow of commerce. A list of the important cities of the middle states immediately calls to mind the great commercial entrepots of the antebellum days: New York, Philadelphia, and Baltimore along the Atlantic Coast and Pittsburgh, Cincinnati, Louisville, Nashville, and St. Louis in the Mississippi Valley all traded extensively across sectional boundaries and were vitally concerned with maintaining the national pattern of trade.

Finally, the cultural patterns of the middle states (particularly those north of the Ohio River), taken together, formed a subculture within the emerging national civilization. The middle states' subculture was cosmopolitan and metropolitan, pluralistic and commercial. It was cosmopolitan in the sense that it was least bound by the parochialisms of an internally-oriented society or the religious and ideological concerns of the sections to the north and south of it. Its leading elements sought ties with the larger world and with Europe as they had since the eighteenth century when both New York City and Philadelphia developed coteries of businessmen and intellectuals who shared the same desire to foster such contacts and to benefit from them. If the Yankees to the north of them were more fertile in inventiveness and more serious in moral matters, as a group the people of the middle states were more concerned with being up-to-date in virtually every realm of human endeavor.

The commercial interests of the middle states' subculture helped to foster this cosmopolitanism. Even in colonial times the middle states had distinguished themselves as the great commercial centers of the nation. The rivalry between New York and the other East Coast port cities in the early nineteenth century only accentuated this tendency. By the mid-nineteenth century the great cities that occupied the middle section of the nation as far west as St. Louis had shown every sign of continuing in this tradition, and even Chicago's challenge of St. Louis was gaining momentum in direct proportion to the former city's conversion into a center of middle states' culture as a result of shifting migration patterns after its Yankee beginnings. In the middle states, commerce was virtually the measure of all things. Public and private efforts were directed toward its promotion and governmental policies were designed to support commercial development to a greater extent than in any other section.

Cosmopolitanism was also buttressed by the essential pluralism of the middle states' subculture. This pluralism also had its roots in the earliest colonial times. The Northern states began as homogeneous settlements and were, by the middle of the nineteenth century, strenuously if hopelessly resisting their change into more heterogeneous communities, while the Southern states, which began with greater heterogeneity, had developed a highly homogeneous subculture. The middle states, on the other hand, had from the beginning attracted highly diverse population elements. People from every land that contributed settlers to North America came to the middle states and continued to do so. Even in the colonial period, the tie between church and state had been weak in the middle states and established churches had well-nigh disappeared by the Revolutionary War. In its place there were a multitude of religious groups and societies that were forced to live together in a manner that was not characteristic of either of its two sister subcultural areas. Pluralism led to a greater tolerance of diversity and a cultivation of diverse habits on the part of many groups, encouraging them all to avoid manifestations of hostility even toward those groups and ideas that differed from accepted norms.

The middle states were metropolitan in the sense that their cities had already become the focal points of their development. In truth, cities were of prime importance in the middle states from the seventeenth century onward. The history of the extension of the middle states' subculture westward is as much a history of the extension of cities as it is one of the extension of farms. The movement toward cities was another pillar that strengthened cosmopolitanism, pluralism, and commerce.

With all of the outlets available to energetic people in the middle states, their subculture did not place a high value on political activity. Politics was not considered to be a means of achieving salvation or necessarily to be the best way to secure social change. It was, rather, a necessary element in the maintenance of society, sometimes even a necessary evil, but not one that required the attentions of the best and most energetic people unless they were people who had chosen to make their careers and fortunes in the political arena. These professionals served as political brokers for the highly diverse interests located in their states and communities. Real success lay in shying away from troublesome issues, ideological concerns or moral postures. Unable to afford such luxuries in their immediate spheres of influence, they had no stomach for them on the national scene either.

All of these factors combined to make the bulk of the residents of the middle states most susceptible to remaining the vital center. Their commercial interests dictated a commitment to peace and union. Their general outlook was tolerant of differences and was characterized by a "live and let live" attitude. And they were usually antireformist or at best were unimpressed by the demands of reformers. Though they wished to preserve the peace by rejecting all extremists during most of the 1850s, in the last analysis a threat to the Union from whatever power could be considered a direct threat to their most vital interests. It was this threat to union that would ultimately move them off the vital center northward.

During the early 1850s, however, the middle states even leaned toward the Southern point of view. Many of the middle states passed black codes designed to prevent the settlement of free blacks within their boundaries. In national elections, the middle states were the ones most likely to stay in the center, to maintain competitive two party politics and to select moderates as candidates.

The very heterogeneity of the middle states, however, was to cause great conflicts within each of them during the prewar decade. While the subculture described above was dominant in all of them statewide, in every one there were substantial areas which were dominated by the equally distinctive subcultures of the North and the South. So, for example, in New York, the middle states' subculture was dominant in the area below Albany down through New York City. Since that was the most heavily populated part of the state, New York as a whole seemed to be shaped by its culture. The northern and western parts of the Empire state, however, had been settled primarily by New Englanders moving westward, people who reflected a very different subculture, and who fought for control of the state for all those years. The situation in Pennsylvania was much the same, except that in the Keystone state only the narrow strip consisting of the two tiers of counties along its northern boundary had been settled by New Englanders. The bulk of the state's area and population were of the middle states' subculture.

In the states directly to the west of Pennsylvania, the situation was made even more difficult by the existence of wide areas settled by elements of the Southern subculture as well as the other two. Ohio, Indiana, and Illinois combined all three subcultures to varying extents and all three competed for power within them. Those three states, more than any others north of the Mason-Dixon line, had reason to support peace and union since civil war on a nationwide scale held every promise of bringing civil war within each of them as well.

Not too different was the situation within the upper tier of the slave states, the ones which would become the border states of the 1860s. In Maryland and Delaware, for example, a combination of the commercial, pluralistic, cosmopolitan, and metropolitan elements of the middle states' subculture had been grafted onto a slave-holding society. As the middle states' patterns began to win out after 1830, slavery ceased to be the force it was in the states to the south, but it still complicated the internal political situation in each. Kentucky and Tennessee, the two states that paralleled Ohio, Indiana, and Illinois across the Ohio River, were faced with the same tragic dilemma of union or chaos. Their consistent support of moderates, Whig Unionists and ultimately Constitutional-Unionists in national politics, reflected the almost desperate efforts of their leadership to preserve the Union. Their failure was to weigh heavily on both states for the next century. Missouri was in a similar position but with the pressures less intense because of its opening to the West. Finally, Virginia was to be so divided because of the overlap that the war was to bring formal division of its territory.

Of all the states dominated by the middle states' subculture in the 1850s, only New Jersey was reasonably free of internal cultural conflicts. Though it had attracted some Southerners in that part of the state located below the Mason-Dixon line, they were rapidly assimilated into the state's dominant patterns. Moreover, the small concentrations of Yankees who located in a few cities within New Jersey had long since been overwhelmed by new immigrants from Europe. Consequently, it was to be the only state which was to maintain the political posture of the 1850s after the Civil War began.

The Polarization of Political Ideas

The polarization in political culture was paralleled by a polarization of political ideas as well. In fact, polarization at the ideological level was to be more influential at levels that touched the man in the street than even students of political ideas will usually claim.

Examination of the polarization of political ideas is made particularly complex because both sides started from common premises that never ceased to be recognizable within their respective positions. The polarization can be traced through three major categories. The most important of these was undoubtedly the polarization of Northern and Southern conceptions of the nature of the federal system, particularly in regard to the place of the states and the character of majority rule in the Union as a whole. The second involved the divergence of opinion as to the proper role and functions of government, while the third, a product of the post-1848 generation, involved the development of new and diverging legalisms that were grafted onto the respective sets of ideas that were developing in the other two categories and served to give sanction to them.

At the root of the polarization of political ideas in the 1850s was the notion that the North and the South were two separate civilizations that had come together briefly in a compact but were now diverging as separate civilizations often must. The recognition that there were significant cultural differences between the North and the South was already strong in colonial times. Perception of these differences was probably reduced to its lowest point during the period of the American Revolution, partly because the common

135

cause united the revolutionaries regardless of section. Perhaps more importantly, the eighteenth century was one of those happy eras in which the intellectual endeavors of men of diverse cultures led in the same direction to create a cross-cultural republic of the intellect that united thinking men in every clime. Nowhere was this intellectual unity stronger than in the emerging United States. Its influence was felt in virtually all segments of American society and in all parts of the country.

By the age of Jackson, however, the intellectual unity of the eighteenth century was thoroughly demolished. Without its overarching unifying tendencies, the diverging social and economic trends of the nineteenth century were able to reawaken notions of cultural difference which far transcended those of earlier times. While voices had been raised even earlier to claim the existence of distinct Northern and Southern civilizations, they did not influence large publics until the intellectual structure of the revolutionary period was breached. When it was, however, the voices were heard in the North as well as in the South.

At the center of the two civilizations idea was the slavery issue. The diverging economies of the North and the South could have been accommodated as complementary to one another had there been a sense of community between the sections. The question of slavery, however, gave both sections a chance to claim civilizational uniqueness; the North by glorifying its abandonment of the slave system and the South by justifying its retention of that system. Playing upon very real cultural differences, spokesmen of radical groups in both sections could magnify those differences to claim, on one hand, that morality and godliness could not exist in a civilization based on involuntary servitude and, on the other hand, to claim that culture and graciousness could not exist in a civilization that was not so rooted.

After 1848, the cultures of the North and South diverged even further by virtue of Northern acceptance of industrialization and Southern rejection of the new world that industrialization created. Politically, the two civilizations idea was reflected in two very practical ways. In the first place, the demands for government action, North and South, began to diverge significantly. Southerners, with a traditionalistic bias, were more amenable to the perpetuation of many aspects of mercantilist policy; rejecting the thrust of entrepreneurial capitalism, they sought government intervention in the economy as agriculturalists always have to take some of the risk out of the business that has traditionally been the most risky of all. Rather than encouraging private enterprise, which might exercise its commitment to the profit motive at the expense of farmers and plantation owners who would be at their mercy, most of the Southern states undertook the economic activities, such as banking and railroad construction, that by 1846 had become the domain of the new capitalists in the North. Southern statism was not motivated by any socialistic conceptions of social justice. On the contrary, few indeed were the enterprises managed entirely by public bodies in the South. Rather, it was believed that the rich and the well-born deserved an opportunity to invest in conjunction with government in worthwhile enterprises designed to serve their society and preserve the economic underpinnings of their political order.

The Southern definition of "worthwhile government activity" was generally confined to the banking and internal improvement fields. In the North, on the other hand, the idea that the internal improvement realm was to be left as much as possible to private initiative was gaining momentum and had virtually swept that section by the 1850s, even though the reality remained one of private reliance on government aid. The role of government was confined to that of subsidizer and stimulator, not owner or manager. (This was neither the first nor the last time that such a gap existed between ideology and rhetoric, on one hand, and reality, on the other.) At the same time, Northerners were devising new and, for them, far-reaching tasks for government. They began to translate the ideas that government had a role to play in educating their children, in setting standards of public health, and in caring for those unable to care for themselves, into concrete programs involving all levels of government. As yet, the programs were in the embryonic stage, but, during the 1850s, those states north of the Ohio River that had not yet done so established statewide systems of public education and created such state welfare institutions as asylums for the insane, the deaf and dumb, and the mentally retarded, and reformitories for delinquent children. These activities were rejected by most Southerners as illegitimate interferences with the rights of parents to determine the future of their offspring and encroachments on the preserve of the individual to determine what he would do with his property and his life. They concentrated on providing government-supported services for the elite, such as state universities to complete the education of the sons of that elite and public improvements to facilitate the commerce of the plantations.

Of course, the divergent approaches to the role of government led to growing literacy in the North and spreading illiteracy in the South, further widening the gap between the sections and convincing Northerners of the moral superiority of their civilization while assuring Southerners that liberty could be preserved only in theirs. By the mid-1850s, even those Southerners who had previously supported federal activities narrowed their support to an interest in internal improvements while, at the same time, many of those Northerners who earlier had been reluctant to encourage more federal activity began an intensive campaign to secure federal aid for agriculture, education, welfare, and science as well as aids to business. Some of the latter demands also received Southern support, but others, such as the tariff, aroused Southern ire as much as they aroused Northern interest.

Partly in response to this divergence of expectations as to the proper role of government, but primarily in response to the slavery issue, there was a polarization in the sections' conception of the nature of the federal system. The true character of this polarization has often been obscured by mythologies that developed in response to the war itself and not in response to the issues that caused the war. Before the war, neither the North nor the South believed that the federal government and the states had to be involved in a mutually antagonistic relationship for the health of federalism. Indeed, the struggle in the 1850s was to determine whether the federal government would serve the states of one section or the states of the other by cooperating with them in securing the political aims of their citizens.

Both sections periodically assumed "states' rights" postures for tactical reasons, the Northerners doing so as frequently as the Southerners. Southerners fell back on the sovereign powers of the states when they wished to discourage Northern abolitionist efforts in their section while Northerners fell back on the same sovereign powers in an effort to frustrate enforcement of the Fugitive Slave Law. On the other hand, Southerners turned to Washington in an effort to force federal action in support of the rights of slave owners throughout the Union just as Northerners turned to the federal government to secure the maintenance of free institutions in the new territories of the West.

Stepping back slightly from the level of immediately tactical pursuits, until the 1850s there was even substantial agreement on the value of union. Northerners and Southerners approached the problems of federalism with the implicit assumption that whatever their interpretations of federal-state relations, they should reinforce the bonds of union rather than diminish them. The most famous act of state defiance of federal authority prior to 1861, South Carolina's attempt to nullify the Tariff of 1832, was more of a unionist than a secessionist effort in that the Palmetto state sought a way to maintain the Union without surrendering what its leaders conceived to be its sovereign rights by invoking the doctrine of nullification. However absurd this tactic might seem to others, it is significant as a reflection of that state's psychological commitment to union even under duress.

In the 1850s, however, the Southern leadership, or at least a substantial portion of it, slowly abandoned their commitments to the Union and replaced them with an earnest desire for secession and the creation of a new Union. The reasons for this are not to be found in political theory though they were reflected in their theoretical formulations. The process of ideologically justifying alienation involved two steps. First, there was the necessity of erecting a theory of absolute state sovereignty, a theory that denied the right of the federal government to intervene in the internal activities of any state except under the most limited and prescribed conditions. Then it was necessary to demonstrate that the federal government, instead of acting as the agent of the states where it was required to do so by the Constitution, was violating their sovereignty by transgressing those limits.

Here it is necessary to step back even further to see a fundamental difference between Northern and Southern conceptions of the Union, differences that date back to the Revolutionary War itself. Whereas Northerners believed the Union had come into existence at the same time the states had become independent, assuming from the first the powers that had been vested in the Crown under the British imperial system, the Southerners started with the assumption that the Declaration of Independence created individually sovereign states which only united subsequently to form the United States. The record of this difference in viewpoint is visible in the very resolves of the state governments in the 1770s and 1780s.

In the first two generations of the Republic, this difference was essentially one of theoretical concern, no more. Both Southerners and Northerners accepted the perpetuity of the federal constitution, even if they differed on the proper role of the federal government in specific cases. Beginning in the 1830s, however, Southerners began to reformulate the old theory of the prior existence of the states and to elevate it into what may properly be termed "a legitimate constitutional heresy" — that is to say, a deviant view of constitutional theory that has no significant basis in history, but which has been so widely accepted by a segment of the American people that it acquires a legitimacy of sorts. Under this legitimate constitutional heresy, states' rights notions were transformed into doctrines of state sovereignty that when carried to their logical extreme authorized any state no longer satisfied with the terms of the federal compact to withdraw from that compact, freely and without penalty. This notion, which would have been foreign to such ardent defenders of states' rights as Jefferson and Madison, was first hinted at by John Taylor of Carolina during the days of the Jeffersonians. Even John C. Calhoun, however, who is noted as the spokesman and apologist for the South, hesitated to embrace such a notion, which he knew to be heretical, until relatively late in his career.

While this heresy was not given a coherent formulation in the North until the 1850s, many Northerners would have accepted it without much hesitation if only because they either rejected the notion of federal coercion of any state or eagerly sought to rid the Union of the slave power. In the 1850s, however, just as this doctrine was becoming part of a new Southern consensus, the people in the North were rejecting it for all time. The reasons for this were twofold. In the first place, the shift of Northern population westward and the rise of a generation of people born in the new states of the North's West meant the creation of a large population of people who knew the Union as a creator of states and not as the states' creature. These people, familiar as they were with beneficent federal activities all their lives, had a loyalty to the Union that would not tolerate notions of its disruption, as well as an economic stake in its maintenance. Northeasterners, on the other hand, even the abolitionists among them, had become relatively optimistic about the chances of their cause in the future and, in feeling that way, had no desire to allow the Union to be disrupted, which would enable the South to maintain slavery for a longer period of time.

The people of the Southwest, the only Southerners who might have been relied upon to share the sentiments of the West, were pulled Southward by the changes in technology that weakened their attachments to the North and by the pressures of a cold war turning hot that touched them more closely than any other Americans.

140

Bibliographic Notes — Chapter 7

The basic bibliography on the coming of the Civil War was used for this chapter as well. For comparisons between Northern, Southern and middle states, see W.J. Cash, *The Mind of the South* (1941); Herbert J. Doherty, Jr., "Mind of the Antebellum South," in Arthur S. Link, ed., *Writing Southern History Essays in Historiography in Honor of Fletcher M. Green* (1965); Paul Goodman, "Ethnics and Enterprise: The Values of a Boston Elite, 1800-1860," *American Quarterly* 18 (1966): 437; Perry Miller, *Life of the Mind: From the Revolution to the Civil War* (1965); Arthur K. Moore, *The Frontier Mind: Kentucky* (1957); Henry Nash Smith, *Popular Culture and Industrialism, 1865-1890* (1967); William R. Taylor, *Cavalier and Yankee: The Old South and the American National Character* (1961); Alexis de Tocqueville, *Democracy in America*, ed. J.F. Mayer (1969).

On Southern politics and society, see J.G. Baldwin, *Flush Times of Alabama* (1853); Minnie C. Boyd, *Alabama in the Fifties* (1931); Jesse T. Carpenter, *The South as a Conscious Minority* (1930); Wilbur J. Cash, *The Mind of the South* (1941); Avery O. Craven, *The Growth of Southern Nationalism, 1848-1861* (1953); Clement Eaton, *The Growth of Southern Civilization, 1790-1860* (1961), *The Mind of the Old South*, rev. ed. (1967), and *History of the Old South*, 2nd ed. (1966); John Hope Franklin, *The Militant South, 1800-1861* (1956); Eugene D. Genovese, *The World the Slaveholders Made: Two Essays in Interpretation* (1969), Thomas P. Govan, "Was the Old South Different?" *Journal of Southern History* 21 (1955): 447; Clayton D. James, *Antebellum Natchez* (1968); Guion G. Johnson, *Antebellum North Carolina* (1937); Weymouth T. Jordan, *Rebels in the Making: Planters' Conventions and Southern Propaganda* (1958); Thomas P. Kettell, *Southern Wealth and Northern Profits* (1860), ed. Fletcher M. Green (1965); R.G. Osterweis, *Romanticism and Nationalism in the Old South* (1949); Thomas N. Page, *Social Life in Old Virginia before the War* (1897); Ulrich B. Philips, "The Central Theme of Southern History," *American Historical Review* 34 (1928): 30; David M. Potter, *The South and Sectional Conflict* (1968); E.M. Ripley, *Social Life in Old New Orleans* (1912); Robert R. Russel, *Economic Aspects of Southern Sectionalism, 1840-1861* (1924); Charles G. Sellers, ed., *The Southerner as American* (1960); William R. Taylor, *Cavalier and Yankee: The Old South and the American National Character* (1961); Frank E. Vandiver, ed., *The Idea of the South: Pursuit of a Central Theme* (1964); T. Harry, Williams, *Romance and Realism in Southern Politics* (1961).

Northern politics and society are examined in Daryl Pendergraft, "Thomas Corwin and the Conservative Republic Reaction, 1858-1861," *Ohio State Archaeological and Historical Quarterly* 57 (1948): 1;

Building Toward Civil War

Samuel Shapiro, "The Massachusetts Constitutional Convention of 1853," *New England Quarterly* 33 (1960): 207; Roger H. Van Bolt, "Indiana in Political Transition, 1851-1853," *Indiana Magazine of History* 49 (1953): 131.

In that context, the Lincoln-Douglas debates brought forth the differences between the Yankee and middle states world views. See Paul M. Angle, ed., *Created Equal? The Lincoln-Douglas Debates* (1958); Richard A. Heckman, *Lincoln vs. Douglas* (1967); Harry V. Jaffa, *The Crisis of a House Divided: The Lincoln-Douglas Debates* (1959), and "Expediency and Morality in the Lincoln-Douglas Debates," *Anchor Review* 2 (1957): 179; Willard L. King and Allan Nevins, "The Constitution and the Declaration of Independence as Issues in the Lincoln-Douglas Debates," *Journal of the Illinois State Historical Society* 52 (1959): 7.

On Jacksonian democracy, its political thought, and the subsequently polarization of political ideas, see Joseph L. Blau, ed., *Social Theories of Jacksonian Democracy* (1947); Louis Hartz, *The Liberal Tradition in America* (1955); Richard Hofstadter, *The American Political Tradition* (1948); Marvin Meyers, *The Jacksonian Persuasion* (1957); Vernon L. Parrington, *Main Currents in American Thought*, 3 vols. (1927-1930); Edwin C. Rozwenc, ed., *Ideology and Power in the Age of Jackson* (1964); Arthur M. Schlesinger, Jr., *The Age of Jackson* (1945); Alexis de Tocqueville, *Democracy in America*, ed. Philips Bradley, 2 vols. (1948); Glyndon G. Van Deusen, "Aspects of Whig Thought in the Jacksonian Period," *American Historical Review* 64 (1959): 305; Benjamin F. Wright, "Political Institutions and the Frontier," in *Sources of Culture in the Middle West*, ed. Dixon Ryan Fox (1934); Arthur M. Schlesinger, *The American as Reformer*, 2nd ed. (1950), with a new preface by Arthur M. Schlesinger, Jr. (1968); Alice Felt Tyler, *Freedom's Ferment* (1944).

On the development of eleemosynary and educational institutions in the North, see Daniel J. Elazar, *The American Partnership* (1962); Robert Bremner, *American Social History Since the Civil War* (1971) — on the shift in the Southern position on federalism, see pp. 351-352, 532-533.

For general reference on the Constitution and constitutional development, see H.C. Hockett, *The Constitutional History of the United States, 1776-1876*, 2 vols. (1939); James Morton Smith and Paul L. Murphy, eds., *Liberty and Justice; Forging the Federal Union: American Constitutional Development to 1869* (1965); Carl B. Swisher, *American Constitutional Development*, 2nd ed. (1954).

On slavery in the territories, see Arthur E. Bestor, Jr., "State Sovereignty and Slavery," *Journal of the Illinois State Historical Society* 54 (1961): 117; Mark DeW. Howe, "Federalism and Civil Rights," *Proceedings of the Massachusetts Historical Society* 77

(1966): 15; Allan Nevins, "Constitution, Slavery, and Territories," in Gaspar Bacon, *Lectures on the Constitution of the United States, 1940-1950* (1953); Robert R. Russel, "Constitutional Doctrines with Regard to Slavery in the Territories," *Journal of Southern History* 32 (1966): 466.

Chapter 8

THE POLITICS OF POLARIZATION

The Continued Polarization of Politics

After the 1856 elections demonstrated that the Republican party was here to stay, the overall situation went from bad to worse. All the pressures of the decade began to converge and press against the slender reed of political adjustment.

The Democrats, their hold on the electorate slipping, fell prey to terrible internal divisions as all the disparate elements that had managed to live together in the same party in the hour of victory rediscovered their basic differences in the hour of incipient defeat. The Douglas-Buchanan feud reached the point where it virtually paralyzed an already weak federal government. Southerners in the administration, realizing that their two generations of control in Washington were coming to an end, sought to do what they could either to consolidate their section's position in the Union or prepare for its successful exit. Northern Democrats fell to quarrelling over the best strategies — whether they would win more by supporting the slave system in the name of the Constitution and the Union or by joining the free-soil movement.

These and other conflicts were exacerbated by the *Dred Scott* decision. When the United States Supreme Court took it upon itself to solve the great question of slavery, it was acting out of the highest motives. (We of another generation who know a Court that has assumed similar burdens, can understand that misapprehension.) The justices' perception of the ability of the national administration as then constituted to act forcefully was sound. But some problems are not to be solved by courts even in a system where the court is a symbol of a hallowed constitution and certainly not when the court's decision flies directly in the face of the thrust of the times.

By denying Dred Scott's appeal for freedom on the grounds that no black could ever sue in any American court because he could never be a citizen or even — legally — a man, the Court not only put into the Constitution a doctrine never intended by the framers, but also placed itself foursquare in the path of the forward thrust of the nineteenth century. By attempting to remove the conflict from the political arena and making it a legal matter, the Court did much to close off the nation's ability to make use of the greatest benefit of problem-solving through the political process, that is, the avoidance of all-or-nothing decisions. The law, speaking as it must in fixed terms, will inevitably, at some point, make an "either-or" ruling. In this case, the either-or decision eliminated the politically constructed barriers that prevented slavery from being extended into free states and emancipation from being forced on the slave states. Whatever the difficulties of this unwieldy compromise, particularly in deciding the disposition of new lands, it did enable the nation to come into existence and survive, "half slave and half free," while a solution to its difficulties might possibly have been worked out. By eliminating not only the barriers, but also the possibility of imposing barriers, the struggle was transformed into an aggressive one on both sides. Perhaps it would have been so transformed in any case. Certainly the events in Kansas a few years earlier suggested such a direction. But violence there could still be repudiated by moderators who could not avoid being polarized by *Dred Scott*.

While Southerners hailed the decision as a vindication of their constitutional theories, hostile Northern reaction was appropriately intense. For if, as the Court said, no American citizen could be denied the right to take his property with him to any part of the Union, the decision put an end to the possibility of maintaining any free soil, even in the free states. This decision — one of the most nationalizing in the court's history — meant that the political efforts of a decade were for naught and that nothing short of a constitutional revolution could lead to the diminution of the slave system.

After 1857, then, the political contest took on a new turn as more and more Northerners felt that slavery had to be eliminated everywhere before it engulfed them, and the Southern leadership felt that they had a last opportunity to extend the rights of slaveholders throughout the Union. This is reflected in the change in the character of political debate. Up to 1857, only the hard-core abolitionists talked openly about eliminating slavery altogether through national action. Abraham Lincoln could say, in an 1854 speech on the Kansas-Nebraska Act in which he characterized slavery as an evil in abstract terms, "The Missouri Compromise ought to be restored. For the sake of the Union it ought to be restored...." After that year, Lincoln had to conclude that "a house divided against itself cannot stand," and that the Union would either become all slave or all free. This view, espoused earlier in almost identical words by the abolitionists with no success, became the rallying call of the Republican party.

In October 1857 this slogan was expanded by William Seward's speech on the "irrepressible conflict," which justified the new rallying cry beyond any but the abolitionists' earlier expectations. From then on, in Lincoln's mind, it was only a question of timing. Thus he could endorse the Republican platform of 1860 which promised to protect slavery in the states where it existed because he did not want to disrupt the Union; that is, the timing was not yet right.

By the same token, before 1857 only the most radical Southerners called for reopening the slave trade and for free extension of slavery throughout the Union. As late as 1856, when South Carolina's Governor James H. Adams suggested such a course to that state's legislature, he was roundly denounced by many influential citizens. That same year, the annual Southern Commercial Convention meeting at Savannah (a center of slave smuggling) voted sixty-one to twenty-four against a similar resolution. After *Dred Scott* both ideas became articles of Southern faith. In May 1859, the Southern Commercial Convention meeting at Vicksburg, Mississippi, reversed its earlier stand by a vote of forty to nineteen and openly called for unrestricted importation of Africans as slaves. Not the least of the reasons given for this reversal was that a plentiful supply of cheap slaves would encourage the extension of the institution to the Pacific without drawing off slaves from the Southeast, thereby forcing squatter sovereignty to work on behalf of the South.

Nothing better illustrates the fate of the moderates after 1857 than the political decline of Stephen A. Douglas. Whereas before *Dred Scott* he was a hero to much of the nation for advocating popular sovereignty, afterward the continued advocacy of that doctrine placed him in the position of undermining the Supreme Court and satisfying neither section. So long as popular sovereignty was politically reasonable, he could be viewed as a great compromiser. Once the slavery issue was transformed into an either-or question, he became a "grubby politician," unwilling to squarely face the issues of his day. When the nation's best political compromiser was so compromised, polarization was complete.

Between 1857 and 1861, the South mounted its last political

offensive in Washington. It was an effort that in the name of states' rights pushed the centralization of power in the federal arena to new heights that would not be paralleled until the Civil War itself. Southerners in Congress and the administration attempted to secure enforcement of the Fugitive Slave Law by establishing the equivalent of a national police force and backing it with unlimited funds and constitutional support from the nation's high court. Within Congress itself, senators suspected of abolitionism or free state sentiments were, wherever possible, denied assignment to important committees. The national government progressively excluded even free blacks living in the Northern states from rights of citizenship guaranteed them by their states of residence. Thus a man like Frederick Douglass, the leading black spokesman in the North, who had been forced to flee to England after the *Dred Scott* decision had put him, an ex-fugitive slave, in jeopardy, was denied a passport by George M. Dallas, the United States Minister to the United Kingdom and a member of a prominent Philadelphia family, on the grounds that he was not and could not be a citizen of the United States.

The Thirty-sixth Congress convened on December 5, 1859, in an atmosphere charged with tension. In the House, a new group of Republicans, including many of the men who were to be in the forefront of their party for the next forty years, took their seats, while in the Senate the men who were to lead both sides in the coming conflict sparred with each other daily. When the Thirty-sixth Congress would pass into history two years later, the nation would already be disrupted.

The disruption of the Democratic party was not fully completed until the spring of 1860 when Southern Democrats demanded national party endorsement of their extreme position on the slavery issue. Northern Democrats, unable to accede to such demands, were able to prevent their ratification but only at the price of Southern secession from the Democratic party. Their defection assured the election of a Republican in the fall and that, consequently, was the crucial step toward the secession of the Southern states themselves.

From Cold War to Hot

While the mainstream of political life in the nation was passing through the stages of cold war, hot conflicts were developing on its edges, conflicts which moved closer to the center of the stream as the decade wore on. These conflicts began in the competition between Northern and Southern interests in the Caribbean and Central America. They came to a bloody climax with John Brown's raid.

The failure of the South to gain new slave territory through the Mexican War led some Southerners to seek an extension of the nation into Latin American lands where they believed the slave system could be extended. Out of their efforts grew the filibustering expeditions to Cuba and Central America of the 1850s. The first of these were directed against Cuba between 1849 and 1851. Vigorously opposed by the North, which wanted no further slave lands to deal with, they were nipped in the bud by a federal administration that, although substantially Southern, was hesitant about tolerating the use of the United States as a base of operations for Cuban adventurers. Even so, some 200 Southerners invaded Cuba during those years. In 1851, some fifty were captured and executed by Spanish authorities and others escaped that fate only when Congress reluctantly voted a "ransom" of $25,000 for their safe return. At the same time, commercial interests in New York and the middle states, in combining with leading Southern planters (neither of whom were likely to resort to violence), did stimulate unsuccessful federal efforts to purchase Cuba from Spain in the Polk and Pierce administrations.

Southern expansionist interests were temporarily deflected westward by the elevation of Jefferson Davis to the cabinet and his efforts to promote a Pacific railroad with a Southern connection. While the Gadsden Purchase was successfully consummated in order to acquire lands for a Southern route, the railroad project itself was caught in the sectional struggle and temporarily buried, not to be exhumed until a free-soil route was assured by the coming of the war. Meanwhile, Southern hopes were kept alive by substantial federal grants of land to the states of Arkansas and Missouri for construction of a Pacific railroad that later became the Missouri Pacific.

Southern expansionist interests then turned to filibustering again, this time to focus on William Walker, who led an unsuccessful expedition to Lower California in 1853. When that failed, he moved on to Nicaragua where he was able to set up a regime in 1855. Walker's government successfully subjugated the country and was virtually recognized by President Pierce in 1856. Northerners viewed the whole enterprise with alarm, many erroneously believing it to be a full-scale Southern plot. This feeling was fanned by Northern businessmen with interests in Nicaragua who did not want to pay taxes to an efficient government when they could bribe an inefficient one at less cost. Led by Cornelius Vanderbilt, who owned the Pan-Isthmanian Transportation Company that prospered transporting gold seekers to California, a coalition overthrew Walker in 1857 after a brisk little war. By that time, the *Dred Scott* decision had worked its poison and Walker, who had been considered something of a black sheep in the best Southern circles, was hailed as a hero in that section for opposing the Yankee commercial octopus. Walker had little trouble raising a new expedition, but it was broken up by the United States Navy. (Later, in 1860, he would be executed in Honduras during another try, through the connivance of the Vanderbilt interests, but by that time he was hardly the first casualty of the Civil War.)

Southern interest in Mexico led to a series of still obscure attempts to secure concessions of territorial rights in that hapless republic. Tied ostensibly to the imperative need for better communications with California after 1849, these efforts involved a number of men who were later to become prominent in the Confederacy, including John Slidell and Judah P. Benjamin of Louisiana. These, too, come to naught, in part because of the opposition of Northern business interests.

Continued troubles with Cuba led Southern expansionists to attempt to provoke war with Spain in 1854. They were frustrated only by the quick actions of Secretary of State William L. Marcy, a New York Democratic politician of the new style who, whatever his political ambitions in normal times, shared the free-soil views of his section. His repudiation of the Ostend Manifesto prepared by Southern sympathizers including James Buchanan, which declared the annexation of Cuba essential to the preservation of slavery, ended the war threat. As news of the manifesto spread through the North, it served as a convincing demonstration of the Free-Soilers' contention that an aggressive Southern "Slave Power" sought to spread its peculiar institution under the protection of the American Constitution and finance it with Northern treasure. Coming in 1855, the Republican party reaped full benefit from it.

By 1855, however, the center of attention had shifted to Kansas Territory, where a hot war was in the making much closer to home, a war in which Americans would begin killing each other directly. The Senate passed the Kansas-Nebraska Act on March 3,

1854. On April 26, a month before favorable House action, popular sovereignty advocates in Massachusetts organized the Massachusetts Emigrant Aid Society. This highly Yankee move applying the organizational principles of the new age to a problem which theoretically was to be settled by letting nature take its course (as it had in previous westward migrations) was another indication of the growing gulf between North and South.

While Southerners waited to move into Kansas from adjacent Missouri in their usual haphazard, individualistic manner, a New England company was organized to achieve Northern supremacy in a territory 1,500 miles away. In July, the first party set out from Boston under its auspices and by the end of the year, 600 settlers had been sent westward to found Lawrence, Topeka, and other settlements. Establishment of Lawrence led to the first armed clash between Northerners and Southerners as a party of Missourians claiming the townsite were repulsed on October 6, 1854, after a brief skirmish. Reincorporated the next year as the New England Emigrant Aid Society, the company was to pour 2,000 settlers into Kansas in two years, founding the territory's major free-state communities and supplying them with the organizational and technological tools for the state's ultimate conquest. While the 2,000 may have represented a small proportion of the actual settlers, their impact far exceeded their numbers, as is often the case where organization makes the difference.

Meanwhile, Missourians, also realizing that popular sovereignty really meant the "firstest with the mostest," acted in a manner more in their style by sending a small permanent expedition to found Leavenworth and dispatching thousands of armed men across the border to secure the election of a proslavery territorial delegate (November 29, 1854) and a proslavery legislature (March 30, 1855). They were even able to intimidate Andrew Reeder, the Pennsylvania-born territorial governor, a Pierce appointee (who had arrived in Kansas the day after the first "battle" of Lawrence), into accepting the fraudulent results. During the summer of 1855, the proslavery legislature adopted a constitution and enacted a spate of legislation designed not only to establish slavery but to keep antislavery settlers out of Kansas.

The free-state advocates, beaten to the punch in the field, retaliated by assembling in local conventions during September 1855 and in a statewide convention at Topeka the next month where they framed a free-state constitution, appointed a military commander, and began importing arms. After the election of appropriate officers for the state-in-the-making in January 1856, Kansas had two competing governments.

Governor Reeder, whose antislavery sympathies had become evident, was removed from office by Pierce in July and replaced by Wilson Shannon, a proslavery Ohioan. Three months later, Reeder was sent to Congress by the free-state men. With this kind of confusion evident, hostilities became almost certain.

The first of the Kansas "wars," the so-called Waukarusa War, began on November 26, 1855. It lasted for eleven days and was limited to a war of maneuver. The proslavery Kansans, though reinforced by 1,500 Missourians, hesitated to attack heavily defended Lawrence, the center of the free-state movement, thus giving Governor Shannon time to negotiate a settlement.

A month later, however, President Pierce recognized the proslavery government and branded the Topeka government as revolutionary, coming out fully behind the proslavery forces. Thus emboldened, the latter prepared to eliminate by force what their president had branded an unreasonable assembly. Pierce's proclamation of February 11, 1856, virtually authorized the violent suppression of the free-state forces. The North retaliated by shipping arms to Kansas that were in use by April 19 when a pro-Southern posse was fired upon. On May 5, the free-state government was indicted for high treason by a pro-Southern grand jury and its leaders went into hiding or exile. Less than three weeks later, on May 21, the Kansas-Missouri forces sacked Lawrence, killing two people who became the first publicized casualties of the cold war turned hot. That was the opening battle of a four-month war. Within a week, full-scale guerilla warfare was being waged by both sides, punctuated by five pitched battles. Before federal troops temporarily restored order by sealing off the Kansas-Missouri border in September, some 200 lives were lost, $2 million in property was destroyed, Shannon had resigned as governor, and the whole country was in an uproar.

By that time, violence had spread to the floors of Congress itself. The national legislature, its Senate Democratic and its House controlled by Republicans, was paralyzed by sectional conflict reinforced by party division. Neither side could get its solution to the Kansas question adopted and neither would listen to the other. In the two days before the battle of Lawrence, Senator Charles Sumner of Massachusetts, one of the most able, resolute, fanatic, and intemperate of the Republicans, denounced the "Slave Oligarchy" and its "rape" of Kansas in a speech that was calculated to antagonize and offend his Southern colleagues to the point where he directly insulted several senators. The day after the battle, Representative Preston S. Brooks of South Carolina, nephew of Senator Andrew P. Butler of that state and one of those insulted by Sumner, entered the Senate chamber and assaulted the Massachusetts senator with a cane. Before the two men could be separated, Sumner was badly battered. Taking full advantage of his injuries, he remained away from the Senate for three and a half years, leaving his empty chair as a continuous reminder of the event. The Democratic minority prevented Brooks' expulsion from the House, but he resigned to go before the voters of his district for a vote of confidence. Naturally, they returned him by an overwhelming margin, "proving" to the North that "all Southerners" condoned violence. Coming at the same time as the Lawrence fight, the two events, reported as sensationally as possible, further exacerbated the sectional division.

By January 1857, the Kansas question settled down to violent stalemate, a cancerous sore on the American body politic and particularly on the Democratic party. In December of that year, in a referendum boycotted by the Free-Soilers, participating Kansas voters approved the proslavery Lecompton constitution for the state-in-the-making. When, in February 1858, President Buchanan urged Congress to accept it and admit Kansas to the Union, he precipitated a crisis in the Democratic party. Stephen A. Douglas led Northern Democrats in opposition to the Lecompton constitution on the grounds that the ways of its drafting and approval violated the principle of popular sovereignty, not to speak of elemental principles of political justice. He and his supporters succeeded in bringing Congress to call for a second referendum in August 1858 at which the constitution was overwhelmingly defeated (11,812 to 1,926).

The return to political fighting, coupled as it was with an increasingly interventionist proslavery administration, meant that no settlement could be reached with the by-then free-state majority in the territory. For three more years, the question remained more or less alive to poison sectional feelings and to help destroy the Democratic party. Under the *Dred Scott* decision, slavery was legal in Kansas. The territory was occupied by federal troops who superintended elections which were carried by the Free-Soilers, while the federal civil officials there and in Washington connived to turn the territory over to the proslavery forces.

Back in the states men were beginning to arm themselves as

well. In the North, antislavery men began storming jails to release fugitive slaves who had been captured by a federal enforcement network that was not to be duplicated until the civil rights struggles of the 1960s. United States commissioners, marshals, and deputy marshals in every federal court district stood ready to search for and apprehend fugitive slaves. Federal troops were available to guard fugitives taken into custody and naval vessels were sent to transport them southward. The presence of federal forces only served to anger the Northerners who felt that the "Slave Power" was not only managing the nation's destiny but interfering with their local rights as well. Stung to action, enrollments in the state militias increased and by 1859 new regiments, companies, and battalions were drilling on village greens and city squares from Maine to Minnesota. The young men, in particular, who sought to escape the tedium of daily life in the provinces and who saw only the glamor of military life as "Zouaves," "Fusiliers," "Hussars," or what have you, were easily recruited into such units. In the South, similar units sprang up. Moreover, Southern state legislatures began appropriating additional funds for arms purchases in preparation for any eventuality — meaning, really, secession.

Meanwhile, in 1859 some of the Kansas fighters found their way east. John Brown, the most able fanatic in free Kansas, embittered by that struggle and emboldened by abolitionist support, decided to assault the heartland of slavery itself to provoke a slave uprising. It made no difference that an overwhelming majority in the North disavowed Brown and his raid; the South saw only the support he received from the "Secret Six" and people like Ralph Waldo Emerson. The two-day battle at Harper's Ferry that resulted from his efforts gave the Southern secessionists, who were beginning to reemerge as the Republican party grew stronger in the North, the issue beyond slavery that they needed while at the same time giving the Northern antislavery fanatics a martyr.

Economic Enhancement of the Trend Toward Division

The economic pattern of the cold war decade added its share to the tenseness of the situation, further separating the needs and interests of the Northerners and Southerners, then exacerbating the problems they faced. Southern agricultural production expanded at an unprecedented rate after 1850, climaxing two generations of great growth, but, except in the border states, was generally confined to raising cotton and tobacco. Slavery was particularly useful in raising both crops, but the availability of slaves distracted even the small Southern farmers (who were numerically in the majority even in the Black Belt) from exploring the possibilities of mechanized agriculture that was spreading in the North and the West. Cotton remained the nation's primary export, increasing its share of the export market from forty-three percent (1836-40 average) to fifty-four percent (1856-60 average), thus encouraging what was to be the South's fatal economic delusion that the European economy stood or fell on Southern cotton. Moreover, the cotton trade was increasingly concentrated in the hands of New York merchants whose role was hardly noticed in good times, but would become painfully evident in bad ones.

At the same time, domestic trade patterns were being reoriented from a north-south to an east-west axis by the spreading rail network and the New York-Great Lakes-Mississippi Waterway, increasing the South's isolation from the rest of the nation. Whereas the Northern and Southern extremities of the nation had been affected by these new transportation systems even earlier, the vital center of the country was forced to make its choice in the 1850s. The bulk of Cincinnati's trade before 1850, for example, was with the South. By 1860, the Queen City had reoriented itself and was trading predominantly with the Northeast. Chicago, a Northern entrepot, was rapidly gaining on St. Louis, which lived off the Southern-oriented river trade. The great increase in the value of New Orleans' receipts from Mississippi River traffic was misleading, since it reflected the great growth of cotton and cane production in the Old Southwest, most of it for export abroad, even as Northern trade declined.

The sectional divergence in manufacturing was also sharpened drastically in that decade. In 1860, only one-seventh of all manufacturing establishments in the nation were in the South. That section had less than ten percent of the total capital invested in manufacturing and produced less than ten percent of the total annual value added by manufacturing. The South was hardly more of a manufacturing area than the free-soil areas in the trans-Mississippi West that were barely settled on their fringes. Not only was Northern industry growing in size, but whole new industries were coming into being. Improved mining technology enabled workers to go deeper into the earth to extract its riches, whether they sought coal and oil in Pennsylvania, copper and iron in Michigan, lead in Illinois and Wisconsin, or gold and silver in California, Colorado, and Nevada. The raw materials thus recovered fed the new factories. The emergence of a machine tool industry enabled the new factories to better process those raw materials. Improved railroad bridge building technologies created a new communications system that stretched from the Atlantic to the Missouri by 1860.

In 1857 a decade of boom times was punctured by a panic and a three-year depression as the unregulated national economy fell victim to its own inherent weaknesses. The failure of the Ohio Life Insurance and Trust Company in August 1857 set off a sharp financial panic reinforced by overspeculation in railroad securities and real estate. Withdrawal of bankers' balances from New York City depositories that autumn to cover the demands of panic-stricken depositors increased the problem to the point where specie payments were temporarily suspended. The commodity price index, which had risen from 84 in 1850 to a high of 111 in 1857, fell to 93 the next year, and then to a low of 89 in 1861 before recovering through the impact of the Civil War.

While recovery came reasonably soon in the Northeast as the new industrial economy recoiled with little difficulty, the rest of the country, dependent upon the more deeply affected agricultural economy, remained in a recession until the war boom. Moreover, the recession was intensified the farther one went from the centers of American finance. These economic difficulties, coming as they did on the heels of Kansas and *Dred Scott*, made people in both sections more fearful and consequently more receptive to the seeds of dissension.

The Equation of Conflict: Multiplication = Polarization

The record of increased sectional conflict in the 1850s is especially interesting because every one of the specific items in the record had its precedent in earlier decades. In the literal sense, the difference between the conflicts of the 1850s and those of earlier years was one of degree, but the escalation of degree had the effect of transforming the character of the conflicts as well. This difference in degree was caused not by the escalation of one issue only, but by the convergence of several divisive issues all serving to exacerbate intersectional conflict. Single issues do not split countries; nor do single events incite revolutions. If that were so, there could be no such thing as a democratic consensus and civil societies could only be held together through the threat of brute force. Every civil society is perennially faced with great polarizing issues which can be "managed" only because the cross-pressures counteracting their divisive tendencies, added together, are stronger. Thus, the conflict of interests between North and South already visible in the Revolutionary generation remained manageable as long as there were more interests uniting the sections than dividing them. Until 1847, North-South differences were held to manageable proportions in two ways. The spirit of nationalism produced by the common tasks of forging and maintaining independence from European domination and acquiring possession of the remainder of the continent to the west of the original states grew in the hearts of people of all sections, with the sectional feeling that also grew not at all in contradiction to this sense of being American. This spirit was reflected in the men elevated to national leadership between 1776 and 1847, regardless of section. Even after the slavery issue had rung the "fire bell in the night" in 1820, the nation's leaders were known nationalists. Adams, Jackson, and Polk stand out among the presidents as articulators of the national dream while Benton, Clay, Webster, and even Calhoun — the great leaders of Congress and their respective political parties and the spokesmen of their respective sections — remain enduring symbols of American nationalism even today.

Just as important, the country had not yet been polarized into two distinct and separate sections in people's minds. When Americans thought of their country's divisions, they did not think of "the North" and "the South," but of "New England," "the Middle States," "the Border States," "the South," and "the West" in one combination or another. There were as many ties and as many differences between the first two as between the first two and the last two. Indeed, the most pronounced feelings of sectional polarization before 1847 were between "the East" (north and south) and "the West" (north and south), even though (or perhaps because) the division between North and South marked by the absence or presence of slavery received explicit political recognition and legal endorsement in the Missouri Compromise by actually drawing a line across the territories, separating the two systems and establishing the free-state slave-state party in the Senate.

After 1847, however, there was a great convergence of pressures along the same lines of cleavage: the sectional lines dividing North and South. The nation no longer had to worry about

European threats or logical extensions of the national domain. Death forced the great nationalistic leaders of the previous generation from the scene. The new leaders raised in their place were products of very different circumstances. Though they sincerely professed nationalism, nationalism was no longer the central issue that concerned them, or the country as a whole, and the other issues that took its place in their hearts were divisive ones. The greater West temporarily disintegrated as a section as North and South each absorbed its respective "West." As the antebellum decade wore on, even the middle and border states whose precise divisions were normally difficult to determine, except for the slavery issue, were forced apart.

Though the economic situation did not change significantly insofar as intersectional relations were concerned — there has been an overemphasis on the purely economic "causes" of the Civil War — changes in the two sections' economic systems led to social changes which did indeed become significant. As the decade wore on, these social changes were to become even more pronounced. More than that, they were progressively invested with a moral character that made each of exceptional value in the eyes of the people of each section.

In sum, the original conflicting interests of North and South were augmented by new ones in the half generation before the war. At the same time, the deleterious consequences of those conflicting interests were becoming less and less restrained by once-substantial cross-pressures that had linked the two sections, their states, leaders, and people, in the past. With each new crisis, tension between the two sections was escalated further, the chances for misunderstanding grew, and the effort required to preserve the Union increased. As the bases of consensus and mutual trust were further eroded with each new conflict, the normal processes of democratic politics ceased to operate effectively.

Bibliographic Notes — Chapter 8

On the Buchanan administration and the split in the Democratic party, see B.G. Auchampaugh, *James Buchanan and His Cabinet* (1926); Ollinger Crenshaw, "The Speakership Contest of 1859-1860," *Mississippi Valley Historical Review* 29 (1942): 323; and Reinhard H. Luthin, "The Democratic Split During Buchanan's Administration," *Pennsylvania History* 2 (1944): 13.

For the Dred Scott decision and its impact, see Thomas B. Alexander, "The Dred Scott Case," *South Carolina Historical Proceedings* (1953); Frederick S. Allis, "The Dred Scott Labyrinth," in *Teachers of History: Essays in Honor of Laurence Bradford Packard*, ed. Stuart Hughes (1954); Philip Auchampaugh, "James Buchanan, the Court, and the Dred Scott Case," *Tennessee History Magazine* 9 (1924): 56; H.T. Catterall, "Some Antecedents of the Dred Scott Case," *American Historical Review* 17 (1924): 56; Edward S. Corwin, "The Dred Scott Decision," *American Historical Review* 17 (1911): 52; Walter Ehrlich, "Was the Dred Scott Case Valid?" *Journal of American History* 55 (1968): 265; H.H. Hagan, "The Dred Scott Decision," *Georgetown Law Journal* 15 (1927): 95; Frank H. Hodder, "The Dred Scott Case," *Mississippi Valley Historical Review* 16 (1929): 3; Vincent C. Hopkins, *Dred Scott's Case* (1951); John C. Hurd, *The Law of Freedom and Bondage*, 2 vols. (1858-1862); Stanley I. Kutler, *The Dred Scott Decision* (1967); Eugene I. McCormac, "Justice Campbell and the Dred Scott Decision," *Mississippi Valley Historical Review* 19 (1953): 565; Wallace Mendelson, "Dred Scott's Case," *Minnesota Law Review* 38 (1953): 16; R.R. Stenberg, "Political Aspects of the Dred Scott Case," *Mississippi Valley Historical Review* 19 (1933): 571; Carl B. Swisher, "Dred Scott One Hundred Years After," *Journal of Politics* 19 (1957); 167.

The struggle for Kansas is chronicled and analyzed in Horace Andrews, Jr., "The Kansas Crusade: Eli Thayer and the New England Emigrant Aid Company," *New England Quarterly* 35 (1962): 497; Lester B. Baltimore, "Benjamin F. Stringfellow: The Fight for Slavery on the Missouri Border," *Missouri Historical Review* 62 (1967): 14; G.R. Gaeddert, *The Birth of Kansas* (1940); Paul W. Gates, *Fifty Million Acres: Conflicts over Kansas Land Policy, 1845-1890* (1954); Ralph V. Harlow, "The Rise and Fall of the Kansas Aid Movement," *American Historical Review* 41 (1935): 1; Robert W. Johannsen, "The Lecompton Constitutional Convention: Analysis of Its Membership," *Kansas Historical Quarterly* 23 (1957): 225; Samuel A. Johnson, *Battle Cry of Freedom: The New England Emigrant Aid Company in the Kansas Crusade* (1954); James C. Malin, *John Brown and the Legend of Fifty-Six* (1942), and "The Proslavery Background of the Kansas

Building Toward Civil War

Struggle," *Mississippi Valley Historical Review* 10 (1932): 285; Robert E. Moody, "The First Year of the Emigrant Aid Company," *New England Quarterly* 4 (1931): 148; Alice Nichols, *Bleeding Kansas* (1954); Floyd C. Shoemaker, "Missouri's Proslavery Fight for Kansas, 1854-1855," *Missouri Historical Review* 48 (1954): 41; Bernard A. Weisberger, "The Newspaper Reporter and the Kansas Embroglio," *Mississippi Valley Historical Review* 36 (1950): 633.

Its spread eastward to Harper's Ferry is discussed in J.C. Furnas, *The Road to Harper's Ferry* (1959); Richard J. Hinton, *John Brown and His Men* (1894); Allan Keller, *Thunder at Harper's Ferry* (1958).

Changing economic conditions and the Panic of 1857 are described in the books on economic development cited in the earlier chapters, plus George R. Taylor, *The Transportation Revolution* (1951); George W. Van Vleck, *The Panic of 1857* (1943).

PART FOUR:

ANALYSIS: GENERATONS, CULTURES, FRONTIERS, AND SECTIONS

Chapter 9

THE GENERATIONS OF AMERICAN POLITICS

The Generational Rhythm

It is no accident that fifteen years is the measure of time between the reemergence of the slavery conflict in the political arena as a result of the Mexican War and the outbreak of the Civil War. One of the purposes of this book is to closely study the generational rhythm of politics. Social time seems to follow certain rhythms connected with the human life cycle. Those rhythms are encapsulated in the progression of generations, periods of between twenty-five and forty years which roughly correspond to the span of full productivity of the average adult. The human drama seems to play itself out through a progression of generations, each of which has its own internal rhythm. This pattern is crystal clear in American history and is nowhere more clear than in connection with the Civil War.

Thomas Jefferson, in his search for a system that would provide the maximum degree of individual liberty, was perhaps the first American to note the existence of that rhythm. In a letter dated September 6, 1789, to his friend and colleague, James Madison, at the outset of the French Revolution, he suggested the following:

> Let us suppose a whole generation of men to be born on the same day, to attain mature age on the same day, and to die the same day, leaving a succeeding generation in the moment of attaining their mature age all together. Let the ripe age be supposed of 21 years, and their period of life 34 years more, that being the average term given by the bills of mortality to persons who already attained 21 years of age. Each successive generation would, in this way, come on and go off stage at a fixed moment, as individuals do now.

> What is true of a generation all arriving to self-government on the same day, and dying all on the same day, is true of those on a constant course of decay and renewal, with this only

difference. A generation coming in and going out entire, as in the first case, would have a right in the 1st year of their self-dominion to contract a debt for 33 years, in the 10th for 24, in the 20th for 14, in the 30th for 4, whereas generations changing daily, by daily deaths and births, have one constant term beginning at the date of their contract, and ending when a majority of those of full age at that date shall be dead. The length of that term may be estimated from the tables of mortality, corrected by the circumstances of climate, occupation, etc. peculiar to the country of the contractors. Take, for instance, the table of M. de Buffon wherein he states 23,994 deaths, and the ages at which they happened. Suppose a society in which 23,994 persons are born every year and live to the ages stated in this table. The conditions of that society will be as follows. 1st, it will consist constantly of 617,703 persons of all ages. 2dly, of those living at any one instant of time, one half will be dead in 24 years 8 months. 3dly, 10,675 will arrive every year at the age of 21 years complete. 4thly, it will constantly have 348,417 persons of all ages above 21 years. 5ly, and half of those of 21 years and upwards living at any one instant of time will be dead in 18 years 8 months, or say 19 years at the nearest integral number. Then 19 years is the term beyond which neither the representatives of a nation, nor even the whole nation itself assembled can validly extend a debt.

On similar ground, it may be proved that no society can make a perpetual constitution, or even a perpetual law....Every constitution, then, and every law, naturally expires at the end of 19 years. If it be enforced longer, it is an act of force and not of right.

Once the sage of Monticello experienced the problems of constitution-making on a large scale, he certainly did not try to encourage polities to begin anew every nineteen years. Yet in proposing his radical scheme, Jefferson did come to grips with an important social phenomenon, one which perceptive statesmen of every age have reckoned with in one way or another — namely, the succession of generations as the measure of location in time.

Biological and Sociopolitical Rhythms

As Jefferson noted, people's own biological heritage provides them with a natural measure of time. We often use the concept of the generation in a common sense way for just that purpose, as when we talk about the "lost generation" or the "generation gap." In fact, social time does move in sufficiently precise generational units to account for the rhythm of social and political action. If we look closely and carefully, we can map the internal structure of each generation in any particular civil society and chart the relations among generations so as to formulate a coherent picture of the historical patterns of its politics.

During a period of no less than 25 and no more than 40 years, averaging 30 to 35 (Jefferson gives 34 as the average), most humans will pass through the productive phase of their life cycles and then pass into retirement, turning their places over to others. Every individual begins life with childhood, a period of dependency in which his role as an independent actor is extremely limited. Depending upon the average life expectancy of his society, he begins to assume an active role as a member of society sometime between the ages of 16 and 30 (Jefferson's average: 21), at which point he has between 25 and 40 years of "active life" ahead of him during which he is responsible for such economic, social, and political roles as are given to mature men and women in his society. Sometime between the ages of 60 and 75, if still alive, he or she is relieved of those responsibilities and is by convention, if not physically, considered ready for retirement.

This pattern can best be viewed by focusing on its manifestations in a particular political system. Figure 9-1 traces the shifts in the aggregate population of the United States as reflected in United States census data from 1850 (the first year that complete data are available in readily accessible form) through 1970. The different lines reflect the replacement of mature populations at age and generational intervals of 30, 35, and 40 years. As Figure 9-1 indicates, the similarity within groups of lines reveals a regularity of biological replacement regardless of the alternate ways a generation can be defined; the similarity between groups of lines indicates a temporal consistency of biological replacement. Moreover, the data reveal a clear pattern of generational succession which corresponds to the shifts in political generations described below.

Human political life reflects this generational pattern on both an individual and a collective basis. For the first eighteen or more years of life, an individual is essentially powerless from a political point of view, having no right to vote, and essentially dependent upon elders for political opinions. After attaining

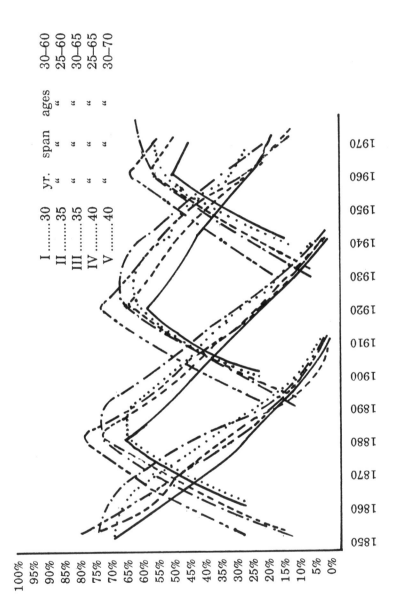

Figure 9-1

REPLACEMENT OF POPULATIONS BY GENERATIONAL INTERVALS

I	30	yr.	span	ages		30–60
II	35	"	"	"		25–60
III	35	"	"	"		30–65
IV	40	"	"	"		25–65
V	40	"	"	"		30–70

166

suffrage, individuals must still pass through a period of political apprenticeship before the right to vote can be translated into the chance for political leadership (the exceptions are few enough to prove the rule). Most people reach their thirties before assuming positions of responsibility of any significance on the larger political scene. It is only then that they become serious contenders for political power and, with good fortune, are able to replace the incumbent powerholders who depart from the scene as a result of physical or political death (which may be defined as the ending of one's serious political career without suffering actual physical death). By and large, the years from one's thirties to one's sixties represent the period in which the potential for political influence is at its maximum. A few people begin to exercise influence earlier and some very exceptional people remain political leaders longer, but rare indeed is a political career that exceeds forty years of meaningful influence past one's apprenticeship.

One empirical test of this phenomenon is the turnover pattern in the United States Congress. Figure 9-2 graphically shows the turnover pattern in the House of Representatives between 1790 and 1877. The overall secular trend has been toward less rapid turnover, but within that trend turnover is highest at generational intervals. As will be noted below, those intervals match the generational divisions that are marked off by the principal events in American history. The situation in the Senate is summarized in Figure 9-3. There, too, the secular trend is the same, and the highest turnover peaks occur at the same generational intervals.

Studies indicate that the voting behavior of the average citizen reflects a similar cycle of participation. A very high percentage of newly enfranchised young people do not bother to vote. The percentage of eligible voters actually exercising their franchise increases significantly for people in their thirties, remains much the same until retirement age, and then declines again. It seems that voters as well as leaders tend to "retire" after a generation's worth of activity.

Jefferson further suggests that every nation or civil society represents a particular sequence of generations based upon a common starting point (the moment when self-government begins). Indeed, the sequence of political generations for any particular society, nation, or group is set at the beginning of its history by its founders. Take the United States. The historical record shows that the founders of polities, state and federal, generally were young people at the beginning of the productive phase of their

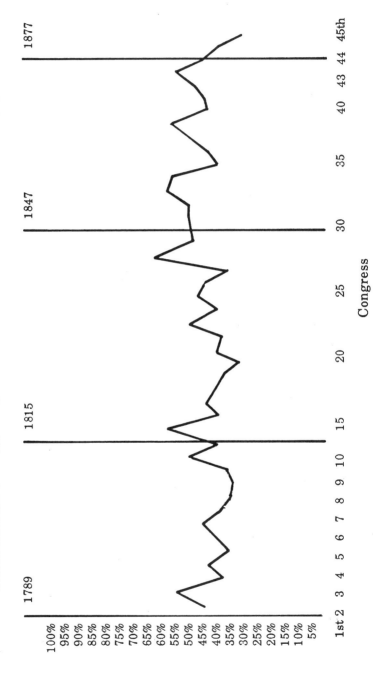

Figure 9-2

PERCENTAGE OF FIRST TERM MEMBERS IN THE U.S. HOUSE: 1789-1879

Figure 9-3

PERCENTAGE OF NEW MEMBERS IN THE U.S. SENATE:
1789-1879

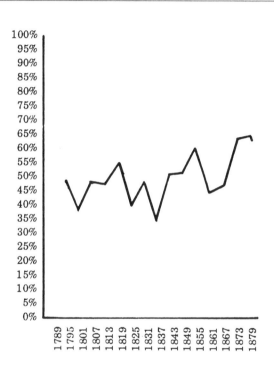

life cycles. They formed a leadership group which in the normal course of events matured, retired, and were replaced according to the cycle which they had, willy-nilly, established. While there are always some new people entering the political arena who attract the public eye, and others leaving the arena, for the most part the same cast of characters is visible over an extended period of time until they seem to disappear within the space of a few years.

Because political beginnings occur in history from time to time, they establish a much greater regularity of generational succession in social and political life than what would be found in the simple processes of human biology, which theoretically should, if other things were equal, maintain a constant "changing of the guard." In this way, the biological basis for the progression of generations is modified by locational factors. Given sufficient data, we could probably trace the generational cycles and patterns back to the very foundations of organized society. In the United States, a civil society whose foundings are recorded in history, we can do just that.

Such changes as occur in any society are intimately tied to the progression of generations. Each new generation to assume the reins of power is necessarily a production, to a greater or lesser degree, of different influences in a historical society (as distinct from a preliterate or primitive one) and is shaped to respond to different problems, heightening the impact of the change and encouraging new political action to assimilate the changes into their lives. At the same time, the biological fact that three or (at the most) four generations are alive at any given time creates certain linkages between generations (e.g., the influence of grandparents on grandchildren) that ensure a measure of intergenerational contacts and social continuity, and also help to shape every generation's perception of its past and future. In this respect, Jefferson's effort to radically separate generations is socially inaccurate, just as it is biologically impossible and politically unmanageable. John Adams, who saw society as a fabric of interlocking generations, was more correct in his understanding of the linkage of generations, as Jefferson came to realize.

Here we come to the linkage between generations of people and generational patterns of events. Any particular event is the end product of the coming together of myriad causal chains, yet a careful and systematic review of history reveals that, for whatever reasons, those end-products of similar contextual import, which at first glance seem to be "accidents," occur at appropriate points within the generational time-frames. In the course of examining the evidence, some possible explanations as to why this is so will be advanced. Through them, the linkage between the two dimensions of the generational rhythm will be suggested. The fact that political events occur within a more or less regular generational rhythm does not mean that the character of such events is fixed; each generation generates its own kind of events, but their meaning in the context of history tends to be much the same.

Generational Progression in the United States

The United States offers one of the most clear-cut examples of the progression of generations because its beginnings were so decisive and its history so well documented. In the first third of the seventeenth century, groups of young adults (primarily in their twenties or early thirties) settled virgin territory at key points along the Atlantic coast and in that way initiated what was to become in time the generational progression of the United States in what was, for all intents and purposes, a free land. Since the first generation of Americans began more or less "even," its people (particularly its leaders) passed from the scene at approximately the same time, thereby opening the door for a new generation of leaders to enter the picture and to begin the process all over again.

The same process was repeated in each area as the frontier moved westward. Those who moved out first from the settled areas to the frontier tended to be young adults at the beginning of their careers, in a position to take the necessary risks and standing to benefit most from them. Thus it was that at every stage of the advancing frontier, new men would pioneer in new areas of settlement, establish their patterns, and pass from the scene at roughly the same time, thereby allowing a new generation to assume the reins.

The Internal Structure of the Generation — Challenge and Response

Within each generation, there is a more or less regular progression of political events revolving around the development of a particular set of challenges confronting that generation and its response to them. It is this recurring pattern of challenges and responses that gives each generation its particular character. While the shape of the challenges is primarily determined by external — or environmental — forces, the mode of handling those challenges and the shape of the response is primarily determined internally.

A generational map of the pattern of challenge and response within each generation will look something like this: the "border" between the old and new generations is marked by several decisive political actions, often involving constitutional change, whose characteristic feature is the simultaneous completion of the major responses of the old generation and the opening of new directions, challenges, and opportunities for the new one. The first half of the new generation is a time for recognizing the new challenges confronting it and the issues it raises, and developing and

171

testing proposals for political action to meet them. At the same time, it is a period of population change, as old voters and leaders pass from the scene of political activity and new ones come into it. During that period, there occur the generation's expressions of public will that point it in the direction which the response will take, generally by raising leaders to office who have indicated that they are ready to respond to the generation's developing challenges. In fact, the response itself builds up in a diffuse way in various public quarters, particularly in the states and localities while the challenge is coming to public attention, and only after it has been tested in many quarters does it emerge as a concentrated national effort.

The second half of the generation begins with a great spurt of governmental innovation on the national plane designed to respond to the now recognized challenge. That effort lasts for three to five years. The remainder of the generation is then occupied with digesting the results of that spurt, modifying the new programs so that they will achieve greater success, and at the same time integrating them into the country's overall political fabric. The end of the generation is marked by political acts that both ratify and codify its accomplishments while also serving to open up the issues of the next generation. By that time, voices calling for political responses to new challenges are already beginning to be recognized. This process may be diagrammed as shown in Figure 9-4.

Generation, Centuries, and Events

Between the founding of the first European settlements along the Atlantic seaboard three and a half centuries ago and the Civil War generation, seven generations of Americans were challenged and responded to events; the Civil War generation was the eighth to face its responsibility in that respect. The pattern of challenges and responses has taken two generalized forms: one during the colonial period when each colony had its own internal politics and was essentially independent of the others, and the other after independence when a common national constitution created a common national politics. In some cases, particularly after independence, when the nation could act decisively, the responses have been very clear-cut indeed. In others, particularly in the colonial period, they were more diffuse. Figures 9-5, 9-6, and 9-7 chart the progression of political events for three selected generations: the first, or founding, generation (Figure 9-5); the

172

Figure 9-4

A GENERALIZED MAP OF
INTRAGENERATIONAL PATTERNS

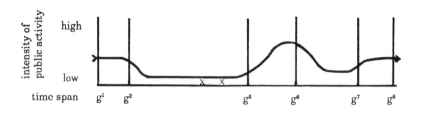

g = generation

g¹ to g²   Formative events that close off the previous generation's issues and activities and open up the issues and activities of the new generation (approximately 3 to 4 years)

g¹ to g⁴   General buildup during which time issues and problems are defined, experimental solutions are undertaken, and new voters injected into the body politic in sufficient numbers to potentially change the party alignment (approximately 10 to 15 years)

g⁵ to g⁶   Years of intensive political response, particularly on the legislative front on the national plane

g⁶ to g⁸   Years of political stabilization and consolidation during which the changes initiated in g⁵⁻⁶ are completed and institutionalized around a new level of public consensus (approximately 10 years)

g⁷ to g⁸   Culminating events that bring to a close the activities of the generation, ratifying its changes and opening the door to the next generation (approximately 3 to 5 years) fifth, or revolutionary, generation (Figure 9-6); and the eighth, or Civil War, generation (Figure 9-7).

The character of the challenges changed from century to century. During the seventeenth century, they were essentially related to the tasks of founding a new society as manifested in the various colonies. By 1713, migrants from the Old World — mostly from the British Isles, the Netherlands, and Germany, but already including a significant number of Africans, and small numbers from virtually every corner of Europe — had founded all but one of the original thirteen colonies, giving birth to at least two generations of native Americans of European descent in the English colonies, and had started those colonies on the road toward becoming a separate nation with its own civilization.

In the eighteenth century, the challenges were essentially related to the tasks of consolidating the supremacy, unity, and independence of those colonies. From the first American recognition of common continental interests during the course of Queen Anne's War (1713) to the conclusion of the "Second War for Independence" in 1815, the century was devoted to forging an independent American nation. These generations created the idea of American nationalism, successfully fought for the independence of the united colonies, and established the United States as a democratic federal republic. The ideas bequeathed by those three generations form the core of the political heritage of all subsequent generations of Americans.

In the nineteenth century, the challenges were essentially related to expanding the scope, wealth, and purpose of the American national enterprise. The century can be said to have begun at the point where America turned its back on European entanglements after 1815 and ended at the point where it reluctantly reembraced them during World War I. Its generations transformed the young republic into an industrialized continental nation with a strong national generation, abolished slavery, settled the West, and created an embryonic world power ready for overseas involvements.

Again, there is a common sense recognition of this in the treatment of American history. The seventeenth century stands out clearly as the century of the founding of American settlement; the eighteenth century stands out as the century in which an independent American nation was forged; the nineteenth century stands out as the century of continental expansion; and the twentieth century is the century of the United States as a world power.

174

Historical centuries do not cover precisely the same time periods as chronological centuries. In American history, as in modern European history, historical centuries have come to an end and new ones have begun some time within the first fifteen years after the chronological dividing point. Thus, for both Britain and America, the sixteenth century ended with the death of Queen Elizabeth (1603), and the seventeenth century began with the opening of the British-American frontier at Jamestown (1607) and the beginning of the conflict between Stuarts and Puritans which was to become the decisive political factor of the next three generations. The seventeenth century ended and the eighteenth century began with the Treaty of Utrecht and the conclusion of Queen Anne's War (1713), which eliminated the Netherlands as a world power and turned the Anglo-French conflict in the New World into a primary consideration for both countries. The eighteenth century ended with the fall of Napoleon and the end of the War of 1812 (1815); and the nineteenth century began with the Congress of Vienna and the American turn inward toward the West (1816). The nineteenth century ended and the twentieth century began with the outbreak of World War I (1914), and the final closing of America's last land frontier (c. 1917).

Figure 9-8 graphically delineates the progression of centuries and generations and relates them to the major forces and factors shaping American history. Six forces or factors are considered: (1) the stages of the continuing American frontier; (2) the country's dominant mode of economic organization; (3) the principal challenges facing the American people in each generation and the central responses to those challenges; (4) the sequence of critical elections; (5) the changing forms and patterns of American intergovernmental relations; and (6) the changing relationships between racial, ethnic, and religious groups. (One note of caution: the figure necessarily portrays the divisions between generations and centuries precisely, when, in fact, the dates must be viewed as approximate. Historical eras can be delineated, but they do not begin or end with such sharpness. Convenience demands that we be more precise for analytical purposes than life ever is.)

Figure 9-5

PATTERNS AND TRENDS IN THE FIRST GENERATION

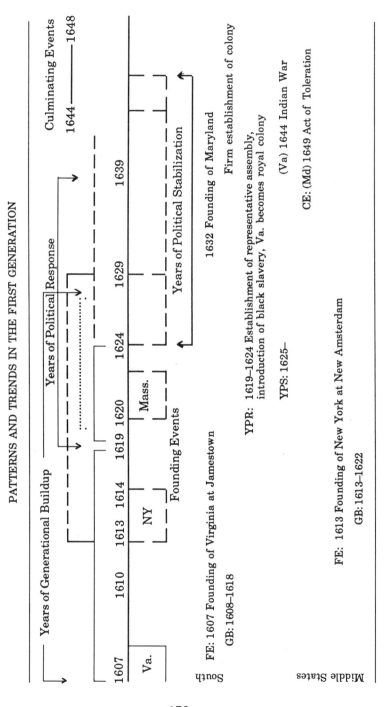

FE: 1607 Founding of Virginia at Jamestown
GB: 1608–1618

FE: 1613 Founding of New York at New Amsterdam
GB: 1613–1622

YPR: 1619–1624 Establishment of representative assembly,
introduction of black slavery, Va. becomes royal colony

YPS: 1625–

1632 Founding of Maryland
Firm establishment of colony

(Va) 1644 Indian War

CE: (Md) 1649 Act of Toleration

176

YPR: 1624–1629 Colonization begun in earnest, first governor appointed, Manhattan purchased, patroon system introduced

YPS: Indian wars and settlement along Hudson

CE: 1647 Stuyvesant governor of New Amsterdam

1622 Permanent settlement in Maine
1623 Permanent settlement in New Hampshire
1629 Founding of Massachusetts

GB: 1620-1630

FE: 1620 Founding of Plymouth

YPR: 1630–1640: Great migration of Puritans to Massachusetts and Connecticut, founding of basic institutions
1634–1639 Settling of Connecticut towns
1636 Settling of Rhode Island
1630–1638 Settling of New Hampshire towns
1639 Conn. formed as confed. of 4 towns

CE: 1643 New Engl. Confed.
1646 Decision of Nonallegiance to England
Cambridge Synod
1647 Rhode Island formed as confed. of 4 towns
Gorgas dies and Maine ends separate development

YPS: 1640–1646 Mass. expels heretics
1641 1st incorp. municipality in NE (York, Me.)

New England

Figure 9-6

PATTERNS AND TRENDS IN THE FIFTH GENERATION

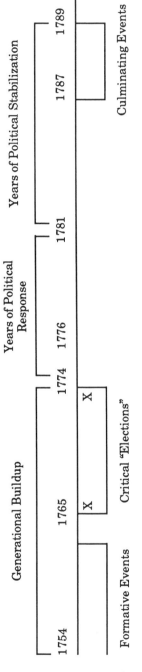

Formative Events (1754–1756)
1. French and Indian War opens last phase of elimination of French threat to colonies (1754)
2. Franklin proposes Albany Plan of Union, first formal proposal for federation of colonies

Generational Buildup (1754–1774)
1. Elimination of French from Canada and American West
2. Developing struggle over British role in government of colonies
3. Crossing of Appalachian barrier with beginning of settlement in Kentucky and Tennessee
4. Succession of intercolonial "Congresses" begin to develop mechanisms for federation

Critical "Elections" (1765–1774)
1. Majority of representatives to Stamp Act Congress are loyalists but potential separatist faction emerges on national basis
2. Potential separatist faction a majority at First Continental Congress

Years of Political Response (1774–1781)
1. War of Independence
2. Break with Britain and Declaration of Independence
3. Formation of United States of America, adoption of Articles of Confederation, establishment of national government
4. Creation of national domain in the West

Years of Political Stabilization (1781–1789)
1. End of Revolutionary War (1781) and signing of peace treaty (1783) acknowledging American independence
2. Organization of Confederation government and its efforts to get a grip on the country
3. Organization of national domain in the West for settlement through the Northwest Ordinances of 1785 and 1787
4. Activation of the Bank of North America to give rudimentary shape to the country's finances

Culminating Events (1787–1789)
1. Constitutional Convention
2. Ratification of Constitution

Figure 9-7

PATTERNS AND TRENDS IN THE EIGHTH GENERATION

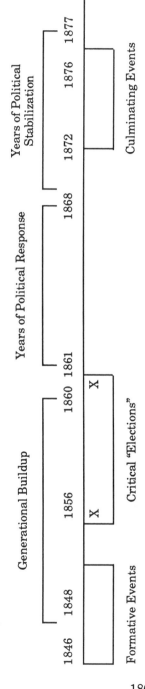

Formative Events (1846-1849)
1. Chicago Rivers and Harbors Congress (1847)
2. Treaty of Guadelupe Hidalgo ceding Mexican lands (1848)
3. Discovery of gold in California (1848)

Generational Buildup (1847-1860)
1. Anti-slavery movement turns to struggle over free soil to polarize North and South
2. Whig party breaks up and is replaced by Republican party
3. Westward movement stimulated by railroad construction and mining booms
4. Industrial revolution becomes countrywide in its impact and its accompanying urbanization, countrywide in its spread, generating new economic and social problems

Critical Elections (1856-1860)

1. Republican party, founded in 1854, mounts its first national contest for the presidency. In losing, it forged the basis for its successful coalition of the future.

2. The Republican party coalition, facing a Democratic party divided three ways, wins in North to gain presidency and become the leading national party, though without a clear majority. It holds presidency until 1884.

Years of Political Response (1861-1868)

1. Secession, Civil War and reunion (1861-1868)
2. Domestic "New Deal" under Lincoln
3. Reconstruction (attempts to break the power of the Southern establishment and to enfranchise the Negroes; XIII, XIV and XV Amendments)
4. Completion of basic political organization of the West

Years of Political Stabilization (1868-1876)

1. End of Reconstruction and renormalization of the Southern position in the Union
2. Implementation of legislative innovations of the early 1860s
3. Struggle for control of Republican party
4. Supreme Court decisions dispose of Civil War issues

Culminating Events (1876-1877)

1. Last Southern states restored to Union and federal troops withdrawn from South
2. Beginnings of agrarian protest movements
3. Disputed election of 1876
4. Power of last Indian tribes capable of resisting white settlement broken

The Bench Marks of American Political History — Critical Elections and New Deals

In the course of mapping the topographic characteristics of a particular landscape, geologists mark off crucial points through a system of bench marks. Crucial points in the passage of time can also be seen to be marked off in some way. In American political history, the crucial points of demarcation are very much in tune with the generational rhythm of events. They are of two kinds: first, the critical elections that determine who shall govern in a particular generation; and, second, the "new deals," or periods of intensive federal legislative innovation, through which government initiates a systematic response to the generation's challenges.

A major element in the response of the generations is the sequence of critical elections that has preceded every major period of national response since the adoption of the Constitution and which has its parallel even in the revolutionary generation. As two generations of political scientists have demonstrated, a critical election is one which brings about major alterations in the party loyalties of major blocs of voters, shifting them from one political party to another. V.O. Key, who first suggested the term, defined "critical election" in his seminal *Journal of Politics* article as one in which "the depth and intensity of electoral involvement are high, in which more or less profound readjustments occur in the relations of power within the community, and in which new and durable electoral groups are formed." These shifts and readjustments which occur as a result of the critical elections lead to the formation of new nationwide electoral coalitions and either to a change in the political ascendency from one party to the other or, within the majority party, from one major element to another. Figure 9-8 links the pattern of critical presidential elections with the overall generational system.

Students of American electoral behavior have clearly shown that there is a tendency for one of the major parties to command the allegiance of a majority of the national electorate for a relatively long period of time — approximately one generation, as we have defined the term. Thus, for example, from the 1930s until the 1970s, the Democratic party was the majority party in the country as a whole. The results of this situation are well known. Between 1932 and 1976 only two Republicans won the presidency, and the GOP controlled the Congress for only two terms. In fact, since 1952, the

GOP as a political party has been unable to overcome the Democratic majority and elect a Republican Congress. The succession of Democratic-controlled congresses — even when Republicans occupied the White House — since 1954 reflect the true extent of the nationwide Democratic majority. The generation that began in 1977 is one of transition, with the GOP more likely to win the White House but unable to dislodge the Democratic majority in Congress and the states.

According to the critical elections theory, a party becomes the majority party when it is able to put together a nationwide coalition comprising a majority of the various permanent and transient electoral groups. Once one of the parties is able to put together such a coalition and thereby capture the majority of the voters, the tendency of the electorate to remain stable in its allegiances will enable it to remain the majority party until positive reasons develop that lead to the dissolution of the winning combination. This dissolution, too, is virtually inevitable. Times and moods change, new problems attract the voters' attention, the opposition party exploits the dissatisfactions that develop and sooner or later makes the necessary inroads in various electoral groups.

As the majority coalition begins to weaken, its constituent electoral groups become alienated from one another. Their changing needs may even bring former confederates into conflict with each other. The members of these electoral groups may begin to find the other party more receptive to their new demands. As issues pass and problems change, whole electoral groups may decline radically in importance and new, still uncommitted, groups may emerge to be wooed and won by the opposition. When the time is ripe for a change, realignment takes place, reshuffling the parties' constituent elements, the myriad electoral groups.

While the beginnings of every alignment can be found in the state and congressional elections, the shift becomes a national phenomenon only through the medium of the quadrennial presidential election. Once every four years, sufficient voter interest is aroused to make embryonic realignments actual. Once the realignments become fixed, they are further reflected in the state and congressional elections that follow. The series of presidential and congressional elections in which the realignment occurs are the critical elections.

The generational thesis helps place the phenomena of critical elections in context, revealing the larger pattern behind their recurrence. The formation and dissolution of electoral conditions is

Figure 9-8

THE GENERATIONAL RHYTHM OF AMERICAN POLITICS: A GRAPHIC OUTLINE

Century and Generation / Dates	Frontier Period	Economic Period	Challenge-Response	Critical Elections	Intergovernmental Relations	Ethno-Religious Trends
17th 1607 / 1 1648	Rural-Land Frontier (East Coast settled)	Colonial Mercantilism	Founding and establishing political institutions		Founding and organizing colonies	Ethnic separation on religious basis. Establishment of churches
2 1676			Establishing local identity		Experiments in federal organization	
3 1713			Building a pluralistic social base			
18th / 4 1756			Eliminating the French from North America			
5 1775 1776 1781 1787	(Appalachians crossed)		Establishing national independence	1768 Stamp Act; 1774 1st Cont. Congress	Formation of Union	Protestant diversification and disestablishment; increased ethnic diversity within framework

	Years	Frontier	Economic System	Political Theme	Party/Year	Intergovernmental	Pluralism
6	1789 / 1815		Semi-Mercantilism	Organizing a new government	1796 Federalists; 1800 Dem-Repub.	Development of intergovernmental cooperation	Informal reestablishment of Protestantism. Influx of Catholics and Jews
19th 7	1816 / 1846	Urban-industrial Frontier (Continent Spanned)	First Transition	Democratization of the American polity	1824 Nat. Dems.; 1828 Jacksonian Dems.		
8	1848 / 1876		Free Enterprise Capitalism	Reorganizing for an industrial society	1856 Democrats; 1860 Republicans	Era of land grants	Period of Eastern and Southern European immigration; Protestant counterattacks
9	1913		Concentrated Enterprise Capitalism	First assault on problems of industrialization	1892 Democrats; 1896 Republicans	Beginnings of cash grants.	
20th 10	1917 / 1946	Metropolitan Technological Frontier	Second Transition	Reformation of the industrial system	1928 Republicans; 1932 Democrats	Grant-in-aid federalism	Discovery of pluralism
11	1949 / 1976		Regulated Enterprise Capitalism	Responding to metropolitan frontier as world leader	1956 Republicans; 1960 Democrats	Concentrated cooperation	Recognition of pluralism
12	1977	Rurban-Cybernetic Frontier		Movement toward power-sharing in the world and less government at home		"New Federalism"	Lifestyle pluralism

closely tied to the generational rhythm. The bare outlines of the patterns are shown in Figure 9-8. Notice that the critical elections generally come about eight years into each generation, after the challenge and the need to develop responses to it have become widely perceived. They serve as the political catalyst for the generational response.

Three times in American history the critical elections have elevated the party previously in the minority to majority status. In the series of elections beginning in 1796 and culminating in 1800, the Jeffersonian Democratic-Republicans replaced the Federalists. In the 1856 through 1860 series, the Republicans replaced the Democrats who had become the heirs of the Jeffersonians, and in the 1928 through 1932 series, the Democrats in turn replaced the Republicans.

Between each shift, the critical elections served to reinforce the majority party, which was successful in adapting itself to new times and new conditions. Thus, from 1824 to 1828, the Jacksonian Democrats picked up the reins from their Jeffersonian predecessors; from 1892 to 1896, the Republicans were able to reconstitute their party coalition to maintain and even strengthen their majority position. In 1956 through 1960, the Democrats were able to do the same thing. The old coalition put together by Franklin Delano Roosevelt and the New Deal, which underwent severe strains in the late 1940s and early 1950s, was reconstituted and reshaped by Adlai Stevenson and John F. Kennedy to give the Democrats an even stronger majority than before, which made the programs of the 1960s possible.

The "realignment" that takes place does not so much involve changes in the allegiance of specific voters but a disruption of the common pattern whereby children tend to vote as did (or do) their parents — along lines determined by issues current during their grandparents' prime. A realignment thus becomes the end result of an event or compact series of events so crucial that they disrupt this "normal" progression and lead a significant percentage of children to reassess their family voting patterns as they come of age and alter them in light of a situation which has made the old issues lose their primary importance. As the parents die (or cease to vote, as is often the case with oldsters), the votes of their children come to represent first the balance in the electorate and then the majority. The shift is first felt in the period of generational buildup, which is precisely the period when this changing of the guard is taking place among political actives and rank and file alike. That is why the critical elections occur during that part of each generation and serve to bring it to an end. By the time of the ratifying election, the new generation of "children" has moved from balance to majority.

The culmination of each series of critical elections is a burst of innovative federal activity, legislative activity of the kind usually referred to in connection with the New Deal of Franklin Delano Roosevelt. Figure 9-8 indicates when each such response has taken place, labeling them with the names by which they are commonly known. Figures 9-5, 9-6, and 9-7 show the responses of three crucial generations. The labels should be generally self-explanatory. Thomas Jefferson and Andrew Jackson are well known for their reforms. It is less well known that Abraham Lincoln presided over a period of domestic reform legislation of major proportions that enabled the country to adjust to the internal revolution the way the New Deal provided the basis for overcoming the social problems of industrialization. Most recently, Lyndon B. Johnson's Great Society carried on the pattern on schedule, as it were.

The generational pattern leading to such bursts becomes quite clear in the eighth generation. During the decade or more prior to enactment of the relevant legislation, members of both houses of Congress were busy hammering out bills acceptable to coalitions sufficiently wide to gain their passage. The Lincoln administration successfully enacted legislation blocked by hostile congressional forces or presidential vetoes through the 1850s, including the Homestead Act, the transcontinental railroad land grants, and tariff reform.

Thus, proper understanding of the progression of time within and across generations and centuries makes it possible to place political and related events in a meaningful temporal context and helps to identify their relationship to one another. Moreover, it offers a means to evaluate the extent to which most political and social studies (which, by their design, tend to be atemporal in character) contribute to our larger knowledge of political systems and behavior by enabling us to place them in their proper temporal context as well.

The Persistence of Alignments

The fundamental issues and alignments that form the hidden dimensions in shaping political behavior show every sign of persisting over three generation periods and then dissipating in the fourth. The issues and alignments revolving around the nature of the federal union and the slavery issue that emerged during the sixth generation of American life — the first generation under the Constitution — persisted through the eighth generation (a century later) when they were resolved in the Civil War, which in turn created a new set of fundamental issues and alignments having to do with economic reform and the adjustment to a pluralistic society that took form in the ninth generation to dominate American politics for a century. Those issues and alignments did not disintegrate until the eleventh generation, after World War II. While this intergenerational pattern is on a different axis from that of the historical centuries, the two are linked in that the starting point of the former comes at the high point of the latter, precisely in the years which are the focus of this volume.

The issues of the past century will no doubt be replaced in the twelfth generation by some of the issues that have surfaced in American life in the 1960s. Indeed, the crisis of the 1960s, which commentators have described as the most divisive since the Civil War, came just when it would have been predicted to come according to the patterns of generational progression, when the set of fundamental alignments fixed by the Civil War era was finally ceasing to bind any appreciable segment of the American people, and a new set of issues of equal intensity was available to move to center stage. This is why the conflict was so intense, the sense of alienation from the American past so deep among the members of the generation then coming to maturity, and the changes in American life so vast. Nearly a generation later its impact is still strong. It is also why a look at the previous breaking point should be of particular interest to contemporary Americans.

The Civil War generation began in the late 1840s, approximately between 1846 and 1848, when the Mexican war elevated new figures to national leadership while older ones reached the end of their careers and passed from the stage during those same years or immediately thereafter. These new men and new issues slowly captured center stage during the first half of the generation, the former acquiring office and status and the latter, definition and meaning, thereby provoking response to the challenges they posed. The Civil War, coming for four years in the middle of the generation, represented the coming together of those responses in a short but decisive period. At its end the results of the war were

concretized during Reconstruction, which brought the generation
to its conclusion with an introduction of a new social and political
balance within the United States that saw a pulling back of the
most extreme demands generated as a result of the war, along
with the entrenchment of its most widely accepted results.

During the half generation that is the subject of this volume, we
saw the new men and their new issues emerge to take the place of
their predecessors. We saw how the challenges which each pro-
voked, respectively and in concert, were translated into political
terms and were expressed through two critical national elections
that changed the party alignment in the United States, and how the
definition of the challenges led to a well-nigh inevitable response,
namely the Civil War.

The ensuing crisis led to far-reaching consequences because
it followed along lines of permanent cleavage already existing in
the country. Hence, in order to understand its impact, it is first
necessary to understand those permanent cleavages and where
lay the fault lines which divided them. Two major interrelated
cleavages came into play here: political culture and sectionalism,
with the shape of the latter strongly influenced by the content and
spread of the former.

Bibliographic Notes — Chapter 9

Antoine Augustin Cournot, in *Considerations sur la marcher des
ides et evenments dans les temp moderne* (Paris, 1872), developed the
principle that governments are articulated through historical events
and suggested how continuity among governments is maintained.
Guiseppe Ferrari, *Teoria dei periodi politici* (Milan: Hoepli, 1874),
emphasized the thirty-year interval and suggested a fourfold classification of governments as preparatory, revolutionary, reactionary, and
conciliatory in a repeating cycle. Wilhelm Dilthey, "Uber des
Studium der Geschichte der Wissenschaften von Menschen, der
Gesellschaft und dem Staat," in Volume 5 of *Gesammelte Schriften*
(Berlin: Teuber, 1924), applied the concept to cultural development.
Leopold von Ranke and his student Ottokar Lorenz emphasized that
governmental periodization was one of the keys to the scientific study
of history, utilizing as tools the study of genealogy and heredity.
Lorenz introduced the concept of the three-government century. See J.
Marias and M. Rintala, "Generations," in *International Encyclopedia*

of the Social Sciences, Volume 6 (New York: Macmillan and Free Press, 1968), pp. 88-96.

After World War I, Jose Ortega y Gasset, in *Man and Crisis* (New York: W.W. Norton, 1962) and *The Modern Theme* (New York: W.W. Norton, 1933), made the succession of governments the basis of his philosophy of social life, adding, among other concepts, the distinction between contemporaries (those alive at the same time) and coevals (those who are part of the same government.).

His work has been continued by his student, Julian Marias. See Marias, *La estructura social: Teoria y metodo* (Madrid: Sociedad des Estudias y Publicaciones, 1964); idem, *El metodo historico de las genereciones* (Madrid: Revista de Occidenta, 1961); idem, "Ortega and the Idea of Vital Reason," in *Dublin Review* 222, 445, and 446; 56-79; 36-54. Sociologist Karl Mannheim, in "The Problem of Generations," pp. 276-320 in *Essays on the Sociology of Knowledge,* also worked on this problem, as did such scholars as Francois Mentre, in *Les governments sociales* (Paris: Bossard, 1920), and Engelbert Drerup, in *Das Generations problem in der griechischen und griechischromischen Kultur* (Germany: Schonongh, 1933). The thesis was applied by Wilhelm Pinder to art, in *Das Problem der Generation in der Kunstgeschichte Europas* (Berlin: Frankfurter Verlags-Anstalt, 1928), and to literature by Julius Peterson, "Die Literarischen Generationen," pp. 130-187 in E. Ermatiner, ed., *Philosophie de Literaturwissenschaft* (Berlin: Junker & Dunnhaupt, 1930), and by Henrie Peyre, *Les governments litteraires* (Paris: Boivin, 1948).

More recent efforts by political and social scientists have focused on the problems of intergovernmental differences and the political socialization of new governments primarily in totalitarian regimes or in reference to parties of the extreme right or left. Sigmund Neumann, in *Permanent Revolution: Totalitarianism in the Age of International Civil War* (New York: Praeger Press, 1965), was the first to apply this perspective in his study of the rise of Nazism. R.A. Bauer, et al., in "Generational Differences," pp. 190-198 in *How the Soviet System Works* (Cambridge, Mass.: Harvard University Press, 1956), included it in their study of the Soviet system. Marvin Rintala, "The Problem of Generations in Finnish Communism," in *American Slavic and East European Review* 17 (1958): 190-202, *Three Generations: The Extreme Right Wing in Finnish Politics* (Bloomington, Indiana: Indiana University Press, 1962), and "A Generation in Politics: A Definition," *Review of Politics* 25: 509-522, focused on right and left in Finland; while Maurice Zeitlin, "Political Generations in the Cuban Working Class," *American Journal of Sociology* 71: 93-508, studied Cuba. S.M. Eisenstadt, *From Generation to Generation: Age Groups and Social Structure* (New York: Free Press, 1956), and Joseph Gusfield, "The Problem of Generations in an Organizational

The Generations of American Politics

Structure," *Social Forces* 35: 323-330, utilized the generational concept in entirely different settings, in Israel and the United States respectively.

The theory of critical elections was proposed by V.O. Key in "A Theory of Critical Elections," *Journal of Politics* 17 (1955): 3-18, and "Secular Realignment in the Party System," *Journal of Politics* 21 (1959): 198-210. See also Walter Dean Burnham, *Critical Elections and the Mainsprings of American Politics* (1970); William M. Chambers and Walter Dean Burnham, eds., *The American Party System: Stages of Political Development* (1967); Gerald Pomper, *Elections in America* (1968); and James Sundquist, *Dynamics of the Party System* (1973).

For a more complete discussion of this theory of the generational rhythm, see Daniel J. Elazar, "The Generational Rhythm of American Politics," *American Politics Quarterly* 6 (1978): 55-94, *Toward a Generational Theory of American Politics* (1968), and *Cities of the Prairie: The Metropolitan Frontier in American Politics* (1970). Elazar tested and applied this thesis to more recent trends in international relations in "Generational Shifts in International Politics" (1981) and to the history of the Jewish people in *A Gazetteer of Jewish Political Organization* (1981) with Stuart A. Cohen, *The Jewish Polity* (1984), also with Stuart A. Cohen, and *Jewish Communities in Frontier Societies* (1983).

Chapter 10

THE CLASH OF SECTIONAL POLITICAL CULTURES

Organizing Power to Pursue Justice

To no small extent, the clash between North and South was a clash of political subcultures, which was especially intense because both sides saw themselves as authentic expressions of their common American heritage as heirs of George Washington and the revolutionary founders of the United States. In other words, both shared the same political culture but understood its meaning so differently as to bring them into conflict.

The United States as a whole shares a general political culture that is rooted in two contrasting conceptions of the American political order, both of which can be traced back to the earliest settlement of the country. In the first, the political order is conceived of as a marketplace in which the primary public relationships are products of bargaining among individuals and groups acting out of self-interest. In the second, the political order is conceived to be a commonwealth — a state in which the whole people have an undivided interest — in which the citizens cooperate in an effort to create and maintain the best government in order to implement certain shared moral principles. These two conceptions have exercised an influence on government and politics throughout American history, sometimes in conflict, sometimes by complementing each other.

The two conceptions are reflected in the matrix of value concepts that forms the larger cultural basis — general as well as physical — of American civilization. This matrix is portrayed in Figure 10-1. Its component value concepts together provide the framework within which the value orientations of the American people are shaped while the differences in emphasis in the interrelationships among them reflect the various subcultures in the United States.

The four elements of the matrix are located between *power* and *justice*, the two poles of politics that between them encompass the

Figure 10-1

THE MATRIX OF VALUE CONCEPTS IN
AMERICAN CULTURE

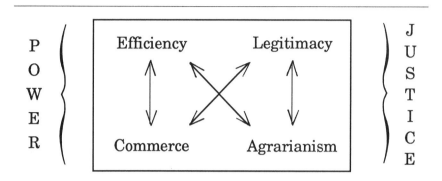

basic political concerns of all civil societies, namely, who gets
what, when and how (power), on the one hand, and the development of the good society (justice), on the other. The major continuing task of every civil society is to shape an immediately practical
relationship between the two poles in a manner that best fits its situation. Indeed, the character of any civil society is in large measure determined by the relationship between power and justice that
shapes its political order. Consequently, a particular civil society's conceptions of the uses of power and the nature of justice are
important aspects of its political culture.

Efficiency may be defined operationally in this context as the
achievement of goals in a manner that involves the least wasteful
or minimum expenditure of resources. *Legitimacy* refers to those
aspects of a polity that are believed to be supported by the underlying values of its citizenry, particularly as embodied in its constitutional system. Both represent tendencies found in every civil
society that are given meaning by each society's culture (general
and political).

Already, prior to the Civil War, in the North efficiency was
measured in predominantly commercial terms as befitted a civil
society which *The Federalist* correctly described as an extended
commercial republic. *Commerce*, in America, embodies the
exchange of goods, services, and *ideas*. In the antebellum South,
on the other hand, commerce was far from occupying the same

position. Efficiency in Southern culture involved the mainten-ance of a planter class with the leisure to engage in public affairs.

A good case can be made that the federal republic was founded to advance and protect commerce and that it has adhered quite closely to that original purpose. This adherence contributed to the mutual alienation of North and South. Both efficiency and com-merce are primarily related to the concerns of power and its man-agement, hence they especially reflected the differences between the new industrial power of the North and the established slave power of the South, throwing them into direct competition and con-flict.

Legitimacy, on the other hand, was and is given meaning in the United States by the particularly American complex of values and aspirations here termed *agrarianism*. The ideal of agrarianism predominant in the antebellum North envisioned the United States as a commonwealth of self-governing freehold-ers, each with a tangible stake in his community and, hence, in American society as a whole, raised to new heights of human de-cency through the general diffusion of knowledge, religion, and morality. While that ideal stemmed from both Puritan and Jef-fersonian roots, in the South agrarianism was transformed into the elevation of the "self-sufficient" plantation as its apotheosus, introducing an elitist dimension as against the egalitarian agrarianism of the North.

As the embodiment of the nation's social and political mys-tique, agrarianism in one form or another has been the major source and test of legitimacy in the United States. Both agrarian-ism and legitimacy are related to the problem of the attainment of justice and are expressions of the continuing effort to create a more just society in the United States.

Each of the four tendencies is pulled in the direction of power or justice and is also modified by every other tendency. Thus, in ev-ery form it has taken, American agrarianism has had a strong commercial aspect, beginning with the American's desire to make a profit from the use of the land even while valuing close-ness to it for moral reasons. By the same token, the values of agrarianism modify commercial efficiency at crucial points so that maximizing profits is not the only measure of efficiency in American life, even as they themselves are tailored at some point to meet the demands of election.

The politically defined limits of commerce in America are set by the demands of agrarian legitimacy. Periodically, the commercial aspects of American society have run wild, only to be pulled back in line, sooner or later, on the grounds that they have been set free illegitimately (e.g., trusts are illegitimate even if they are efficient from a commercial point of view). This common sense of legitimacy is defined in what are essentially agrarian terms. At such points, political action is forthcoming to reshape the commercial order so as to reintegrate it in accordance with the principles of agrarian legitimacy. At the same time, what is commonly deemed legitimate is itself shaped by the attachment to commerce as a key aspect of American civil society.

In the antebellum years, North and South had their own particular combination of these four elements, leading to different conceptions of what constitutes justice and how to organize power to attain it. But both remained within the overall American framework. Consequently, as polarization increased, each came to see its understanding of the American way of life as the only legitimate one and the other's as a life-threatening heresy.

The extremists on both sides, the abolitionists in the North and secessionists in the South, came to the conclusion that the differences were so great that two separate ways of life were involved, that it was a myth to think they had anything sufficiently in common to tie them together as Americans. But for most Americans the differences were still less important than the similarities. In great part this was because, while the extremists were polarized into two camps and ultimately the nation would be as well, the common political culture of Americans was expressed through three political subcultures. The moralistic political subculture of New England and its westward extensions gave rise to abolitionism and even for those who were not extreme abolitionists, support for the idea of Free Soil, that is to say, the prevention of the westward extension of slavery and the "Slave Power," became an article of faith. The traditionalistic South produced the radical secessionists, but even among other Southerners there was a commitment to the Southern way of life.

It remained for the individualistic residents of the middle states, whose commitment to the commercial character of the extended American republic was almost entirely a commitment to the whole American marketplace as the sole judge of who could participate, who held the country together as it polarized. It was only when they came to the conclusion that one side refused to respect the rules of the game, the sole criterion for participating in the marketplace, that they, too, were polarized. And the Civil War came.

The national political culture is a synthesis of three major political subcultures that jointly inhabit the country, existing side by side or even overlapping. All three are of nationwide proportions, having spread, in the course of time, from coast to coast. At the same time each subculture is strongly tied to specific sections of the country, reflecting the streams and currents of migration that have carried people of different origins and backgrounds across the continent in more or less orderly patterns. Each of the three reflects its own particular synthesis of the marketplace and the commonwealth dimensions of the American way of life.

The Individualistic Political Culture

As an ideal type, the *individualistic political culture* emphasizes the conception of the democratic order as a marketplace. In its view, government is instituted for strictly utilitarian reasons, to handle those functions demanded by the people it is created to serve. A government need not have any direct concern with questions of the "good society" except insofar as it may be used to advance some common conception of the good society formulated outside the political arena, just as it serves other functions. Since the individualistic political culture emphasizes the centrality of private concerns, it places a premium on limiting community intervention — whether governmental or nongovernmental — into private activities to the minimum necessary to keep the marketplace in proper working order. In general, government action is to be restricted to those areas, primarily in the economic realm, which encourage private initiative and widespread access to the marketplace.

Nineteenth-century individualistic conceptions of minimum intervention increasingly were oriented toward laissez-faire, with the role of government conceived to be that of a policeman with powers to act in certain limited fields. In the twentieth century, the notion of what constitutes minimum interference has been drastically expanded to include such things as government regulation of utilities, unemployment compensation, and massive subventions to maintain a stable and growing economy — all this within the framework of the same political culture. The demands of manufacturers for high tariffs in 1890 and the demands of labor unions for workmen's compensation in 1990 may well be based on the same theoretical justification that they are aids to the maintenance of a working marketplace. Culture is not static. It must be viewed dynamically and defined so as to include cultural change in its very nature.

The character of political participation in systems dominated by the individualistic political culture reflects this outlook. The individualistic political culture holds politics to be just another means by which individuals may improve themselves socially and economically. In this sense, politics is a business like any other that competes for talent and offers rewards to those who take it up as a career. Those individuals who choose political careers may rise by providing the governmental services demanded of them and, in return, may expect to be adequately compensated for their efforts. Interpretations of officeholders' obligations under this arrangement vary among political systems and even among individuals within a single political system. Where the norms are high, such people are expected to provide high quality government services for the general public in the best possible manner in return for the status and economic rewards considered their due. Some who choose political careers clearly commit themselves to such norms; others believe that an officeholder's primary responsibility is to serve himself and those who have supported him directly, favoring them even at the expense of the public. In some political systems, this view is accepted by the public as well as the politicians.

Political life within an individualistic political culture is based on a system of mutual obligations rooted in personal relationships. While in a simple society those relationships can be direct ones, societies in individualistic political cultures in the United States are usually too complex to maintain face-to-face ties. So the system of mutual obligations is harnessed through political parties that serve as "business corporations" dedicated to providing the organization necessary to maintain it. Party regularity is indispensable in the individualistic political culture because it is the means for coordinating individual enterprise in the political arena and is the one way of preventing individualism in politics from running wild. In such a system, an individual can succeed politically not by dealing with issues in some exceptional way or by accepting some concept of good government and then striving to implement it, but by maintaining his place in the system of mutual obligations. He can do this by cooperating according to the norms of his particular party, to the exclusion of other political considerations. Such a political culture encourages the maintenance of a party system that is competitive, but not overly so, in the pursuit of office. Its politicians are interested in office as a means of controlling the distribution of the favors or rewards of government rather than as the means of exercising governmental power for programmatic ends.

Since the individualistic political culture eschews ideological concerns in its businesslike conception of politics, both politicians and citizens look upon political activity as a specialized one, essentially the province of professionals, of minimum and passing concern to laymen, and with no place for amateurs to play an active role. Furthermore, there is a strong tendency among the public to believe that politics is a dirty — if necessary — business, better left to those who are willing to soil themselves by engaging in it. In practice, then, where the individualistic political culture is dominant, there is likely to be an easy attitude toward the limits of the professionals' prerequisites. Since a fair amount of corruption is expected in the normal course of things there is relatively little popular excitement when any is found unless it is of an extraordinary character. It is as if the public is willing to pay a surcharge for services rendered and only rebels when it feels the surcharge has become too heavy. (Of course, the judgments as to what is normal and what is extraordinary are themselves subjective and culturally conditioned.)

Public officials, committed to "giving the public what it wants," are normally not willing to initiate new programs or open up new areas of government activity on their own recognizance. They will do so when they perceive an overwhelming public demand for them to act, but only then. In a sense, their willingness to expand the functions of government is based on an extension of the quid pro quo "favor" system that serves as the central core of their political relationships, with new services the reward they give the public for placing them in office.

The individualistic political culture is ambivalent about the place of bureaucracy in the political order. In one sense, the bureaucratic method of operation flies in the face of the favor system that is central to the individualistic political process. At the same time, the virtues of organizational efficiency appear substantial to those seeking to master the market. In the end, bureaucratic organization is introduced within the framework of the favor system;

large segments of the bureaucracy may be insulated from it through the merit system but the entire organization is pulled into the political environment at crucial points through political appointment in the upper echelons and, very frequently, the bending of the merit system to meet political demands.

The Moralistic Political Culture

To the extent that American society is built on the principles of commerce in the broadest sense of the term and that the marketplace provides the model for public relationships in this country, all Americans share some of the attitudes that are of first importance in the individualistic political culture. At the same time, substantial segments of the American people operate politically within the framework of two political cultures whose theoretical structures and operational consequences depart significantly from the individualistic pattern at crucial points.

The *moralistic political culture* emphasizes the commonwealth conception as the basis for democratic government. Politics, to the moralistic political culture, is considered one of the great activities of man in his search for the good society — a struggle for power, it is true, but also an effort to exercise power for the betterment of the commonwealth. Consequently, in the moralistic political culture, both the general public and the politicians conceive of politics as a public activity centered on some notion of the public good and properly devoted to the advancement of the public interest. Good government, then, is measured by the degree to which it promotes the public good and in terms of the honesty, selflessness, and commitment to the public welfare of those who govern.

In the moralistic political culture, individualism is tempered by a general commitment to utilizing communal — preferably nongovernmental, but governmental if necessary — power to intervene into the sphere of private activities when it is considered necessary to do so for the public good or the well-being of the community. Accordingly, issues have an important place in the moralistic style of politics, functioning to set the tone for political concern. Government is considered a positive instrument with a responsibility to promote the general welfare, though definitions of what its positive role should be may vary considerably from era to era.*

Since the moralistic political culture rests on the fundamental conception that politics exists primarily as a means for coming to grips with the issues and public concerns of civil society, it also embraces the notion that politics is ideally a matter of concern for every citizen, not just for those who are professionally committed to political careers. Indeed, it is the duty of every citizen to participate in the political affairs of his commonwealth.

Consequently, there is a general insistence that government service is public service, which places moral obligations upon those who participate in government that are more demanding than the moral obligations of the marketplace. There is an equally general rejection of the notion that the field of politics is a legitimate realm for private economic enrichment. A politician may indeed benefit economically because of his political career, but he is not expected to profit from political activity and in fact is held suspect if he does.

Since the concept of serving the community is the core of the political relationship, politicians are expected to adhere to it even at the expense of individual loyalties and political friendships. Consequently, party regularity is not of prime importance. The political party is considered a useful political device but is not valued for its own sake. Regular party ties can be abandoned with

---

* As in the case of the individualistic political culture, the change from nineteenth- to twentieth-century conceptions of what government's positive roles should be has been great, i.e., support for Prohibition has given way to support for wage and hour regulation. At the same time, care must be taken to distinguish between a predisposition toward communal activism and a desire for federal government activity. For example, many moralistic types opposed federal aid for urban renewal without in any way opposing community responsibility for urban redevelopment. The distinction they make (implicitly at least) is between what they consider legitimate community responsibility and what they believe to be central government encroachment, or between "communalism" which they value and "collectivism" which they abhor. Thus, on some public issues we find certain moralistic types taking highly conservative positions despite their positive attitudes toward public activity generally. Moralistic types may also prefer government intervention in the social realm — i.e., censorship or screening of books and movies — to similar government intervention in the economy, holding that the former is necessary for the public good and the latter, harmful.

relative impunity for third parties, special local parties, or non-partisan systems if such changes are believed helpful in gaining larger political goals. Politicians can even shift from party to party without sanctions if the change is justified by political belief. In the moralistic political culture, rejection of firm party ties is not to be viewed as a rejection of politics as such. On the contrary, because politics is considered potentially good and healthy within the context of that culture, it is possible to have highly political nonpartisan systems. Certainly nonpartisanship is not instituted to eliminate politics, but to improve it by widening access to public office for those unwilling or unable to gain office through the regular party structure.

In practice, where the moralistic political culture is dominant today, there is considerably more amateur participation in politics. There is also much less of what Americans consider corruption in government and less tolerance of those actions that are considered corrupt, so politics does not have the taint it often bears in the individualistic environment.

By virtue of its fundamental outlook, the moralistic political culture creates a greater commitment to active government intervention in the economic and social life of the community. At the same time, the strong commitment to communitarianism characteristic of that political culture tends to channel the interest in government intervention into highly localistic paths so that a willingness to encourage local government intervention to set public standards does not necessarily reflect a concomitant willingness to allow outside governments equal opportunity to intervene. Not infrequently, public officials will themselves seek to initiate new government activities in an effort to come to grips with problems as yet unperceived by a majority of the citizenry.

The moralistic political culture's major difficulty in adjusting bureaucracy to the political order is tied to the potential conflict between communitarian principles and the necessity for large-scale organization to increase bureaucratic efficiency. Otherwise, the notion of a politically neutral administrative system creates no problem within the moralistic value system and even offers many advantages. Where merit systems are instituted, they tend to be rigidly maintained.

The Traditionalistic Political Culture

The *traditionalistic political culture* is rooted in an ambivalent attitude toward the marketplace coupled with a paternalistic and elitist conception of the commonwealth. It reflects an older, precommercial attitude that accepts a substantially hierarchical society as part of the ordered nature of things, authorizing and expecting those at the top of the social structure to take a special and dominant role in government. Like its moralistic counterpart, the traditionalistic political culture accepts government as an actor with a positive role in the community, but it tries to limit that role to securing the continued maintenance of the existing social order. To do so, it functions to confine real political power to a relatively small and self-perpetuating group drawn from an established elite who often inherit their "right" to govern through family ties or social position. Accordingly, social and family ties are paramount in a traditionalistic political culture, even more than personal ties are important in the individualistic political culture, where, after all is said and done, a person's first responsibility is to himself. At the same time, those who do not have a definite role to play in politics are not expected to be even minimally active as citizens. In many cases, they are not even expected to vote. Like the individualistic political culture, those active in politics are expected to benefit personally from their activity, though not necessarily by direct pecuniary gain.

Political parties are of minimal importance in traditionalistic political cultures because they encourage a degree of openness that goes against the fundamental grain of an elite-oriented political order. Their major utility is to recruit people to fill the formal offices of government not desired by the established power holders. Political competition in a traditionalistic political culture is usually conducted through factional alignments, an extension of the personal political characteristic of the system; hence political systems within the culture tend to have loose one-party systems if they have political parties at all.

Practically speaking, the traditionalistic political culture is found only in a society that retains some of the organic characteristics of the preindustrial social order. Good government in that political culture involves the maintenance and encouragement of traditional patterns and, if necessary, their adjustment to changing conditions with the least possible upset. Where the traditionalistic political culture is dominant in the United States today, political leaders play conservative and custodial rather than initiatory roles, unless strongly pressed from the outside. Whereas the individualistic and moralistic political cultures may or may not encourage the development of bureaucratic systems of organization on the grounds of "rationality" and "efficiency" in government, depending on their particular situations, traditionalistic political cultures tend to be instinctively antibureaucratic because bureaucracy by its very nature interferes with the fine web of informal interpersonal relationships that lie at the root of the political system and have been developed by following traditional patterns over the years. Where bureaucracy is introduced, it is generally confined to ministerial functions under the aegis of the established power-holders.

The characteristics of the three political cultures are summarized in Table 10-1.

Returning to the matrix of value concepts that undergirds the overall American culture, we can see the political subcultural variations manifesting themselves in two ways:

1. in the differences in the shades of meaning attached to each of the four tendencies, for example, the differences between the communitarian agrarianism of the moralistic New England town, the individualistic agrarianism of the middle states, and the plantation agrarianism of the traditionalistic South.

2. in the degree of emphasis placed on each of the four tendencies, for example, the greater emphasis on commerce and commercial efficiency in the individualistic middle states, the particular conception of aristocratic (read oligarchic) agrarian legitimacy based on caste in the traditionalistic South, and the special kind of populist agrarian efficiency of the moralistic Northwest.

More generally, we see that the individualistic political culture draws most heavily from the value orientations of commerce, the moralistic political culture from those of agrarianism, and the traditionalistic culture emphasizes those of legitimacy (as its representatives understand the concept). Each of these different emphases weighs the matrix as a whole in a different direction even while preserving all its elements intact, thereby reflecting subcultural rather than cultural differences. Hence we are reminded that, while the differences among the three subcultures are measurably real, they are not as extreme as they would be if they were reflections of different *cultures*.

The Clash of Sectional Political Cultures

Table 10-1

CHARACTERISTICS OF THE THREE POLITICAL CULTURES

Concepts	Individualistic	Moralistic	Traditionalistic
	GOVERNMENT		
How viewed	As a *marketplace* [Means to respond efficiently to demands]	As a *commonwealth* [Means to achieve the "good community" through positive action]	As a means of maintaining the *existing order*
Appropriate spheres of activity	Largely economic [Encourages private initiative and access to the marketplace] Economic development favored	Any area that will enhance the community although non-governmental action preferred. Social as well as economic regulation considered legitimate	Those that maintain traditional patterns
New programs	Will not initiate unless demanded by public opinion	Will initiate without public pressure if believed to be in public interest	Will initiate if program serves the interest of the governing elite
	BUREAUCRACY		
How viewed	Ambivalently [Undesirable because it limits favors and patronage, but good because it enhances efficiency]	Positively [Brings desirable political neutrality]	Negatively [Depersonalizes government]
Kind of merit system favored	Loosely implemented	Strong	None [Should be controlled by political elite]

POLITICS

Patterns of Belief

How viewed	Dirty [Left to those who soil themselves engaging in it]	Healthy [Every citizen's responsibility]	A privilege [Only those with a legitimate claim to office should participate]

Patterns of Participation

Who should participate	Professionals	Everyone	The appropriate elite
Role of parties	Act as business organizations [Dole out favors and responsibility]	Vehicles to attain goals believed to be in the public interest [Third parties popular]	Vehicle of recruitment of people to offices not desired by established powerholders
Party cohesiveness	Strong	Subordinate to principles and issues	Highly personal [Based on family and social ties]

Patterns of Competition

How viewed	Between parties; not over issues	Over issues	Between elite-dominated factions within a dominant party
Orientation	Toward winning office for tangible rewards	Toward winning office for greater opportunity to implement policies and programs	Dependent on political values of the elite

The "Geology" of Political Culture

The three political subcultures arose out of very real sociocultural differences found among the peoples who came to America over the years, differences that date back to the very beginning of settlement in this country and even back to the Old World. Because the various ethnic and religious groups that came to these shores tended to congregate in their own settlements, and because as they or their descendants moved westward they continued to settle together, the political patterns they bore with them are today distributed geographically. Indeed, it is the geographic distribution of political cultures as modified by local conditions that has laid the foundations for American sectionalism. Sectional concentrations of distinctive cultural groups have helped create the social interests that tie contiguous states to one another even in the face of marked differences in the standard measures of similarity. The Southern states have a common character that unites them despite the great material differences between, for instance, Virginia and Mississippi or Florida and Arkansas. Similarly, New England embraces both Maine and Massachusetts, and Connecticut and Vermont, in a distinctive way. These sectional concentrations can be traced for every part of the country, and their effects can be noted in the character of the interests shared by the states in each section.

Not only must the element of geography be considered in portraying the overall pattern of these political subcultures, but also a kind of human or cultural "geology" that adds another dimension to the problem. In the course of time, different streams of migration have passed over the American landscape in response to the various frontiers of national development (see below). Those streams, in themselves relatively clear-cut, have left residues of population in various places to become the equivalent of geological strata. As these populations settled in the same location, sometimes side by side, sometimes overlapping, and frequently on top of one another, they created hardened cultural mixtures that must be sorted out for analytical purposes, city by city and county by county, from the Atlantic to the Pacific.

Quite clearly, the various sequences of migration in each locale have determined the particular layering of its cultural geology. At the same time, even as the strata were being deposited over generations and centuries, externally generated events, such as depressions, wars, and internal cultural conflicts, caused upheavals that altered the relative positions of the various groups in the community. Beyond that, the passage of time and the impact of new events have eroded some cultural patterns, intensified others, and modified still others, to make each local situation even more complex. The simple mapping of such patterns has yet to be done for more than a handful of states and communities, and while the gross data that can be used to outline the grand patterns as a whole are available in various forms, they have been only partially correlated. However, utilizing the available data, it is possible to sketch with reasonable clarity the nationwide geography of political culture.

The Continuing Frontier

The geography of political culture is directly related to the continuing American frontier. Since the first settlements on these shores, American society has been a frontier society, geared to the progressive extension of man's control over his environment and the utilization of the social and economic benefits gained from widening that control, that is, pushing back the frontier line. The very dynamism of American society is a product of this commitment to the conquest of the ever-advancing frontier, a commitment that is virtually self-generating since, like a chain reaction, the conquest of one frontier has led to the opening of another.

The frontier process emerging from the meeting of civilization and raw nature is a dynamic one; men approach the untamed area with a view to bringing it under their control because it appears to offer indefinite possibilities for expansion as well as a chance to begin again from the beginning, to implement goals that appear difficult or impossible to implement in the civilized areas about them. A frontier situation possesses the following elements: (1) the exploration of that which was previously unexplored and the development of that which was previously undeveloped; (2) a psychological orientation toward exploration, development, growth, opportunity, and change — often typified by the "boom" spirit; (3) an economy that is growing in scope and changing in character; (4) manifold opportunities for exploration and pioneering, coupled with a strong element of risk; (5) widespread freedom for people to engage in frontier-like activities and generally to have free access to the developing sector; (6) substantial movement of populations in search of opportunity or improved living conditions; (7) an emergent or "unfinished" society that is continually responding to the advancing frontier by changing its social and settlement patterns; and (8) the creation of new opportunities on many levels of society as a consequence of pushing back the frontier.

It is this frontier situation that has created the major social and economic changes that have, in turn, forced periodic adjustments in the nation's political institutions, changes of particular importance to the role and functioning of federalism and to the character and particular concerns of intergovernmental relations.

Since the first settlers arrived in 1607, the American frontier has passed through three stages. First came the *rural-land* frontier — the classic American frontier described by the historians — lasting roughly from the seventeenth through the nineteenth centuries. It was characterized by the westward movement of a basically rural population interested in settling and exploiting the land and by the development of a socioeconomic system based on agricultural and extractive pursuits in both its urban and rural components.

Early in the nineteenth century, the rural-land frontier gave birth to the *urban-industrial* frontier which began in the Northeast and spread westward, in the course of which it transformed the nation into an industrial society settled in cities and dedicated to the spread of new technology as the primary source of the nation's economic and social forms. The dominant characteristic of this frontier was the transformation of cities from service centers or workshops for the rural areas into independent centers of opportunity, producers of new wealth, and social innovators possessing internally generated reasons for existence and growth. At first overlapping the rural-land frontier, the urban-industrial frontier became dominant by the last third of the century.

Moving beyond the confines of this book, it is important to note that the chain reaction continued beyond the urban-industrial frontier. By the mid-twentieth century, the latter had given birth, in turn, to the *metropolitan-technological* frontier, which is characterized by the radical reordering of an industrial society through rapidly changing technologies and a settlement pattern that encourages the diffusion of an urbanized population within large metropolitan regions. These radically new technologies, ranging from atomic energy and automation to synthetics and cybernetics, and the accompanying suburbanization of the population, influenced further changes in the nation's social and economic forms in accord with these new demands. Like the first two frontier stages, the metropolitan-technological frontier has also moved from east to west since the 1920s, becoming nationally dominant after World War II. It reached its high point early in the 1960s and in the late 1970s, giving way to a *rurban-cybernetic* frontier in its early stages.

Each successive frontier stage has opened new vistas and new avenues of opportunity for the American people by developing new economic activities, creating new settlement patterns, and mastering new social problems growing out of the collision of old patterns and new demands. Consequently, each frontier has generated new political concerns revolving around the accommodation of the challenges and opportunities within the civil society.

We have seen how the advancing land frontier provided the proximate cause of the exacerbation of the North-South conflict over slavery and the arena in which the initial stages of that conflict were intensified. In doing so, the frontier was playing its characteristic role, just as fifty years earlier the first stages in the opening of the urban-industrial frontier in the form of the invention of the cotton gin moved the South off its increasingly abolitionist course to one in which slavery became the bedrock of its economy.

While the final expansion of the land frontier westward played its role, the full emergence of the urban-industrial frontier in the Northeast and Near West in the antebellum years further sharpened the division between North and South. Moreover, because urbanization and industrialization were particularly successful in the middle states where the market-oriented individualistic culture welcomed the new urban-industrial order, that second frontier stage contributed to the polarization of North and South. No matter how much the middle states may have sympathized with the Southerners against high-handed and fanatic Yankees, in the end their interests were with the industrializing North rather than with the atavistic plantation-centered agrarianism of the South.

Streams of Migration

The basic patterns of political culture were set during the period of the rural-land frontier by three great streams of American migration that began on the East Coast and moved westward after the colonial period. Each stream moved, in the persons of the westward migrants, from east to west along more or less fixed paths, following lines of least resistance which generally led them due west from the immediately previous area of settlement (Map 10-1).

Across the northern part of the United States thrusting westward and slightly southwestward is an area settled initially by the Puritans of New England and their Yankee descendants. The

Puritans came to these shores intending to establish the best possible earthly version of the holy commonwealth. Their religious outlook was imbued with a high level of political concern in the spirit of the ancient Israelites whose ideal commonwealth they wished to reproduce. From the first, they established a moralistic political culture.

After five generations of pioneering in New England, where they established several versions of their commonwealth in the several New England states, the Puritans had developed a set of deeply rooted cultural patterns that had become, for all intents and purposes, indigenous to their part of the New World. Then, moving westward into New York state, the Yankees began their great cross-country migration. Across New York, northern Pennsylvania, and the upper third of Ohio, the Yankee stream moved into the states of the upper Great Lakes and Mississippi Valley. There they established a greater New England in Michigan, Wisconsin, Minnesota, and Iowa, and they attempted to do the same in settling northern Illinois.

Beginning in the mid-nineteenth century, they were joined by Scandinavians and other northern Europeans who, stemming from a related tradition (particularly in its religious orientation), reinforced the basic patterns of Yankee political culture, sealing them into the political systems of those states. Pressing westward, Yankees settled the Willamette Valley of Oregon and eastern Washington and were the first "Anglos" to settle California. As Mormons, they settled Utah; then as abolitionists they settled Kansas. They became the leaders of the permanent settlements in Colorado and Montana and even moved into northern Arizona. In all these states, they were joined or followed by the same Scandinavian-northern European group and in each they established the moralistic political culture to the extent that their influence enabled them to do so. Within those states and the smaller ones colonized from them the moralistic political culture flourishes today.

Groups of quite different ethnic and religious backgrounds, primarily from non-Puritan England and the interior Germanic states, settled the middle parts of the nation, beginning with the Middle Atlantic states of New York, New Jersey, Pennsylvania, Delaware, and Maryland. The majority of these highly diverse groups, which, in the course of living together on the Atlantic coast for three to five generations, established the basic patterns of American pluralism, were united by one common bond in particular — the search for individual opportunity in the New World.

211

Map 10-1

MIGRATION OF CULTURAL STREAMS ACROSS
THE UNITED STATES

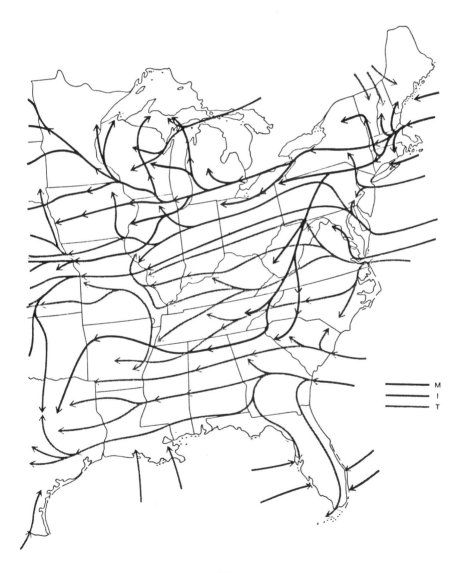

Unlike the Puritans who sought communal as well as individualistic goals in their migrations, the pursuit of private ends predominated among the settlers of the middle states. Though efforts
were made to establish morally purposeful communities, particularly in Pennsylvania, the very purpose of these communities was
to develop pluralistic societies dedicated to individual freedom to
pursue private goals, to the point of making religion a private
matter, an unheard-of step at the time. The political culture of the
middle states reflected this distinctive emphasis on private pursuits from the first and, by the end of the colonial period, a whole
system of politics designed to accommodate itself to such a culture
had been developed with distinctive state-by-state variations,
modified by moralistic traits only in Pennsylvania and by traditionalistic ones in Maryland and Delaware.

These groups also moved westward, across Pennsylvania into
the central parts of Ohio, Indiana, and Illinois, then on into Missouri. There, reinforced by immigrants from Western Europe
and the lower Germanic states who shared the same attitudes, they
developed extensions of their pluralistic patterns. Since those
states were also settled by representatives of the other two political
cultures, thus giving no single culture clear predominance, pluralism became the only viable alternative. So the individualistic
political culture became dominant at the state level in the course of
time while the other two retained pockets of influence in the northern and southern sections of each state.

After crossing the Mississippi, this middle current jumped
across the continent to northern California with the Gold Rush (an
activity highly attractive to individualistic types). Its groups subsequently helped to populate the territory in between. The areas of
Nebraska and South Dakota bordering the Missouri River attracted settlers from Illinois and Missouri; later the Union Pacific Railroad populated central Nebraska and Wyoming; and
Nevada was settled from the California gold fields, founding a
band of states (or sections of states) following the path described
above, in which the individualistic political culture is dominant.

The people who settled the Southern states were seeking individual opportunity in ways similar to those of their brethren to the
immediate north. But, while the latter sought their opportunities in
commercial pursuits, either in business or in a commercially
oriented agriculture, those who settled the South sought opportunity
in a plantation-centered agricultural system based on slavery
and essentially anticommercial in orientation. This system, as

214

an extension of the landed gentry agrarianism of the Old World, provided a natural environment for the development of an American-style traditionalistic political culture in which the new landed gentry progressively assumed ever greater roles in the political process at the expense of the small landholders, while a major segment of the population, the slaves, were totally excluded from any political role whatsoever. Elitism within this culture reached its apogee in Virginia and South Carolina where generation after generation of leading settlers consciously worked at the creation of an "aristocracy." In North Carolina and Georgia a measure of egalitarianism was introduced by the arrival of significant numbers of Scotch-Irish migrants whose traditional culture was strongly tempered by moralistic components.

This peculiarly Southern agrarian system and its traditionalistic political culture were carried westward by the Southern stream. Virginia's people dominated in the settlement of Kentucky; North Carolina's influence was heavy in Tennessee; and settlers from all four states covered the southern parts of Ohio and Illinois as well as most of Indiana and Missouri. South Carolinians and Georgians, with a mixture of other settlers, moved westward into Alabama and Mississippi. Louisiana presented a unique situation in that it contained a concentration of non-Anglo-Saxons rare in the South, but its French settlers shared the same *political* culture as the other Southerners, regardless of their other cultural differences. Ultimately, the Southern political culture was spread through Texas, where it was diluted on that state's western fringes by individualistic-type European immigrants; and Oklahoma, where a similar dilution took place in the north; into southeastern Kansas, where it clashed directly with the Yankee political culture; and later across New Mexico to settle better than half of Arizona and overlap the Yankee stream in southern and central California.

The only major departures from the east-west pattern of cultural diffusion during the settlement of the land frontier came when the emigrants encountered the country's great mountain systems. The mountains served to diffuse cultural patterns because they were barriers to easy east-west movement. Thus, in the east, the Appalachian chain deflected the moralistic Scotch-Irish southward from Pennsylvania to the mountain areas of Virginia, the Carolinas, and Georgia where they were isolated for generations. There, they created special cultural pockets dominated by their traditional culture. Where they settled in the Piedmont

regions of those states, they developed a synthesis of traditionalistic and moralistic elements that had varying degrees of influence on the political cultures of those states.

In the west, the Rocky Mountains served to block the neat
westward flow of the cultural streams and divert people from all
three streams into the valleys from north to south in search of fortunes in mining and specialized agricultural pursuits. There, the
more individualistic types from all three subcultures diffused
from Montana to Arizona, created cultural pockets in all the
mountain states of the west that in some cases — Wyoming, for
example — altered the normal regional patterns of political culture.

The development of the urban-industrial frontier coincided
with the arrival of other immigrant groups that concentrated in
the burgeoning cities of the industrializing states. These groups,
primarily from Ireland, Italy, central and eastern Europe, and
the Balkans, also moved from east to west but settled in urban
pockets, adding new cultural strata to communities scattered
throughout the country. Most of these settlers, though bound at first
by traditional cultural patterns, soon adopted more individualistic attitudes and goals that brought them into the individualistic
political culture. Since most of them settled in cities, their cultural
impact was less universal in scope but more concentrated in force.
In some states (such as Massachusetts) they disrupted established
cultural patterns to create new ones; in others (such as New York)
they simply reinforced the existing dominant individualistic
pluralism; and in still others (such as Illinois) they served to tip
the balance between competing cultural groups.

Sections and Spheres

Sectionalism, as both the concept and the reality have developed in America, embodies the interaction between geography and
history that has forged the set of social patterns which make up the
specific universe of each sectional entity. Each of the eight sections and three spheres into which the United States of today is divided is a grouping of contiguous states tied together by long-term
common interests shaped by common historic patterns. Unlike the
country's regions that encompass essentially homogeneous areas,
each of these spheres and sections is a complex entity combining
highly diverse states, communities, and subregions that remain

linked by an enduring framework of complementary attributes that enables them to satisfy common needs. The frontier emphasizes the workings of humans in time — as embodied in the advances of succeeding generations — to change space; sectionalism reflects the crystallization of actions at specific times in specific spaces. Appropriately enough, Frederick Jackson Turner formulated the classic theory of sectionalism as a corollary to the frontier hypothesis. He saw the twin forces of sectionalism and the frontier as the most important sources of political, economic and social development, as well as political conflict, in the American scheme of things. In his most forceful formulation of the sectional idea, he said:

> The United States is, in size and natural resources, an empire, a collection of potential nations, rather than a single nation....Within this vast empire there are geographic provinces, separate in physical conditions, into which American colonization has flowed, and in each of which a special society has developed, with an economic, political and social life of its own....Between these sections commercial relations have sprung up, and economic combinations and contests may be traced....American industrial life is the outcome of the combinations and contests of groups of States in sections. And the intellectual, the spiritual life of the nation is the result of the interplay of the sectional ideals, fundamental assumptions and emotions.

American sectionalism is based on a pattern of cultural and economic spheres; the greater Northeast, the greater South, and the greater West (Map 10-2). The greater Northeast includes all or the major parts of three sections: New England, the Middle East, and the Near West (or Old Northwest). It embraces the nation's urban-industrial heartland and in the 1850s contained over fifty percent of the country's population in hardly more than ten percent of the country's land area. It is the area where most of the patterns of American civilization originated and where most of the nation's power is concentrated. The sphere developed from a series of "seed" settlements along the East Coast above the Potomac River and includes the area due west of those settlements to a point just beyond Lake Michigan. Its western limits coincide with those of the natural eastern woodland, past which begin the great prairies. The greater Northeast was preeminently shaped by the urban-industrial frontier which superseded its commercial and

217

agricultural economy as a major developmental force early in the nineteenth century.

The greater South, in many ways the most easily distinguishable of the spheres, also began from a number of seed settlements along the Eastern seaboard, but south of the Potomac River, and ultimately advanced westward to include all or major parts of the former slave states plus certain peripheral areas to their north originally settled by Southerners. It embraces three sections: the upper South, the lower South, and the western South (see Map 10-2). In the antebellum period, it was clearly distinguishable by the mandatory slavery of blacks within its territory. It is still held together by a perceived common concern (positive or negative) with "the Southern way of life" as expressed through the mythology of the "lost cause."

The greater South is clearly identifiable in every one of the common statistical measures. Agriculturally, the sphere is marked by the prevalence of cotton or tobacco farming supplemented by widespread timber farming and cattle feeding and sustained by an annual rainfall of more than forty-five inches in all the states that are wholly or partly within the sphere. It is religiously distinctive in a way that no other major part of the United States is, with a marked predominance of Southern Baptists from the Atlantic to West Texas. Much larger and considerably more varied in the spread of urbanization and economic activity than the Northeast, historically the South has been dependent on the Northeast in economic matters. At the same time, the relatively even spread of population in its rural areas — which support isolated homesteads and settlements even more easily than the Northeast — gives the sphere a distinctive population and settlement pattern that has reduced the pressure for the development of large cities. The South was substantially shaped by the land frontier as it was originally manifested in that sphere throughout the nineteenth century, even after the plantation agrarianism of antebellum days gave way to an industrial version of the plantation system when the urban frontier moved southward.

In its broadest sweep, the greater West has been delineated by many geographers and historians to include the entire area west and south of the Appalachian Mountains settled during or after the Revolutionary period primarily or initially by pioneers who were already products of American culture rather than unassimilated immigrants from the Old World. There is much in this definition to recommend it; however, the character of the settlements

Map 10-2

THE THREE SPHERES: SELECTED CHARACTERISTICS

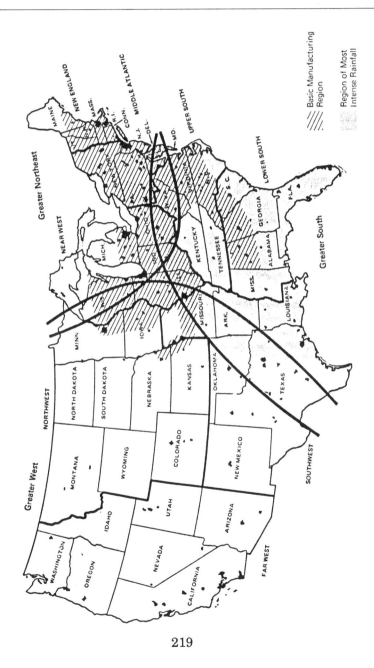

established in the eastern and southern reaches of that vast territory was so firmly fixed by their first settlers into patterns operative in the other spheres that it makes better sense to exclude those parts from the sphere as here defined.

In the South's west, any fundamental Western qualities and influences had to take second place to the influences generated by a slave-based civilization. The continued overwhelming impact of the race question, still the central "problem" of the South, and the other characteristic economic and social features of Southern life have so diluted the impact of Western ways that, for political purposes at least, the latter must be considered to be secondary.

Similarly, the territory immediately west of the Alleghenies, while partly the product of typically Western influences, was so influenced by the first generation of Easterners who came over the mountains to settle and, a century later, by the great European migrations that responded to the urban frontier on both sides of the mountains, that its Western characteristics had to take second place to those of the East. The urban planning of cities of this "Near West," which reaches from the Alleghenies to the Wabash River, illustrates this fact clearly. Though surveyed in the Western manner under the rectangular land survey system established by Congress in 1785, the cities of Ohio and Indiana were laid out in the then dominant Eastern (or Southern) patterns. In most, their local streets were developed in the interstices of the system of roads which converged on the center of town rather than in a grid tied to survey lines. Others were consciously modeled after the Philadelphia city plan. Like their coastal sisters, most of those cities grew primarily as a result of local influences — as products of colonization companies, as local trading centers, or as local milling centers — not as a result of larger regional or even national concerns like those that stimulated the cities of the true greater West. Moreover, the cities of that section were transformed by the urban frontier in much the same way as their East Coast sisters, becoming centers of heavy industry based on the availability of coal, with only sectional differences based on their proximity to iron ore. Thus the cities at the western end of the greater Northeast grew as parts of the Northeastern industrial belt from the very beginning.

The authentic greater West includes all of two sections: the Far West and Northwest, and part of the Near West. It can be said to include all free-soil territories which had not emerged from the land frontier stage of their development by 1850: the free states west of the Mississippi River plus major parts of Illinois, Wisconsin, and Michigan. This is the area in which the national democratic ideals of the nineteenth century were given concrete expression. In the process, the greater West endowed itself with a unique character of its own. Primarily products of Jacksonian democracy and its influences, in the radically new physical environment of the greater West these national democratic ideals were combined with an entirely new technology. The combination stimulated an economic system in which laissez-faire ideas predominated but which was strongly influenced by corporate organization and governmental intervention from the beginning. The same combination gave rise to a populist approach to politics characteristic of the Jacksonian and post-Jacksonian eras that was intrinsically different from the traditional or elitist approaches characteristic of the other spheres. The greater West also gave birth to as unstructured a social system as the modern world has ever seen; a system that allowed, and even expected, great and rapid mobility both vertically and laterally within it. The sphere as a whole was populated through an implicit if unwitting system of recruitment that placed a premium on those with a psychology of individual initiative in economic pursuits and social conformity in most others. Along the borders of the three spheres (generally speaking, between and along the points of intersection of the semicircles in Map 10-2) lie three transition zones — the Ohio Valley, the western South, and the western Great Lakes — that share the characteristics of two or more spheres and have particularly diverse and complex patterns of culture and politics. These were the regions most torn by the events leading up to the Civil War, the regions where the struggles of the 1850s were played out.

Bibliographic Notes — Chapter 10

The principal source for this discussion of American political culture and its subcultures is Daniel J. Elazar's *Cities of the Prairie* (1970), and *American Federalism: A View From the States* (1984); and Daniel J. Elazar and Joseph Zikmund, II, eds., *The Ecology of American Political Culture* (1975).

For an analysis by political scientists of the American national political culture in a comparative setting, see Gabriel A. Almond and

Building Toward Civil War

Sidney Verba, *The Civic Culture* (1963). Two treatments of the origins of the American political culture are Daniel J. Boorstin, *The Americans: The National Experience* (1965); and Seymour Martin Lipset, *The First New Nation: The United States in Historical and Comparative Perspective* (1963).

Since the patterns of the political subcultures are tied closely to the patterns of the general subcultures in the United States, it is possible to gain some impressions of the spread of the former from data prepared to illustrate the spread of the latter. One of the best sources for that data, though somewhat dated, is Charles O. Paullin's *Atlas of the Historical Geography of the United States* (1932). The correlations between religious affiliation and political culture are clear and striking. Edwin S. Gausted's *Historical Atlas of Religion in America* (1962) includes maps showing the spread of religious denominations as of 1950, which are also very useful in following the patterns of political culture.

The basic statement of the frontier theory is still that of Frederick Jackson Turner and can best be found in his *The Frontier in American History* (1920). For an introduction to other aspects of frontier theory, see Nelson Klose, *A Concise Study Guide to the American Frontier* (1964). A good restatement of the theory is that of Ray Allen Billington in *America's Frontier Heritage* (1967). The history and significance of the American land frontier has been set forth in great detail by Turner and his students. See, for example, Turner, *The Frontier in American History*, and Ray Allen Billington, *Westward Expansion: A History of the American Frontier* (1949).

Much less has been written about the urban-industrial frontier. Two good studies are John Kouwenhoven, *Made in America*, rev. ed. (1962) on the role of the new technology of the mid-nineteenth century; and Anselm Strauss, *The Image of the American City* (1961), on the urbanization aspects of the urban-industrial frontier. Walt W. Rostow's *The Stages of Economic Growth* (1960) provides a theory of economic growth that strongly supports the hypothesis presented here. The frontier aspects of the contemporary metropolitanization process have hardly been treated at all. The best discussion available is that of Samuel Lubell, *The Future of American Politics* (1952).

For a full statement of this frontier thesis, see Daniel J. Elazar, *Some Social Problems in the Northeastern Illinois Metropolitan Region* (1961) and *Cities of the Prairie* (1970).

Turner is also the starting point for the study of American sectionalism; see Frederick Jackson Turner, *The Significance of Sections in American History* (1932). See also Wilbur R. Jacobs, ed., *America's Great Frontiers* (1969); Richard Franklin Bensel, *Sectionalism and American Political Development, 1880-1980* (1984).

Epilogue

THE CHALLENGE TO FEDERAL DEMOCRACY

Lincoln and the American Covenant

During the dark February of 1861, on his way east to Washington to be inaugurated as the sixteenth president of the United States, Abraham Lincoln undertook the first whistle stop tour in the nation's history. He did so for two reasons: to convince the nation of his own strength and resolution and to get a first hand sense of the strength and resolution of the American people in the face of the impending crisis. In the course of his circuitous trip by railroad from Springfield, Illinois, to the nation's capital, he spoke over eighty times in some sixty cities and towns in seven states. In those talks, which ranged from the briefest of back platform remarks to public addresses before the legislatures of Ohio, New York, New Jersey, and Pennsylvania, and in his first inaugural address, drafted before he left Springfield and then revised in Washington to embrace the sense of his extemporaneous expressions en route, the president-elect effectively defined the great political question confronting the American people during the 1861-1865 period, and its larger implications in light of the American vocation.

Lincoln believed the great political question to be: "Shall the Union and shall the liberties of this country be preserved to the latest generation?" Characterizing the relationship between the states as "a family relation" and "a regular marriage" in which the states acquired a "particular sacredness" by virtue of their position in the Union and the Union a sacredness by virtue of its role as perpetuator of the liberty of "these States and all these people," he framed his words to define the American political system as one embracing "the Constitution, the Union, and the perpetuity of the liberties of this country," each intimately connected with the other in a single web. Furthermore, he set forth a conception of the nation as being formed, in the biblical manner, through a covenant, at once perpetual from the first yet perennially renewed. Lincoln saw this covenant as three-sided, between "that Supreme Being

223

who has never forsaken this land"; "his almost chosen people"; and their government, "an humble instrument in the hands of the Almighty." To him it was a covenant animated by "the sentiments embodied in the Declaration of Independence," "giving liberty, not alone to the people of this country, but hope to the world for all future time."

Lincoln's position and the challenge implicit in it made a great deal of sense to that segment of the American people which remained loyal to the Union, so much sense that they were to respond by sacrificing themselves or their loved ones on hundreds of battlefields for four long years on behalf of the Constitution, the Union, and the liberties of the people. Both the challenge and the response have been generally acknowledged by the generations of Americans who have lived to enjoy the reaffirmation of the national covenant, yet, in the passage of time and the emergence of new issues, some of Lincoln's meaning, so clear to his contemporaries, has been lost.

The great political issue of the Civil War was more than the preservation of a united nation pure and simple. It was the preservation of a nation united in a particular way, a way that was at once faithful to the terms of the American Constitution, protective of the liberties of the American people, and loyal to the American vocation. Lincoln correctly indicated that the preservation of the Union in any other way would not be worth the effort. The great issue, then, was the fate of the American federal system specifically and of federal democracy as a system of government generally.

Federal democracy is the unique American contribution to the art and science of government. American democracy is federal in two ways. It is founded on a network of covenants or compacts and is thus federal in the seventeenth century usage of the term (*foedus* is the Latin word for covenant), and it is based upon constitutionally established forms of power-sharing or federalism as we know it. As a form of democratic republicanism, federal democracy differs from Westminster parliamentary democracy where power and authority are constitutionally concentrated in a single parliamentary center and delegated from that center as parliament pleases, and from Jacobin democracy, involving rule by an elite, usually self-selected, speaking in the name of the general will. Federal democracy allows, nay, requires the people to design their own institutions embodied in constitutions and then to share in their governance by delegating powers to each of those institutions commensurate with its tasks. Federal democracy is far more dynamic than any other form of democratic government, in part because it rests upon a fundamental consensus embodied in the constitution of the body politic and reinforced by its political culture.

Lincoln clearly understood that the Union rested upon the existence of an American consensus. During the Civil War he tailored his own actions so as to evoke the people's attachment to that consensus in order to preserve the Union. His remarks during his preinaugural tour gave us some important clues to his understanding of the consensus, its power and its limits.

In speech after speech, he repeatedly expressed three thoughts concerning the process of American government. First he emphasized that the honors rendered him by the crowds and dignitaries were homage to the office of the presidency, not to the man, that they would (and should) have been rendered to any of his opponents had they been elected, and that similar homage would (and should) be rendered the man elected to the office on other occasions simply because he was president-elect. However, he also emphasized that as the man chosen to be president by the majority, he had an obligation to live up to the commitments he made to that majority in soliciting their support, provided they did not run counter to the Constitution. Third, he made it a point to remind his listeners that any president was a mere transient figure in the life of the nation who could be replaced with another man more to the liking of the people every four years if they no longer wished him to serve or his policies to be maintained.

There was an important twist in Lincoln's words as he emphasized these three things, one with an important meaning. His eagerness to disclaim any homage for himself is deceptively modest and well calculated. In his effort to show people that they were not hailing Lincoln the man but Lincoln the president, he really was trying to indicate how his reception as the legitimate president-elect, despite his minority victory from the Sangamon to the Potomac, was properly nonpartisan and reflected the underlying procedural consensus that must exist — and did in the North — if the Union, or any popular government, is to survive.

At the same time, he had to indicate the limits of his or any president's (even one with less than a majority of the popular vote) responsibility to rely upon an immediate consensus in formulating policy by reaffirming his obligation to those who elected him. Consensus is immediately necessary, he seemed to say first, on

the procedures of government even where there is immediate dis-
agreement on substantive questions. But, he went on, there must be
room for conflict over policies and personnel within the consensual framework and for the participants in that conflict to gain
partial (but no more than partial) victory if they secure the proper
majority.

Here Lincoln's expression became more careful. He knew that
victory in any particular phase of the conflict must be limited, of
course, by the terms of the Constitution itself, which not only de-
termines how transient majorities are to be formed but also limits
the power of such majorities while they exist. Lincoln was well
aware of the limits of his "majority," yet he spoke of it in two ways.
On the one hand, he acknowledged the constitutional limits on
transient majorities (including the kind that forms to elect presidents) by reiterating his powerlessness and even unwillingness
to interfere with slavery within established states, but, on the other
hand, he spoke of his mandate as stemming from a real majority,
indeed, "*the* majority" (Lincoln's emphasis). In part, Lincoln was
reaffirming a basic constitutional principal of federal democracy, that a real majority was a federal majority — a majority of
the people in a majority of the states — as the decisive measure in a
presidential election and as a more accurate measure of majorities than a simple nationwide popular vote.

In another sense, he was including those Northerners, both
Democrats and Republicans, who shared his opposition to the extension of slavery and his desire to preserve the Union in a
majority that was consensual, not transient or based upon partisan voting for this or that candidate. Lincoln was to make every
effort to invoke the consensual majority in the North even at the
expense of antagonizing some elements in his transient, partisan
majority. In the process he was to subtly alter the immediate con-
tents of the national consensus.

Lincoln apparently made his argument entirely on behalf of a
procedural consensus, that is to say, that the Southerners were
wrong to secede simply because their candidates had failed to win
the presidency. Yet the thinking members of his audiences, undoubtedly familiar with his earlier remarks on the subject of
slavery, would know that Lincoln (like the founding fathers) also
believed that in the long run there must be substantial substantive
agreement in certain fields as a prerequisite for immediate consensus on procedures. He had made that clear in his "House Divided" speech where he stated that the nation cannot forever exist

"half slave and half free." Thus his immediate concern for the procedural concealed but did not diminish his recognition that the problem of substantive consensus had to be faced. No doubt this accounts for his adamant refusal to consider the various "compromises" advanced by moderates between December 1860 and March 1861 to induce the Southern states to remain in the Union. The common feature underlying these compromises was an attempt to introduce further procedural guarantees into the federal Constitution to protect forever Southern, that is, slaveholding interests within the Union. Lincoln clearly recognized that the division between the opponents of slavery and the slaveholders was too pronounced and too strongly reinforced by other social and economic factors to create the substantive consensus necessary to make the procedural guarantees more than a shallow mockery of the democratic process.

Lincoln's perceptiveness was validated by the Civil War itself. Northerners and Southerners both accepted the procedural elements of the American consensus, as the similarities between the federal and the Confederate political systems showed. But, as their differences over the interpretation of the substantive aspects of the consensus grew, the procedures could no longer tie them together. Only when the possibility of raising the substantive questions was sufficiently limited (only by force of arms — hence superficially) was reunion to be possible. Obviously, military force could only limit the possibility; the substantive issues remained to partially reassert themselves after the end of Reconstruction. Some would not be resolved for three more generations.

The Crisis and the Challenge of War

One great virtue of territorial federalism is that it distributes political power geographically in a way that is usually more neutral than any other; one that can be most accommodating to the pressures of socioeconomic change while preventing disastrous socioeconomic cleavages by cutting across potential lines of cleavage. The particular character of the American Civil War as a "war between the states" reflects the coincidence of the nation's geographic and socioeconomic cleavages at the moment of their greatest intensification. Normally, it has been the task of American politics to prevent such coincidences while at the same time resolving reasonable conflicts of interest within the framework of the American consensus. In his message to the special session of Congress, symbolically delivered on July 4, 1861, Lincoln stated the problem in its rawest form:

> Our popular government has often been called an experiment. Two points in it our people have already settled — the successful *establishing*, and the successful *administering* of it. One still remains — its successful *maintenance* against a formidable (internal) attempt to overthrow it. It is now for them to demonstrate to the world that those who can fairly carry an election, can also suppress a rebellion — that ballots are the rightful, and peaceful, successors of bullets; and that when ballots have fairly, and constitutionally, decided, there can be no successful appeal, back to bullets; that there can be no successful appeal, except to ballots themselves, at succeeding elections. Such will be a great lesson of peace; teaching men that what they cannot take by an election, neither can they take it by war — teaching all the folly of being the beginners of a war (emphasis in original).

In sum, despite the shared frame of reference, North and South, the survival of federal democracy as a successful system of government was by no means certain in 1861. A shared frame of reference alone was not enough. A consensus has to be translated into meaningful actions if it is to serve as a unifying force. The way to do that is through politics and in the 1850s American politics proved unequal to the task.

The growing separation of Northern and Southern interpretations of aspects of their common frame of reference, abetted by an assault on the consensus itself by radical groups in each section, was to lead to a crisis of the first magnitude. The Civil War, its prelude of secessionist heresies and its aftermath of reconstruction, challenged the American federal consensus as a whole and every element in that consensus in detail. A challenge of such magnitude would not and did not come over the secession question, which was a manifestation rather than a cause. Rather, it came from a compounding of questions that both contributed to and emerged from the secession crisis itself and their amalgamation with questions rising from seemingly unrelated problems emerging in the post-1846 generation.

Three crucial components can be traced in the challenge of the Civil War. The first and seemingly most obvious one was the challenge to the unity of the nation. This challenge was brought to center stage by the secession of eleven of the Southern states. As Lincoln indicated, meeting this challenge became the central purpose of the war itself.

The second challenge actually antedated the secession crisis, rooted as it was in the development of powerful antislavery sentiments in the North that were not to be denied, sentiments that were strongly reinforced by the growing differences between the economic systems of the North and the South. This was the challenge of reform. Could the American federal system maintain itself and still respond to social and economic changes? This question went to the heart of the problem of maintaining long-time political stability in the face of the necessity for political change, which is the crucial test of any political system.

This challenge came, not from the North-South confrontation, but from the pressures of Northern reformers — abolitionists and their sympathizers who believed the morality of their cause superseded the limits of constitutionalism. Their demands were directed against other Northerners who placed primary emphasis on maintenance of the federal union and its constitution, as well as against the Southern "Slave Power." In their demands for the abolition of slavery they became the first to raise the fundamental question of the compatibility of reforms that would alter the national consensus with the maintenance of the Union. The answer to that question would have momentous consequences for the future development of the country.

Once the war had begun, the survival of federalism as the basis of a stable political system was itself challenged. On the one hand, there was the question of the survival of noncentralized government in the event of a Union victory. On the other hand, there was the equally important question of the possibility that both federal entities would fall apart into smaller pieces in the event of a Confederation victory.

The full implications of this third challenge were not felt until after the Union victory had become inevitable and the problems of reconstruction became of utmost importance. With the Northern radicals at the peak of their power and in need of strong centralized government to further their own revolutionary aims, and the constitutionalists in their section divided by the conflict itself, the political leverage available on behalf of the traditional patterns of noncentralized government was drastically reduced. Radical power was further strengthened by strong public recognition that national authority would have to be used to provide some means of reorganizing Southern governments in such a way as to safeguard the rights of the freed blacks and break the power of those they held responsible for the war. Even if the radicals themselves would accept the retention of traditional federal forms, there remained the vital question of whether the expansion of the national government induced partly by the war, partly by the pressures of industrialization, and partly by the demands of the Republican coalition had not, in itself, irrevocably altered the erstwhile federal balance.

When Lincoln, on his way to Washington and his destiny, spoke of preserving the Constitution, the Union, and the liberties of the people, he was expressing his view of the full meaning of the federal principle. When he spoke of the union of the states as a regular marriage which endowed the partners with particular sacredness, he was expressing the essence of the American covenant idea, both as a relationship and as an ideal. Shortly after speaking of these things, he was to face the desperate necessity of making hard choices in an effort to save them for future generations. As he well knew, his choices would be but one element among many in the ultimate determination of the future of the United States.

Lincoln's delineation of the central elements in the American political system is an important guide for later generations seeking to understand how the American people met the three great political challenges of the Civil War. Americans did so, not by acting in one voice but by speaking in many, often contradictory, voices until sufficient national agreement as to the substantive meaning of the American consensus could be reforged and normal political techniques could once again resume their importance in effectuating the principles of federal democracy.

INDEX

ABOUT THE AUTHOR

Dr. Daniel J. Elazar is a leading political scientist and authority on federalism and American government. He is Professor of Political Science at Temple University in Philadelphia, where he directs the Center for the Study of Federalism, and President of the Jerusalem Center for Public Affairs, an independent "think tank" focusing on Israel and Jewish public policy issues. Professor Elazar also holds the Senator N.M. Paterson Professorship in Intergovernmental Relations at Bar-Ilan University in Israel, where he heads the Institute for Local Government. In 1986, President Reagan appointed him a citizen member of the U.S. Advisory Commission on Intergovernmental Relations, the major intergovernmental agency dealing with problems of federalism.

Professor Elazar has written or edited over 50 books and many other publications ranging from an analysis of local governments in the Midwestern United States to a handbook surveying and classifying federal systems and autonomy arrangements throughout the world. Among them are *The American Partnership; American Federalism, A View from the States* (now in its third edition); *Cities of the Prairie* and *Cities of the Prairie Revisited; Exploring Federalism*; and *Israel: Building a New Society*. He is the editor of *Publius: The Journal of Federalism*, and of the *Jerusalem Letter/Viewpoints*, a newsletter on Jewish public affairs.

Books by Daniel J. Elazar

The American Partnership (1962)
American Federalism: A View From The States (1966; 1973; 1984)
The American System: A New View of Government in the United States
(ed.) (1966)
A Classification System for Libraries of Judaica (co-author) (1968; 1979)
The Politics of American Federalism (ed.) (1969)
Cooperation and Conflict: A Reader in American Federalism (co-editor)
(1969)
Cities of the Prairie (1970)
The Politics of Belleville (1971)
The Federal Polity (ed.) (1973; 1978)
The Ecology of American Political Culture (co-editor) (1975)
Community and Polity: The Organizational Dynamics of American
Jewry (1976)
Federalism and Political Integration (ed.) (1979; 1984)
Republicanism, Representation and Consent: Views of the Founding Era
(ed.) (1979)
Self-Rule/Shared Rule: Federal Solutions to the Middle East Conflict (ed.)
(1979; 1984)
Covenant, Polity and Constitutionalism (co-editor) (1980)
Kinship and Consent: The Jewish Political Tradition and Its Contempo-
rary Uses (ed.) (1981; 1983)
Governing Peoples and Territories (ed.) (1982)
Judea, Samaria and Gaza: Views on the Present and Future (ed.) (1982)
Jewish Communities in Frontier Societies (co-author) (1983)
From Autonomy to Shared Rule: Options for Judea, Samaria and Gaza
(ed.) (1983)
Balkan Jewish Communities: Yugoslavia, Bulgaria, Greece and Turkey
(co-author) (1984)
The Jewish Communities of Scandinavia: Sweden, Denmark, Norway
and Finland (co-author) (1984)
Understanding the Jewish Agency: A Handbook (co-editor) (1984; 1985)
The Jewish Polity: Jewish Political Organization From Biblical Times to
the Present (co-author) (1985)
Federalism and Consociationalism (ed.) (1985)
Jewish Political Studies: Selected Syllabi (co-editor) (1985)
Israel: Building a New Society (1986)
Cities of the Prairie Revisited: The Closing of the Metropolitan Frontier
(co-author) (1986)
Israel at the Polls, 1981 (co-editor) (1986)
Building Cities in America: Urbanization and Suburbanization in a
Frontier Society (1987)
Exploring Federalism (1987)
Project Renewal in Israel: Urban Revitalization Through Partnership (co-
author) (1987)
Federalism as a Grand Design: Political Philosophers and the Federal
Principle (ed.) (1987)
Canadian Federalism: From Crisis to Constitution (co-editor) (1987)
Local Government in Israel (co-editor) (1987; 1988)
The American Constitutional Tradition (1988)
The New Jewish Politics (ed.) (1988)
The Other Jews: The Sephardim Today (1989)
People and Polity: The Organizational Dynamics of World Jewry (1989)

Morality and Power: Contemporary Jewish Views (ed.) (1989)
Maintaining Consensus: The Canadian Jewish Polity in the Postwar World (co-author) (1990)
Constitutionalism: The Israeli and American Experiences (ed.) (1990)
Israel's Odd Couple: The 1984 Elections and the National Unity Government (co-editor) (1990)